But Seriously

JOHN
McENROE
But Seriously

WEIDENFELD & NICOLSON

First published in Great Britain in 2017
by Weidenfeld & Nicolson

1 3 5 7 9 10 8 6 4 2

© John McEnroe 2017

A CIP catalogue record for this book
is available from the British Library.

ISBN HB 978 1 4091 4795 4
TPB 978 1 4091 4796 1

Typeset by Input Data Services Ltd, Somerset

Printed and bound in Australia by McPhersons Printing Group

Weidenfeld & Nicolson

The Orion Publishing Group Ltd
Carmelite House
50 Victoria Embankment
London
EC4Y 0DZ
An Hachette UK Company
www.orionbooks.co.uk

TO PATTY –

My soul mate, my partner in crime—
we *were* meant for each other

A man's gotta do
what a man's gotta do
when a man's gotta do
what he's got to.

Edie Brickell and Steve Martin, *Bright Star*

PROLOGUE

I wake up in a sweat. My pillow's damp and I don't know what day it is. Did I miss the match? Am I playing later? For a few seconds I don't even know where I am. Then it hits me. I already played the match. I already lost it. Jesus, it was back in 1984 and I'm still haunted by it. Even now, more than thirty years later, I'm as hot as I was in the fifth set and I can taste the red clay on my tongue.

It was a match I should have won and it turned into the worst loss of my career. I'd been playing my best tennis ever, I was undefeated that year, and although serve-volleying wasn't the obvious way of winning the French Open on the slow clay of Roland-Garros, I was playing Ivan Lendl. Ivan had so far lost four Grand Slam finals in a row and I sure as hell wasn't planning on breaking that run for him by handing him his first title. In fact, I was planning on beating his ass.

At first, that's exactly what I did. After two sets, I was up 6–3, 6–2, and I was all over him. The crowd was behind me, "*Allez, John! Allez.*" As far as I was concerned, I was in control, I had this in the bag. But as it got hotter, the crowd started losing focus.

1

Then my friend Ahmad Rashad—a great former wide receiver for the Minnesota Vikings—who was there rooting for me, got up to leave. "You got this, Mac! I'll see ya back at the hotel." Shit, the last thing I needed was a jinx. It's an unwritten rule in sports that friends and family don't leave until the match is over. Not that I'm blaming Ahmad for the loss, but that's when little doubts started creeping in for the first time. I still thought I was going to win but those negative thoughts began to get to me.

Everything suddenly became a distraction. At the next changeover I couldn't help but notice the noise from a nearby cameraman's headphones. Someone was obviously trying to get this guy's attention. The third set had barely started when, I swear to God, I heard something like, "When the match is over, we'll focus on John and then stick with him through the trophy ceremony. He's got this, so make sure he's in the shot." In English. In Paris. It was the American TV cameraman listening to the producer's instructions in his headphones, but they were so loud I could hear them too. Unbelievable! Now I was feeling even more jinxed. So I walked to the guy's chair, grabbed the headphones off his head, and screamed as loud as I possibly could into his mic: "SHUT UP!" I knew immediately that my frustration wasn't a good enough reason for me to do this, and while I didn't care about the cameraman, I did care about the crowd. I needed them. But they sure as hell didn't need me and my bad attitude. That was the point when they turned on me. They just wanted the match to go on—who could blame them—and what better way than to change corners and root for my opponent? After all, that French crowd was known for being fickle. I tried to block them out. I was still the best tennis player in the world and there was no way I was losing to Lendl.

I failed to break his serve at 2–2 in the third, despite him being 0–40 down. No matter. I still had my mojo. I was still convinced I could win this thing, all I needed to do was stick with my game plan: serve-volley, and break him—as soon as possible. Except he won the set 6–4.

I had to pull it together. I reminded myself I was two sets to one up; better than him. "Don't panic. Don't let the heat get to you. Don't let these people get to you. They know I can beat this guy. I know I can beat this guy." But it didn't happen.

In the fourth set, I found myself serving, 4–3, 40–30. I'd broken him and was five points from the title. I really thought I could close it out. But in the heat of the moment, my normally soft hands pushed my first volley a fraction beyond the baseline. Somehow, in the blink of an eye, the set was over. He'd won it 7–5 and we were now two sets all.

In the fifth, the heat became stifling, Lendl's confidence ignited, and the crowd got behind him. My legs felt more and more like Jell-O and, with my strength draining fast from my body, I lost my grip on the match. I tried and tried, but in the end, I was the one walking to the net with my head down, while Lendl was smiling goofily, his hands up, jumping around as he sealed his first Slam title.

Does it surprise you that I still have that nightmare, all these years later? It wakes me up every year when I'm in Paris, commentating on the French Open—at least once, usually twice. But every time I have this bad dream, it's a little easier to get over. Maybe I've gained some perspective on this dark moment in my career. Maybe time does heal all wounds. But any way you look at it, this was the closest I ever came to winning this clay-court major.

Thankfully I've had a couple of small chances for revenge since then (although let me be clear: nothing could EVER EVER EVER make up for what happened that day). The first was in October 2010. And it was in Paris. That morning when I awoke

I didn't have to have the nightmare, because after eighteen years, I was finally going to be playing Ivan Lendl again. For me, it was a big deal to meet him on court once more. My chance to get one back on him. I'm not kidding. That 1984 Roland-Garros defeat still burned my guts. We'd come up against each other on a number of occasions since then; sometimes I'd won, mostly I'd lost. We'd last played each other on the main tour back in 1992 in Toronto, but by then we were both on the downward slope of our careers, so it hadn't felt like a proper opportunity for payback. Once I started on the seniors circuit, there was a long period where Ivan was kept off the court because of a clause in an insurance policy that looked like it would stop him from ever playing again. But somehow that got ironed out. So now, in the city where I'd suffered the most painful loss of my career, I finally had the chance to lay that ghost to rest—the one that had been haunting me for twenty-six years.

The setting, Stade de Coubertin, was totally different from the famous red clay of Roland-Garros, even though the two stadiums are only a stone's throw apart. Coubertin is a big enough indoor sports venue that they played the year-end Masters there in 1971 and 1980. But it's also a gray, nondescript building on the edge of the giant Paris ring road. On top of that, I remember the air conditioning wasn't working that evening; packed to full capacity, that place was about as hot as I've ever known a stadium to be. It was an oppressive atmosphere, literally and psychologically. The crowd were into it because they know the game pretty well in France and they understood this was a big match for me.

Generally, on the seniors tour, players get along fine, despite whatever differences they may have had in the past, and there's an element of camaraderie and even light-heartedness in the locker room. Not here. There was an intensity in each of us because we both knew we were going to play as hard as we could.

I wasn't going to lose a point if I could help it—I wanted to make him suffer and show him who was the boss. When Ivan arrived at the stadium, I was on the trainer's table getting a massage. He entered the room, and without so much as a "hello," he said in his heavy accent: "So, John, are we going to make each other look good, or are we going to kick each other's asses?" I paused for a moment and replied, "I'd prefer the latter."

I never thought that, when at long last I found myself on court against Ivan again, I'd be the fitter of the two of us. The guy had been a machine when he was younger. He was known for his fitness. I was the opposite, known for playing doubles as a way of getting fit. Here we were now, and I was clearly in better shape and moving better than him, although God knows he'd worked hard to come back after a long period out of the game and had lost in the region of forty pounds in the months leading up to the match, which is a lot in anyone's book. Trouble was, he still had another twenty pounds to go.

When we started, because of the heat, I could hardly breathe. I kept telling myself that if I felt this bad, he must be feeling a whole lot worse. Except that he was serving bigger than I'd expected—or maybe I was returning worse. The fact was, I was tighter than I'd anticipated because I wanted to beat Ivan to a pulp so badly and I'd got myself pretty worked up.

Toward the end of the first set, when the match was still a close one, something weird happened. Ivan Lendl, this guy—this robot—who was known for his total lack of a sense of humor, started tossing out jokes to the crowd. I hadn't seen that coming, and it threw me to hear Ivan, of all people, asking the crowd why I was taking the match so seriously: "Hey, John, you're playing too fast. It's only a game, relax!"

By the time I'd won the first set 6–4, I guess he realized he was going to lose, because he started acting like he didn't care what happened. His attempts at humor seemed designed to make me look lame and pathetic for wanting to win, but really he was trying to protect himself from humiliation. And it was totally bizarre to have him suddenly try to be this comedian on court.

Then, just as I was smelling victory and moving in for the kill—at 3–2 in the second set—Ivan retired. Without warning. He'd hurt his calf. The public wasn't too thrilled. I felt cheated, like he wouldn't give me the satisfaction of a win. Oh, and to add insult to injury, Ivan told me as he defaulted that if he'd been in better shape, he would have beaten me.

It was still incredibly satisfying to have won, because even if he hadn't bailed on me, I knew I had him. My post-match celebrations made it clear how I felt—I seem to remember doing quite a lot of fist-pumping as I saluted the crowd. Ivan had long retreated to the locker room when I ended the on-court interview by saying that this was a historic moment for me: "I never thought we'd play again . . . and who would've thought I'd be able to say that I was fitter than Ivan Lendl?"

Afterward, Ivan came up to me. "In two months I'll beat you, you know. I'll be ready then. Trust me." Jesus, this guy could be so annoying! But the gauntlet had been thrown. We met on court twice more over the next four months, and both times there was drama.

I'm not sure what it was about Ivan Lendl that brought out an allergic reaction in me. But I do know we were polar opposites; about the only thing we had in common was being members of the human race. I've often heard it said that we react badly to people because they remind us of a part of ourselves that we don't like, or because they possess a character trait that, subconsciously or consciously, we admire and even wish we possessed.

Yes, I admired his dedication and envied his fitness. It's true that Ivan had a work ethic that no one else had, at least in those days, apart from Guillermo Vilas. But Vilas didn't do the whole diet and monastic life thing, whereas Ivan was the first player who seemed to have no life at all outside tennis. I give a lot of credit to the guy for sticking at his regime for so long. It paid off in the end, and he certainly changed the game of tennis: today's players have levels of fitness and commitment that are off the charts. And much as I hate to admit it, that is a good thing. But it seems like the sport has lost some of its personality in the process.

Either way, what better prospect at the start of a new year than facing Ivan Lendl across the net again? This time we were in Adelaide, in early 2011—the week before the Australian Open. And as well as the usual line-up of doubles matches, Ivan and I were scheduled to play singles. Hopefully, this time he'd hold out until the end of the match.

The promoters knew the match-up would sell a few tickets. To be honest, there aren't a whole lot of seniors matches that people will pay to see—including most of mine. They don't give a damn if I play Mikael Pernfors or Andrés Gómez, for example, even though they were great players and they still do a good job, probably better than some of the other guys I get to play against—probably better than me! Of the players of my generation, the ones people wanted to see me take on were Björn and, before he got too old, Jimmy Connors.

My Adelaide match with Lendl almost didn't happen—it was raining hard and we were wondering if we should play in those conditions. I had been suffering with a long-standing hip problem which at times was so bad I doubted whether I could go on playing. The last thing I needed was to slip on a wet court and injure myself even more. Luckily, the rain stopped and the court dried out so the match could go ahead. This time I beat him pretty easily in an eight-game pro-set. The crazy thing was, he was still trash-talking to me the whole time. I think he was annoyed that it wasn't as easy as he'd expected to come back in his late forties and play well. It was like he didn't want to give me credit for playing consistently for the previous ten, fifteen years.

A month later, we were at Madison Square Garden for what was billed as "The Showdown": me against Lendl, followed by Sampras against Agassi. The promotional picture had photos of Pete, Andre and me as we looked in 2011. In my case in particular, I was that old guy with the gray hair. But for some reason, Lendl's picture was from about 1985. Wait a minute, I thought, why do three of us look old while he's looking like he just turned twenty-five? Could it be because the co-promoter of the event was Jerry Solomon, who happens to be Ivan's agent? Credit to him, though, because 17,000 people paid good money to see us play two matches, apparently featuring the ghost of Lendl past.

Not that I ever needed motivation when I played Ivan, but playing in front of a crowd that size was always going to make it even more special. I'd played at the Garden many times when the ATP finals had been held there in the past. This was my home turf, and it was exciting to be going back now, because it had been a long time since I'd last hit a ball there. Plus, I was fit, and I was 2–0 against him, so I couldn't wait.

Just before my match, I was on court having a workout with Pete; I figured if I could keep up with him, I could beat Lendl. As it turned out, I was hitting the ball well and feeling good. I was about to finish up when I decided to move up to the net for a few volleys. Pete hit a ball short, I charged, but as I did so—and I swear this is the only time in my career this ever happened—my foot somehow got stuck underneath me, and I turned my ankle. I knew immediately I'd sprained it. Badly. So I headed straight back to the locker room. My ankle started swelling up like a balloon in front of my eyes. I was in so much pain I was in tears. I wasn't sure I could play, but the only thing I could think about was that I couldn't pass this one up. After all, what if I never got to play here again?

Meanwhile, I was overhearing conversations going on around me, supposedly behind my back and out of earshot, between the promoters, agents and players, all trying to figure out what the hell to do. At one stage, I heard one of the promoters going, "If John doesn't play, we're going to put in Justin Gimelstob. He's offered up his services to play." Are you crazy? That loudmouth? Justin Gimelstob, whose career high in the singles world rankings was 63? He was calling the match for the Tennis Channel and I could tell they were desperate, but the thought of a Sampras, Agassi, Lendl . . . and Gimelstob event was enough to make me tie my laces up as tight as possible and announce, "OK, guys, I'm playing."

When my agent, Gary Swain, told Ivan I was going to have my ankle taped up so I could play, Ivan said, "I'm going to kill him." We were in the locker room, about to go out, when I heard Agassi saying to Lendl, "Are you going to help John out, or are you going to be a fucking pussy and beat his ass?" I think that flustered Ivan. Even though I knew he wanted to kill me, he wasn't sure what to do because it's actually tough to play an injured player. Do you play it safe or do you act like an asshole and just go for it?

Anyway, I got this incredible start. Ivan seemed to be playing it safe, so whenever I had a shot, I went for it. My mind was freed up, everything I tried was a winner. Here I was, on one leg, yet I was controlling every point. In a way, it was beautiful. Meanwhile, he freaked; 2–0, 3–0, 4–0, we were playing first to eight. At 6–3 and two breaks up, I retired. I decided that it was classier to let him "win," even though he was getting his ass kicked, because I knew that for him it was embarrassing and he was getting pissed. Anyway, by then, he knew who was boss.

I know what you're thinking: "Jeez, what happened to Mc-Enroe's competitive edge?"

1

*"I'd rather live in his world than
live without him in mine"*

Gladys Knight and the Pips, "Midnight Train to Georgia"

In 2002, when I ended my first book, I was just beginning the process of working out what I was going to do with my life now that I could no longer compete at the highest level as an athlete. Would it still be tennis—playing on the seniors tour, commentating, a bit of coaching—or something else, like art-dealing, or TV, or film? Or something totally different? I had no idea which way my life was heading, but I knew if I wanted to have new experiences that would fire me up the same way being on a tennis court had done, I was going to have to take some major risks.

I've always needed to feel challenged, to push myself, and I've tried out a lot of different stuff in the intervening fifteen years. Some of it's worked and some of it hasn't, but in life as in sports, it's often the big defeats that teach you the most. If you're too scared of falling flat on your ass, you'll never get out of your chair. And I hope that what I've learned from some of the more laughable calamities I'm going to describe for you on the pages that follow has given me a new perspective on the successes that came before.

That's why this second book is going to be much more than a chronological record of everything that's happened to me since the last one came out. The same way a tennis match alternates between service games and having to wait on the baseline preparing yourself for what your opponent might throw at you, I'm going to intercut a straightforward account of my life as it's unfolded with stories about the past experiences that made me the person I am today.

Hopefully, over the past few years I've made some progress in grudgingly figuring out how to become a better person, and am now known for more than just hitting a tennis ball and getting upset and yelling at linesmen and umpires. But I'll leave that for you to judge. Either way, I'll be dropping so many names in this book it'll make your head spin! (Only kidding . . . sort of.) And the first of those names is my wife's.

I've been with the singer Patty Smyth since 1994. We've been married for twenty of those years and are closer now than ever, which I figure is pretty amazing these days.

Patty has done so many incredible things for me, not least loving and helping me try to bring up our six kids, three of them from my first marriage. When my first book came out, the youngest was only three, the oldest, seventeen. Now they're all grown up—even the youngest will be off to college soon. We've had some ups and downs between the good times, the same as any family does, but at a point where Patty and I are going to be seeing even more of each other, the fact that I'm looking forward to that is a testament to how much we have in common. And if there's any credit for the faint possibility that I might have become a slightly better, less selfish person over the last twenty years or so, the bulk of that should go to Patty. My life was at a low ebb when I met her, and things could've turned out very differently if she hadn't been there to help me through the next few years. She's a very strong character—even more opinionated than me, if that's possible—and probably the only person who can tell me stuff I don't want to hear in such a way that I'll actually listen and take it on board. OK, maybe not without an argument, but we've learned over the years to listen and to compromise. Sometimes I'll even back down and agree that she's right. I guess it's called getting older and wiser.

Since it was kind of the beginning of me becoming who I am now, I wanted to start off by letting her put the record straight (as she sees it) about how we first got together. Even if the differences between her account and the one in my first book aren't as dramatic as she thinks they are, at least this'll give readers the chance to see what I put up with.

Patty's Perspective

John and I fight constantly about when we first met—and it's a battle that continues, because he tells the story completely differently to how I remember it. Obviously everyone has their own perspective, and people's memories can play tricks, but he does try to rewrite history, so it'll be good if I can get my version (which of course is 100 percent the truth) down in print.

The funny thing for me was how different our lives were, and yet how much we had in common—not just through the showbiz world we were both involved in, but also because we'd both been brought up in Queens. I traveled the world to meet a guy who grew up fifteen minutes from me. There's probably a reason for that, because there is something about the landscape you're raised in—the sights, the sounds, the smells—and ours had been very similar. Maybe too similar, to the point where, if we'd met too soon, it might've been a problem.

John McEnroe

I had seen John once in a club in 1984, right before my album *The Warrior* came out. Tina Turner was playing and lots of people were there, so I didn't speak to him; I think he had a girlfriend at the time. In fact, I know he did, because my friend Robert Molnar, who is in fashion and knows all the girls, was sitting with him. Anyway, John was at a table near me and he had one of those Palestinian scarves on that were kind of rock 'n' roll back then.

That's the only time I remember seeing him, which was weird in itself, because we both lived in New York, we were both into music and comedy, and we knew a lot of people in common, but we had never properly met, not once. I think there was a long while where it was meant not to be. Because if we had bumped into each other too soon I would probably have been, like, "I'm not talking to him, he's an asshole." I needed to get my ass kicked a little for us to be ready for each other, and so did he.

The first time I met John was in LA, at a party on Christmas Day 1993. My friends told me he was going to be there and they were super-excited about it, because so many people in LA are so into that celebrity thing. John always says it was a "blind date," but he doesn't know what a blind date is, which is kinda sad. First off, a blind date is where two people meet at a restaurant or someplace: a) they come alone; and b) they don't know who they're meeting. Whereas in our case—and I know he doesn't remember this, because his memory is terrible, but it did happen, and I know because I was mad that she had said this to him, or to anyone—one of my friends had told him in advance: "She's had a bad breakup and she's still getting over it, she's hurting right now." This was true, but at the same time it was nobody's business. Whatever. Let's just say I wasn't looking to get involved with anyone at that point. I might have registered, "Oh, OK, John McEnroe's going to be there," but a lot of people were going to be there.

So, I go with my daughter to this Christmas party, and I remember very clearly John walking in. He had three kids and they were like monkeys on him, because they were little then—two and a half, six and seven. He had one on each arm, and then one's wrapped around his leg, walking into the room.

We met and we talked, and I liked him.

Now I was always a chick who had a lot of guy friends. When you're in bands and you're in the music business, it's all guys—there aren't many girls. So I'd make friends with guys all the time. For example, the film director Anthony Minghella. I'd met him at my friend Carrie Fisher's house. She was like, "He's married!" She kept saying that to me. And I'm like, "That's OK, I'm not interested in him romantically!" Anthony was so funny, we laughed so much, but I had no interest in him at all. I remember Carrie couldn't wrap her head around that.

When I met John that day, I initially thought, "Oh, he's a nice guy." We talked, and then I got nervous, because I realized I actually LIKED him. He was definitely focusing his attention on me, which was making me nervous, so I went inside to make some coffee. It took so long to figure out how to make coffee in this hippy house, and I think I was purposely staying away from John for a while.

Anyway, John got a little jealous, because I was hanging out with Bing Crosby's son while we were trying to make the coffee. And it was when I came back over to him and we talked for a second time that he said this weird thing: "I'm not doing anything for New Year's Eve." That was his big line! It seemed kind of lame, and in any case I was leaving the next day for Key West—it ended up being one of the worst holidays I ever had, but that's another story. Anyway, I didn't want to leave John hanging too much when he'd put himself out there, so I tried to reciprocate to let him keep his dignity intact, and because I thought we might actually meet.

So I told him, "I come to New York all the time, maybe I'll stop by to see the gallery." That, to me, was the cue for him to give me his card or to say, "Yeah, why don't you take my number down?" But he didn't, because he was a bit dull around the edges when it came to that sort of thing. He'd gotten used to women throwing themselves at him. If you're rich, famous and happen to be hot, that's the triple crown. It didn't even occur to him to give me his card. And I would never ask for a guy's number—I'd never do it. Besides, I didn't want it that bad, because I was still licking my wounds. But I do remember feeling like something real had happened, that we had really clicked. John seemed like a sweet person. He was talking to me about his divorce and how hard it was and how he cried at night. He was very sincere, and to me—having lived in LA for four years—that was refreshing.

The following summer, I was having lunch with the girl who had set up our meeting at the Christmas party, and I asked her: "Hey, whatever happened to John McEnroe—does he come to LA anymore? When you see him again, tell him I said 'Hi,' and that I really liked him, I thought he was nice." That was it. But she got all excited and called him right away. Then it was two whole weeks before I heard back from her: "John said I could give you his number." So I said, "You know what? I don't want his number. Tell him if he comes to LA and he wants to call me, he can."

At the time I was thinking, "He's a nice guy and maybe we'll be friends." Never did I think that I would wind up marrying him, or be struck with this thing that would totally take over my life. Anyway, six weeks later, he calls me—I found out afterward that he had beaten Agassi in an exhibition soon after Andre had won the US Open, so I have Agassi losing to thank for that phone call, because that's what gave John the courage to pick up the phone.

I think John was in Arizona on a short changeover, which gave him an excuse not to stay on the phone if he got nervous. He said, "Hi, this is John McEnroe, I'm coming into town and I thought maybe we could go out." The funny thing was, I told him I was going to a lesbian party and if he wanted he could go with me—which is so politically incorrect now, but it was just my way of being glib. There was a long pause before he answered—a pregnant pause, a pregnant lesbian pause. The whole thing ended up being like the first half hour of a romantic comedy where all these obstacles are in the way.

It wasn't John that was the problem so much as the whole idea of being with anyone. John is the one that brought me back, because I was in this no-man's land: "I'm fine—I have a good life, I've been lucky, I have great friends, there is no such thing as love, real love, or monogamy. This is life, and I'm OK with it." And that's when I met him, and that's the reason why it was possible for us to end up being together, because I was fine with where I was at, and I think it was good for him to have to overcome some resistance.

So we had that first date at the lesbian party, and John fell asleep in the middle of it, in the living room, because he was totally jet-lagged, and he'd probably smoked a little pot and had a beer. Buck Henry, who was there too, looked at John and said, "Too bad about your date." We laughed so hard over that—it was hilarious, because I'd been so excited to bring a date. Here I was at a party, and I was like, "I've got a date! This is so cool." At least, it was until he fell asleep.

As I said before, John had been spoiled. Even when we were

arranging to go to the party, he asked me, "Do I have to come pick you up?" He was like that. Even he admits he got a bit seduced by the whole Hollywood side of things for a while. He'd lived in this crazy bubble since he was a kid. He was famous and constantly feted by the most interesting and glamorous people in the world. All he had to do was play tennis— he didn't have to learn about the give and take of everyday life.

When he asked about picking me up, I said, "Why don't you just meet me there, then?" He was like, "OK, I'll come and meet you . . . but will you drive us home?" And I still went! Anyway, later that night we hung out for a bit at my house, but he left at the end of the evening. The next day he came over to take me and Ruby for lunch, and afterward he had to go and play Michael Chang.

I remember going to Carrie Fisher's house that afternoon. I was so nervous, I couldn't eat. I was like, "I'm just going to do it. I'm going to go with it and be with him." I wasn't thinking far beyond that. I was so excited that I actually wanted to be with somebody, because it had been such a long time since I had felt that.

And then he came back. I wasn't planning on seeing him that night—well, we'd said we would try to get together if he got home early, but he didn't get home till 11.30. But that was the night Vitas Gerulaitis—who was John's very good friend—died in a terrible carbon monoxide inhalation accident. And John was calling me from the car.

He said, "I want to come over." I told him, "It's late, and I'm in my pajamas already, I can see you tomorrow." But he said, "I have this feeling about you and me, and I need to see you." And I said, "I don't know, I mean, what's the hurry? We have time . . ." That was when he told me that Vitas had died, and I said, "OK, you can come over." So he came, and we were together from that night on.

It was terrifying at first, because at that time I knew how to be alone but I didn't know how to be in a relationship, and John wanted us to be a couple right away. Within a few weeks, when I was still in LA and he was still in New York, he was asking me, "Do you want to have more kids?" And I said, "Yeah." I always wanted to have more kids, so I closed my eyes and sort of stepped in. It was like this River of John, and I waded out into it, and the current carried me away.

It was weird at the time, because the women who'd been there when we met that first time in Malibu were all saying, "You can't do what he wants, you can't go and see him, you have to play it cool." But I told them, "I'm not playing anything, I don't want it that bad. If it works out, great, but I'm not pretending anything. I'm just going to go, and if I want to see him, I want to see him, if I don't want to see him, I'm not going to see him."

So even though I didn't believe in true love anymore, or that you could have this sort of connection with somebody, all of a sudden I knew: "I'm going to go with this, because he's not going to do anything bad. If it doesn't work out, it's not going to be because he does something horrible to me, or winds up being crazy."

One of the things I really liked about John was that he was very forthright and very direct. I mean, he knew what he wanted, which was unusual for LA. From the beginning he was working on me to move back to New York, that I shouldn't be on the West Coast anymore. Now there was a part of me that wanted to go, cross the country right away and be with him, but the other part, the sensible part, was saying, "I can't do that, John, I have a child." I was afraid, because I had my daughter Ruby to think about, and I needed more time. We almost broke up because of that—he knew what he wanted and I was hesitating, in his mind, where in reality I was only trying to be smart about it.

Maybe it would have been OK if I'd moved back East immediately, but I couldn't do it: I couldn't give up my whole life. Because that was what I had to do. In the end, though, I did it. It took me about a year, but I gave up everything. I gave away all my stuff, I moved into his house in Malibu first, and then I was pregnant within six months. Even then, I was still trying to catch up with what had happened. He knew it was the right thing, whereas I was: "I don't know what I'm doing, but I hope it turns out OK!"

When we first met, obviously I knew who he was, but I wasn't a big tennis fan. I didn't follow the sport. He wasn't the first famous person I'd been around, so I wasn't expecting that side of it to be a big deal. But I had no idea how profoundly known John is everywhere. I mean, in African villages, they know him. Deep in Indonesia, they know him. It's weird. I'd say to him, "How do they know who you are? They don't have TVs here."

The other big adjustment was that a lot of people around me were freaked out by me being with John. Everyone started acting different, even my own family. I don't know if it was because they thought they were losing me to another world, but whatever it was, it was bizarre the way people changed. So we had this very intense connection that was just me and him, and nothing but mayhem and chaos around us. In a way, I think that worked out well, because it helped me understand what he was used to.

I hadn't been involved with anybody with that level of fame before. I'd hung out with a lot of famous people—Carrie Fisher was Princess Leia, for Christ's sake—and I'd noticed how people would be weird around them, sometimes, but this was a whole other level.

It was a challenge at the start. I always tell a story, which John's son Kevin loved the first time he heard it, about when we started dating. Very early on, in the first couple of months, John asked me to go with him to the French Open. I got on that plane with him, thinking it was a big step forward in our relationship, and he didn't say one word to me for the entire flight. He didn't talk to me or even look at me, because that's how he travels: he goes into his own world. He was on the road all the time then, and this was his way of dealing with it. But I didn't know what the problem was, so I was like, "Oh, my God, I've made a terrible mistake—this is horrible, who is this person?"

I was so mad by the time we got there that I started shouting at him—"You didn't say a word!"—and he had no idea that he'd done anything wrong. He was totally unaware. That was a big thing, in the beginning—John being oblivious. So there's definitely been an element within our relationship of it being an educational process. But one of the great things about him is that he will take direction. He always wants to be better at everything—better at tennis, better at being a father and a husband, and just a better person in general. That's part of his DNA, wanting to learn, and I find that very attractive in him, because a lot of people aren't like that, especially as they get older. And I have to say that John has taught me a lot as well.

If you asked me something about him that could be improved, it's that even now, he's a little self-centered. When I first met John, his immediate instinct was always to think about himself, and that's been a hard habit to break. He's way better than he used to be, but it's still there—even spatially. He's such a space-hog. I guess it's a sports thing, in that winning at tennis is all about controlling the space of the court, but when he's walking across a room, he'll physically barrel past you. I'm like, "Hey, man, you can't give me the right of way in our kitchen?"

It gets me mad sometimes, but he's just not thinking. He doesn't mean any harm by it, and he does try to put these things right. Nowadays he'll open the door for me in the car, though sometimes he doesn't. Or if I'm putting my coat on, he might remember to help me, or he might not. I often wonder about that, and I think maybe he didn't get taught certain basic things about manners by his parents. He was so young, emotionally, when he went out into the world that it's taken some of those things a long time to evolve.

I'm a huge Gladys Knight fan, and Gladys is a huge John McEnroe fan, and the reason John knows all the lyrics to "Midnight Train to Georgia" is because it contains his all-time favorite line: "I'd rather live in his world than live without him in mine." He loves that, because it's basically what he was asking me to do. What he was saying was: "I want you in this world, it's my world, and I want you in it, I want you to be happy in it, I want you to take care of me, and I'll be taking care of you."

2

"Good news. I fed my anger monkey a banana this morning and he's feeling much better"

Adam Sandler as Dave Buznik in *Anger Management*

Was I planning to kick-start 2002 in the way I did? No. But this opportunity fell firmly into the category of "the kind of challenges I do not pass up." Over the previous couple of years I'd had a lot of meetings with TV people. They'd noticed that my commentary was going down well, and that I was never short of an opinion. So some of these guys were tooting my horn and telling me that I could become more involved in television, possibly even with my own show if the right vehicle could be found.

These things take a long time. Out of ten meetings, one or two might lead to something. I was looking forward to spending the holidays quietly with family and friends when, right in the middle of what was meant to be an away-from-it-all Christmas vacation, I got a call from LA: did I want to host this game show, which ended up being called *The Chair*, to be aired on ABC, shooting to start early January? Of course I was interested. Game shows can be popular, and this one was being talked up as a potential big deal. The concept had originated, I believe, in New Zealand. From what I understood, it could be in the wheelhouse for me. But did it have to be so goddam urgent? Yes, apparently so, for the simple reason that Fox was about to start with a rival show, called *The Chamber*, and no, ABC did not want to lose out to them.

So in the space of a week, I found myself signed up for this show and flying back to LA a couple of days after New Year. At that stage, I'd been thinking that, outside of the commentating, the TV thing wasn't going to work for me. I'd had so many meetings to discuss so many ideas that never seemed to happen that I wasn't exactly holding my breath over a career in TV. If it happened, great; if it didn't, I knew tennis was always going to be a big part of my life.

The Chair's concept was that contestants—sitting . . . wait for it . . . *in a chair*—would have to answer seven multiple-choice general-knowledge questions, winning increasing amounts of money with each correct answer, up to a total of $250,000. However, they could only answer if their heart rate was below a certain threshold. As host, I was the one asking the questions, visible to the contestants in two ways: first, I was standing above them, and second, if they couldn't bear to look straight at me, they could see a huge image of my face projected on a screen above my head.

The chair which gave the show its title was surrounded by a ring of lit torches to up the temperature and, hopefully, the contestants' already-racing heart rate. If their heart rate redlined, going above the permitted level, they were not allowed to answer, and any money they had earned would be reduced by $100 a second while they waited for their heart rate to drop. In addition, there would be two "heart-stopper" moments of fear or surprise during the contestant's appearance, "guaranteed" to set their heart racing even faster.

In theory, it all sounded like an entertaining and original

concept: trying to get your heart rate down, maintaining a semblance of calm in a tough situation. We can all relate to that feeling—God knows I've had it in enough tennis matches, that moment when you get sweaty palms, your legs feel like lumps of wood and even breathing becomes difficult—so I thought it would make good TV. And in case you're wondering, I was assured by the producers that the contestants would be thoroughly checked over in advance for any heart problems, to make sure that coming face to face with me would not bring on a heart attack!

The doubts began to creep in almost immediately. To me, it seemed obvious that a lot of the things planned for the show weren't going to work. Some were gimmicks that seemed doomed to total and utter failure—for example, having me look down on the contestants from this giant screen like some evil wizard, yelling and screaming at them. In the first few shows, the producers kept telling me, "Scream at them. You know—'You idiot, you moron!' that sort of thing!" to which I really did reply, "You cannot be serious! That's such a dumb-ass thing to do." I mean, what a cliché, right? Plus, it clearly wasn't doing the contestants any good: they were already wound up so tight, sitting in that hot seat in front of a live audience, that every time I said "hello" to them, their hearts would leap out of their chests.

We started filming in early January with the first show going out less than two weeks later. At first, the majority of contestants failed to get below the right heart rate. One after the other they were eliminated as time ran out (the $5,000 they were given as a starting amount would drain away in, well, fifty seconds) before they could manage to bring their rate down from a pounding 140, 150 beats per minute. There was a lot of "Bring on the next contestant!" cheeriness on my part, but it was clear to me the show wasn't working. It got to the stage where I was even saying to them, "Hey, calm down." Me, of all people!

Some contestants were downright cocky when they came on but soon got the smile wiped off their faces. On one episode, this poor guy had as one of his big selling points—and I guess it was the reason he was picked to go on the show—that *allegedly* he was very sexy. Talk about setting yourself up for a fall! When I pressed him as to why exactly women found him sexy, I watched with a mixture of pity and amusement as his heart rate shot up and he lost his ability to speak. He lasted fifty seconds before having to take the walk of shame.

Another guy came on and immediately started to act all tough, trying to cut me down to size, like *I* was too big for my breeches. "Hey, I'm cool," I answered back jokingly, not rising to the bait. "Nah, you're pretty wound up, John," he countered. "Well, if I'm so uptight," I replied, "why is *your* heart rate 175?" Truth was, I felt sorry for this guy with his faux-bravado. The fact was he could barely breathe, he was so nervous.

As contestant after contestant failed to make any progress, the producers freaked out. Eventually they scrapped the time limit and told me that we could sit there for as long as it took until people calmed down enough to have a question thrown at them. In the broadcast version, they would edit this dead screen-time, but from then on during shooting we would literally sit there, waiting, waiting, sometimes as much as twenty minutes. "Jeez," I'd be thinking, "what am I doing here? This is so bogus!"

To make things worse, the so-called "heart-stopper" moments were about as frightening as a dog wagging its tail. One idea involved an alligator being let loose near the contestant. Scary, right? The poor beast was so tied up he couldn't move—in fact, he could hardly breathe—and was freaking out more than the contestant. Then there was the swarm of bees—a thousand bees were shot down from the ceiling. Scary? You've got it. Of the thousand bees, I swear, nine hundred and ninety-nine were dead.

We soldiered on despite growing misgivings, and shot thirteen episodes in total, spread over three weeks. The show was due to go out weekly, Wednesdays at 8 p.m. on ABC. Unbelievably, the first week we had about 12 million viewers and 15 percent higher ratings than Charlie Sheen's *Spin City*, which was the show we were replacing because it was on a hiatus. And when one review proclaimed *The Chair* "a huge hit," I nearly fell over. Ratings soon started to come down, but we were holding up well, because the show was broadcast at a time when parents were watching with their kids. But after about four weeks, the men in suits told the producers that we were being moved to 9 p.m. against *Everybody Loves Raymond*, the number one show in the country at the time, no less. I thought: "Wait a minute, this is supposed to be a family show, but young kids are in bed by that time. Why don't you just have us walk the plank?!"

In the end, they only aired nine out of the thirteen shows we'd taped, even though the numbers we were getting on the last episode would be considered amazing nowadays, enough to give us a top-ten show. Maybe I was crazy, but I believed in this show and thought it could be a hit if done properly, so when I was offered the chance to take the show over to Britain later that year, I figured it was worth one last try. I'd been something of a hit the previous summer when I'd joined the commentary team at Wimbledon. My supposedly "brutally honest punditry, combined with a surprisingly laid-back manner" apparently made me a suitable person to bring a new dimension to quiz shows on the esteemed BBC.

In this less extreme British version, the "heart-stopper"

moments were eliminated, the emphasis placed on the more intellectual and psychological aspects of surviving the chair. My opening remarks "keeping the lid on your heart rate means the difference between winning and losing, something I should know a bit about" were followed by a montage of me acting up on court—boy, was this tedious for me—which the live audience never failed to enjoy. How long, I wondered, was this going to define me? Or, more to the point, how long was I going to *let* it define me? Did I want to stop doing that angry shtick or should I simply accept that it was a part of me, for better or for worse? To be honest, at that stage I still hadn't figured it out.

I was surprised at the amount of time that was wasted on set in the BBC version of the show, with people who were supposed to be working seeming to spend hours doing not very much at all. I'd walk around asking what was happening and find half the crew in the bar because union rules said they had to have a tea-break—and let me tell you, they were not drinking tea. Eventually, I thought "to hell with it," and had a beer or two with them. If you can't beat 'em, join 'em, right? Plus I figured they might be on to something: so what if we weren't working the whole goddam time—why not relax a little?

The fact that for days the chair itself wouldn't even work— it didn't go up or down—was a bad omen from the start. The show saw out its ten-week run but seemed to have no prospect of coming back. On the plus side, I learned a lot from the experience, in particular that it was best not to take everything so seriously or else I'd end up tearing my hair out. I must have taken that lesson on board, because fifteen years later I've still got a bit of hair left on my head.

The Chair had been no walk in the park, but there were some things about making my first TV show as a host that I'd really enjoyed on both sides of the Atlantic: the buzz, the adrenaline of the shoot, the response of the audience. Some aspects of it reminded me of tennis. I liked the way you had to improvise your responses in the moment because there was a limit to how much you could prepare. The main difference for me was that on the court—or in the commentary box—I had a clear idea of what I was doing, I knew my trade. The game show format was new to me, so I was learning. OK, it didn't work out; but as an athlete, I've had to learn to view that sort of situation not as a failure but as a chance to improve.

Over that spring, I had meetings with various people including Brad Grey—founder of Brillstein-Grey, one of Hollywood's biggest agencies, and later head of Paramount Pictures and a major player in Hollywood—who approached me at a party. My own agency assigned me a TV agent, Chuck Bennett, and at one stage we heard that ABC—who had the rights to the NFL *Monday Night Football*, one of the highest-rated programs on TV—were looking to add someone who was not an American football specialist to the mix. They wanted a "personality" who knew a bit about football, which sounded perfect for me. What made it even more appealing was that initially they talked about using three or four different people to do four games each over the course of the sixteen-game season, which would have allowed me to keep up with my other commitments.

But the next thing I heard, comedian Dennis Miller, who happens to be a good friend of mine, got the job all to himself. As it happened, he only lasted two years, so maybe it was just as well I didn't get the gig—even though I was pretty pissed when I found out.

I read the news that he'd got it in the morning paper before playing an exhibition match with Jimmy Connors. As we were in the limo on the way to the arena I called Chuck and asked if he'd actually put my name forward to ABC. Chuck hemmed and hawed and said, "You wouldn't have gotten it anyway, John, they were looking for someone in entertainment, not sports." I fired him soon afterward, and from then on Gary Swain became my TV agent too. I don't think Chuck is losing too much sleep about this now, after running IMG Models for more than twenty years and leaving the company with a payout of tens of millions. You don't have to thank me, Chuck!

Monday Night Football soon went back to an all-football booth, and I carried on keeping my ear to the ground for the next opportunity. That's the thing: you go knocking on doors, you try to make sure your name is being considered, you wait for the callback, and in the end, so much of it comes to nothing. You have to keep putting yourself out there.

I didn't have to wait too long for my next chance to stand in front of a camera. I'd had a cameo role in Adam Sandler's *Mr. Deeds*, which had recently come out and was a big hit. Obviously blown away by my one, scene-stealing moment—throwing eggs at passing cars—the producers got down on their hands and knees and begged my agent to allow them to cast me in his next movie, appropriately called *Anger Management.*

OK, what really happened was that because of the success of *Mr. Deeds*, I thought it would be cool if I could be in the next one, especially as none other than Jack Nicholson would be starring. I mean, who wouldn't want to have the opportunity to shoot a scene with such a legend? I'd enjoyed my previous experience of filming with Adam, and it had turned out well, so when I next ran into him, I joked, "*Anger Management*? I gotta be in this movie. It's right up my alley. Come on, man, you can't even think about doing this movie without me . . ." And as he's such a nice guy, he agreed.

It wasn't easy to find a time when I was free to join the shoot in LA and film my scene with Jack Nicholson. We finally managed to find one right at the end of May. What made it a little tougher was that I had to fly out there from New York, and the following day I was contracted with NBC to commentate on the French Open in Paris. This was quite a lot of traveling to take on so I told Adam, "Listen, don't force it, if this is going to be a pain in the ass, don't worry about it." "No, no, it'll be great," he reassured me, and sent me the script.

In the film, Adam was playing a mild-mannered guy who has to have anger management counseling following a huge argument on a flight—something that I've come close to doing a few times, especially when I've been seated next to one of those people who the moment the plane lands yell into their cell phone that they've landed.

Once on set, I realized that a lot of the writing was getting done at the last minute, or that Adam was improvising there and then. He told me to go see Jack in his trailer. Jack was playing the anger management counselor, and it soon became clear to me that he hadn't even looked at the script and that he too would be winging it on set. It gave me a lot more respect for these guys, seeing the way they can turn up and ace it, no matter what.

In my scene, I'm cast as myself, I'm in an anger management help-group and end up shouting at Jack Nicholson: "I play tennis, you dumb-ass!" "I think we're going to need another session or two, Johnny Mac. You're back in the group," responds Jack, calmly. "Are you insane, Doc? You said I was out!" I shout right back. "You're in!" he explodes. "Out!" And so on. You get the picture. It was fun, going face to face with Jack, both of us red-faced and screaming at each other. It hadn't even taken me long to learn my lines!

I thought it went well, Adam seemed happy, and as we needed very few takes I went off to Paris thinking that had been yet another positive experience and looking forward to taking my family to see me on the big screen sometime the following year. I knew I didn't want to do movies on a full-time basis, but maybe I could do a few more, when the projects seemed right and fun. It would be a good way to throw a few curveballs in my life over the next few years.

My hopes of occasionally making a mark in movies took a blow in April 2003 when the film was finally released. I got a call from my oldest son, Kevin: "Hey, Dad, I saw *Anger Management* last night." "Oh yeah? How was my scene?" I was psyched to hear all about it. "Your scene? You don't have any words!" "What?" "Yeah, you're just in this crib at the end, getting a time-out like every other baby, but you don't say anything." What? No way!

A week later, I was in New York, at one of my favorite Mexican restaurants, hanging out with a couple of friends. We were standing at the bar, having margaritas, and the tequila buzz had kicked in nicely, when my phone rang and it was Adam: "Hey, Johnny—" "What the fuck happened, man?" I cut in, before he could get another word out. "Oh, well . . . I don't know . . ." And then, he just said it: "You didn't kill, Johnny, you didn't kill." There was a lot of background noise, I was with my two friends, I had to shout to make myself heard, so the conversation ended fast, let me tell you.

When I got home, I told Patty what had happened, and she was mad at me. "Why did you do that?" "Do what?" "Why did you get pissed at Adam?" "I didn't!" Not for the first time she was pointing out that I should perhaps have toned down my reaction. Poor guy. The truth was that I was angry, and I was buzzed from the margaritas, but it was his movie and he could do whatever he wanted with it. The worst part was that after watching the movie I realized he was right. I hadn't killed. In fact, my contribution was pretty mediocre.

But at least things worked out better in the European version of the film, where most of my scene did make the cut. Thank God tennis is big in Europe. So instead of me, they'd edited out the famous American basketball coach Bobby Knight, because they assumed no one in Europe would know who he was. This was a minor consolation for me, but I wasn't in another Adam Sandler movie for five years. Obviously there is a funny side to your wife ripping you a new one because you couldn't stop yourself from losing your shit when your childish tantrum cameo got cut out of the film *Anger Management*. I can see that now, although I couldn't necessarily see it then.

3

"It's 'War-hole,' actually . . . as in 'Holes'"

David Bowie, "Andy Warhol"

When I first met him, coming up through the junior ranks at the age of twelve or thirteen, Vitas Gerulaitis was already the coolest guy at the Port Washington Tennis Academy (the go-to place on the East Coast for would-be tennis stars of the future). To be honest, he was probably the coolest guy I'd met in my entire life at that point. Alongside the long curly blond hair, he had this incredible charisma that girls loved, and I remember thinking, "Man, I've got to be like this guy."

Later on, once we'd both broken onto the circuit, Vitas was still the perfect role model. He wasn't just welcome at Studio 54—the famously decadent New York nightclub which David Bowie, Robin Williams, Elizabeth Taylor, Pierre Trudeau and everyone else who was anyone wanted to go to at the height of the disco era—the guys on the door acted like their evening wouldn't be complete without him: "Yes, Mr. Gerulaitis. No, Mr. Gerulaitis." They'd roll out the red carpet for him, and he'd be hanging out with Andy Warhol, Cheryl Tiegs, Bianca Jagger and all the coolest people of the time, whereas I'd be outside practically begging to be let in. "I'm six in the world," I'd tell them, and they'd go "So? . . . Hey, McEnroe, get the hell out of here!" In fact, I don't think they even knew my name—my memory has added that in the hope of making me feel better.

Vitas was always kind to me, though—he'd never brush me off when I'd be bugging him about when we could go to Studio 54 again. And boy did he set me a good example once we were inside. He used to stay out till all hours of the night. He wore me out. By 3 or 4 a.m. I'd be like, "Listen, we've got to get out of here, I need to practice tomorrow." And he'd say, "No, no, it's fine." He seemed to know the world and to be confident within it. So when he took me down to Soho to have a look around some art galleries, I assumed that was a normal thing for tennis players to do—we had some money now, so it was natural for us to want to spend it. What's the first thing you do when you earn some money? You get yourself a place to live, you buy a nice car and a stereo (at least in those days you did), then you get some art to put on the walls.

We went to a bunch of galleries and then ended up at some kind of photo-realist show, where we both bought a couple of pieces. I wasn't particularly thinking of art as an investment then, but if it made me some money down the road, it'd be hard not to like it even more. It was just kind of fun because there was so much less at stake. After I stopped playing the main tour at the end of 1992, when I was at a loss about what to do next, it seemed a good idea to get more involved in the art world and maybe even become an art dealer while I continued to collect. In my first book, I described the way I got in on the ground floor and learned the business from the bottom up—which was a challenge I really enjoyed. I had a fair amount of success too, but by the early 2000s, other commitments—mainly tennis—were taking more of my time and I realized I'd be better off changing the gallery I'd established in Soho to open by appointment only.

Even though I was still active in the art market (and continue to be to this day), I needed to take a step back from being a professional art dealer. I'd started to feel like, "To hell with this, I'm not hanging around here anymore—these artists are even more high maintenance than tennis players." The other reason I got turned off by the art world—which was that art had become too much of a business—probably doesn't make sense at first sight. "You're buying and selling paintings: how can that not be a business, you dumb-ass?" Don't get me wrong. I'm not an "Art for art's sake" type of guy. I loved the fact that it was a business as well. But that shouldn't be *all* it is. And that's what it seemed to be turning into.

I love art and as a result know a little more about it than the average person, but I'm no expert. What I would say is that when you look at some of the biggest artists in the world right now, people like Damien Hirst, Takashi Murakami, Richard Prince, Jeff Koons—what's keeping them a step ahead of the competition isn't only their art, it's the fact that each and every one of them is a brilliant businessman who knows how to maximize the return from their talents.

Of course, that wasn't always the case, and there's no question these artists have produced great art at some point in their careers. Richard Prince, for example, was shunned by the art world for much of his career, but he stuck with his beliefs about the art of appropriation, and gradually people came around to it. And if you take Damien Hirst, when he first did that thing with the dead shark, he went to Australia, hired shark fishermen, had the shark shipped back to England and put it in a glass tank filled with formaldehyde . . . a lot of thought and effort went into it. It was cool.

At a certain point, though, artists always seem to get to this stage where they are replicating a formula. And why wouldn't they, if people are willing to pay for it? I thought Hirst's medicine cabinet pieces were great in the beginning—and I still like them—but after a while it seemed he was just running them off to make an easy buck. And some of those dot paintings he gets the people who work for him to do are ridiculously bad. But then at the same time he'll make $50 million selling his own art and spend it on a Francis Bacon. So I have to respect that and give him credit for supporting the art world, even if I'm not too wild about some of the stuff he's done lately.

If you compare Hirst with someone like John Currin, who is considered one of the top figurative painters in America, if not the world, their approaches are totally different. Currin probably only does twenty paintings a year, so if you're one of the twenty people that owns one, then you're part of a select group. I would think that would be a little more meaningful. But that doesn't seem to be what it's about these days—it's like the herd mentality has taken over. So you end up with one of the two thousand flowers Warhol apparently painted in his life—they're not my favorites; in fact, I find them boring—so everyone can say, "Hey, I've got a flower." "Hey, I've got one too." So you've both got flowers. Wow, that's *great.*

Collecting art has become a lot more complicated over the years. When I first started buying, I did it on the basis of acquiring things I liked—that I would want to put on the walls in my house. I thought that was my biggest strength—that I didn't have some kind of dogma I'd learned from studying art history holding me back. With hindsight, that probably hurt me quite a bit, financially. If I had listened to people that knew, who told me to buy certain things at certain times, pieces that I wasn't sure about, I would have done even better. I started to do that after a while, so I wasn't a total moron, but I'd still get stubborn sometimes. And that would cost me.

I'll give you an example. When I was in college at Stanford, I became friends with a guy named Doug Simon, whose grandfather Norton was a famous collector and philanthropist in the art world, who eventually had a museum named after him in Pasadena. One time on a weekend off from Stanford, Doug and I came down to LA and we stayed at his grandfather's house. I don't think his grandfather was even there, but he had all these Picassos and Matisses—it was unreal. I felt like his house was a museum. Fast forward five years, to say 1983, and Doug and I had become even better friends—in large part because of the art, which I was getting very interested in.

At that point, there was a Jean-Michel Basquiat show at the Gagosian Gallery. Back then, he was just another up-and-coming artist. If you'd told me he would go down in history as one of the transformative artists of the late twentieth century and Larry Gagosian would become arguably the biggest art dealer in the world, I'd have said "You cannot . . ." Well, you get the picture. At that time, Larry—who has since become a friend of mine—was starting out doing shows in LA, and Doug's wife, Tina, was working with him. Doug came to me and said, "You've got to buy one of these Basquiats." I went to have a look. They were $9,000, and I said, "They're terrible, they suck."

I used to do that a lot. I'd see a Lichtenstein and think, "That's total crap," and now it's worth tens of millions. With those Basquiats—even though I've got one now which I love—at first I didn't like them. I didn't get it. Doug told me, "Buy one. Trust me." But I said, "I wouldn't pay a thousand dollars for this piece." And I didn't. I thought his work looked childish, you know? I don't even remember the specific one Doug showed me, but good or bad, it's probably worth $5 million now, which would make me like it a hell of a lot more than I did at $9,000, I'll tell you that.

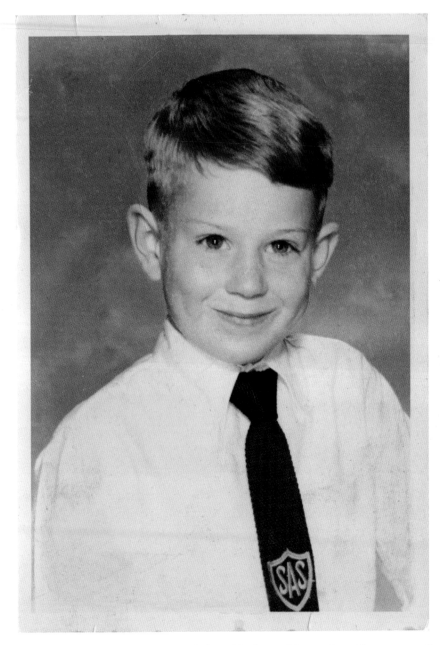

Who'd have thought this angel-faced kid would turn into the terror of Centre Court?

Establishing my commitment to doubles from an early age. My doubles
partner (Fritz Buehning, the guy in the upper left of the picture) now works
at my tennis academy.

Me at the US Open the last year it was played in Forest Hills – back when fashion mattered.

Me, Vitas Gerulaitis, Guillermo Vilas, and Björn Borg in the days when men (well, the first three of us at least) had the balls to wear short shorts. (Bob Straus)

Taking a break with Peter Fleming at Wimbledon in 1985 – who says doubles can't be fun? (Action Images/MSI/Monte Fresco)

Vitas and me modeling the double-denim look, or the "Canadian Tuxedo," as fashion insiders know it. I'm still proud to wear it today, much to my children's disbelief!

Björn Borg and me on the cover of our HBO documentary.

I longed to look as cool as my great Swedish friend and rival, but I could never quite pull it off.

Me looking unusually respectable with my mom and my late father, who always had my back.

One guy I never fully came around to was Andy Warhol, who to my mind was the godfather of that whole "getting your assistants to make the paintings" thing. I know Da Vinci and Rembrandt had a lot of help in their studios, but that doesn't seem the same to me as Jeff Koons having twenty-five people working on "his" art—or Murakami, or Hirst. Does Richard Prince even bother to do his joke paintings himself anymore? I don't know. Who cares? Maybe that's the joke, and if other people don't care, well, that's up to them.

My personal opinion of Warhol when I first came into the world he inhabited was that he was mediocre. But on top of that, he was annoying. He was always there at every party I was ever at, taking your picture late at night even when you were super fucked up. I remember thinking, "Who is this weirdo with the fake hair? Why is he waving his camera around when we're here at three in the morning? Isn't there a place where that could be off limits?"

I've heard he averaged two or three parties a night for thirty-five years—the guy was at everything! When the hell did he work on his art? When I was on the road forty weeks a year, I couldn't be going to as many parties as Andy did—nor did I want to be. But certainly those times when I was in my late teens or early twenties and you'd head over to someone's house at one o'clock in the morning and it would be kind of a mellower scene, and there would be forty or fifty people there, some of whom would be the Mick Jaggers of this world, so you could potentially loosen your collar and try to find a good-looking model or whatever . . . At that point, Warhol always seemed to be up in everyone's face with his camera, being a pain in the ass. I couldn't tell you how many times he took my picture, but even if it was only one, that was more than I wanted him to take.

I'd always known Andy was an artist, but his reputation had

taken a hit over the years and I'd heard he was doing portraits for $15,000 a pop. The problem was I couldn't relate to him as a person, and while I later came to understand and appreciate some of his work, especially the electric chairs and the car crashes, at the time I thought his art was totally lame. But what did I know? I was only a kid. So a few years later, in 1987, when he dies and all of a sudden everyone's going, "He's one of the world's greatest, unbelievable . . ." I'm like, "He *is*?"

Not long before Warhol died, I'd played a charity tennis event in Tahoe for a friend of mine whose mother had multiple sclerosis. I wanted to do something to support the charity, and one of the items being auctioned was the chance to have a portrait of yourself painted by Andy Warhol. Maybe as a joke on myself because of the way I felt about him, or maybe thinking that being part of this process might change that opinion, I paid thirty thousand dollars to have him do a pair. I was still married to Tatum O'Neal then, so that's what he was going to do—paint the two of us together.

He came over to the apartment I still live in now and took some Polaroids. All the while he was doing that, he kept saying, "It's great, it's amazing." You had no idea what this guy was thinking, because everything was "great" and "fabulous" the whole time. I guess if he only said it was good, you knew it was horrible, and if he only said he liked you, you knew he thought you were a total asshole. It's possible the guy was brilliant and I just couldn't see it, but I thought he was weird.

Anyway, once he'd taken his Polaroids he said, "I'll get back to you," and then he went off to, I presume, silk-screen the pictures using a certain angle or color—whatever he'd decided to do. We'd already paid the money and eventually we were going to end up with two Andy Warhol paintings—that was the plan. After that, a year went by and we still hadn't got the painting. So

I said to Tatum, "Call him and find out what the hell's going on," and she does. His people told her, "He's working on them—in fact, he's taking a special personal interest in them—they'll be great, don't worry about it."

A couple of months later, he dies. There's still no sign of the pictures, so Tatum rings his people again to check what's happened. Luckily, it turns out they have been finished, and they send them both over.

Five more years pass, and Tatum and I are getting divorced. At that point I say to her, "You should take one of these Warhol portraits, and I'll have the other." It made sense for us to have one each, but things weren't too happy between us and she told me, "Forget it—I don't want one." I guess she didn't want to look at me.

Now, at the time—this is 1992, and Warhol died in 1987—the paintings hadn't gone up much in value. I'm going to put them at fifty grand each. And by the way, who the hell would want a picture of me and Tatum at that stage, right? We weren't love's young dream anymore—we were getting divorced. So I thought the best thing to do would be to give one of the pictures to each of my kids. The problem was I only had two Warhols, and I had three kids with Tatum.

Around this time an old friend of mine named Richard Weisman alerted me to the fact that sometimes Warhol would run off extra copies of his portraits. Richard put me in touch with the Warhol Foundation, where I got in contact with Tim Hunt—brother of the late James Hunt, the British Formula One racing driver—who worked there. I asked him, "Is there a third portrait? I'd like to buy it if there is, so I can give one to each of my kids." Tim said he'd look into it and the process went on for what seemed like years, until I finally found out that there wasn't another picture, only the beginnings of a drawing of me and Tatum. That sounded interesting, but when I saw it, it was only half or even a third finished. Believe me, I wanted it to be good—"Why don't I get the drawing? That would solve the problem?" But when I saw it, it was horrible . . . terrible—and it wasn't even signed. So no way was I buying it.

The ridiculous part of all this was that my kids didn't seem to want the pictures that much. It was just me being stubborn and trying to resolve the issue. A few more years passed, I'd say we're up to the mid 2000s now, and interest in the portraits—and Warhol's work in general—had grown. Someone asked me if they could have one for a show, and they said it was probably worth $100,000. I thought, "Great, if you can get a hundred grand for it from someone, go right ahead." So they took one, but it didn't sell.

Then someone else who knew I had the pictures asked if they could borrow one for an exhibition of portraits by Warhol and various other people. This happened a few times, and the value kept going up: one minute someone thought they were worth $75,000 the next it was $200,000. Either way, no one bought them. I was starting to get confused. I mean, OK, Björn Borg didn't need them, but you'd think Jimmy Connors might have wanted one for his bathroom!

Eventually I put one of the paintings up for auction with Sotheby's in London, who'd told me they could get half a million dollars for it. They weren't far wrong, because someone bought it for $440,000. I think Sotheby's took a $31,000 commission—I don't know how that amount came up, but I wasn't complaining because the sale made over 400 grand.

The best way of dealing with the fact that I'd finally sold this goddam painting seemed to be by donating the entire proceeds of the sale to charity. And this was where Andy Warhol managed to embarrass me one last time from beyond the grave. The cause I decided to donate it to was Habitat for Humanity, which is the charity Jimmy Carter started. They go to places all over America, and the world, and help poor people build their own houses. It's a great organization. And I think somehow, because I'd given them all this money, I got the idea that I was going to get a call from them.

I was seventeen when Jimmy Carter was elected, and at that time I thought he was one of the coolest guys ever. I never got to meet him, and I realize that in some ways he was considered to be a disastrous president, but outside of the White House he has turned out to be a great person who has done some amazing things. So I ended up convincing myself that now after all these years I was finally going to have a private meeting with Jimmy Carter. And then I got this invite that said, "Jimmy and Rosalyn invite you to Plains, Georgia with 250 other people for a retreat." And I'm like, "Really?"

Patty set me straight about this, as she often does. She told me, "You shouldn't expect anything, or it means you gave the money for the wrong reason." I realized she was right. When you expect it, that's when it's not going to happen. I mean, who the hell was I to expect something just because I gave a donation? It was an interesting lesson and I was humbled by it. I thought mine was going to be the biggest single gift, until I saw the budget. Some people were in for $50 million, and mine was one of God knows how many donations at that level—enough to get a letter from Jimmy Carter that began "To whom it may concern . . ." Hey, a handwritten note would've been nice, but no hard feelings.

I still have the other painting—it's in storage somewhere; I don't think Patty would want that above the mantelpiece, even in the unlikely event that I did. And you know something, I'm happy I did something good for charity, but I still wish I hadn't sold it and instead had got a third painting so I could've given one to each of the kids I had with Tatum. It was my daughter Emily who expressed the greatest interest early on; one time she even asked me, "Could I hang it in my dorm room at college?" I told her, "No, doing that would probably not be the best idea!" But at least she wanted it, plus both my sons have been giving me a hard time lately, so she's the clear favorite to get it at the moment.

4

"I love Paris in the springtime . . ."

Cole Porter

Even while I was pursuing other career options and interests at the start of the 2000s, I had no intention of turning my back on my work as a commentator.

For me, being in the commentary box is an opportunity to have a voice in the game. It won't surprise you that I've got a few things to say—on doubles, on the lack of serve-volleyers in today's game, on wooden racquets, on let-cord serves, on gamesmanship, on . . . Do you want me to go on? As self-appointed "Commissioner of Tennis," it is my duty to do that.

At first I would get upset when people told me I was a better TV commentator than I was a player—it took me years to realize they were paying me a compliment. I started behind the microphone back in 1992, when the dominant style of commentary was incredibly dry and boring (or at least, I thought it was). My timing was good, because tennis on TV was crying out for a change of style. Again it was Vitas Gerulaitis who showed me the way. Vitas had begun working for USA Network not long before I did, and his informal style certainly paved the way for me to hit the ground running with a more relaxed approach.

But what I was doing still felt a bit different from what had gone before—especially once I got a contract with NBC. I liked being able to talk about the game in what I hoped was a conversational way, as if I was sitting round with some friends, talking about what I was watching.

It wasn't till 2000 that I started working for the BBC. They'd been asking for years but NBC waited for the new century to start before they agreed to share me. "Just be yourself," was the message from the men in suits. And that's what I did, and I guess it's worked because I'm still in that BBC booth at Wimbledon every year.

The various television networks I commentate for have different ways of doing things. The main difference between the American ones—CBS, NBC, USA Network and ESPN—and the BBC is that there are no ad-breaks for the BBC. For the American networks, I've got to get my thoughts in during play, whereas for the BBC I have the luxury of talking at the change of ends. The only downside is you always have to obey the BBC's golden rule, which is: Do not, under pain of death, talk during an actual point. Holy Moses, I swear it's more fucking important to them than not swearing on air.

When it comes to my commentating style, I try to be honest, though I'm always respectful—I hope—of the players I'm watching. Whatever the level of tennis, I know it takes guts to be out there. I don't make it about me, either, so I won't speculate about what I would be going through if I was on court, or compare what's happening on court with what I might have gone through in a similar match. I won't reminisce what it was like for me, say, in my final of 1980–whatever, because half the viewers weren't even born then. And anyway, who cares? Viewers want some insight into what they're watching, not some old fart going on about what he might have gone through thirty years before with his wooden racket. Which isn't to say I don't think what I did with that Dunlop wasn't pretty cool at times. I just don't want to keep reminding people.

My commentating commitments give the year a familiar structure, built around the Grand Slam tournaments—the French Open at Roland-Garros, Wimbledon, the US Open. I didn't start working on the Australian Open till 2003, so up till then my Grand Slam commentary season started in Paris. As the song suggests, there are worse places to be in the spring-time, but men's tennis was in a bit of a dry spell in 2002, with no one player dominating and no particular rivalry to set the juices flowing.

The French Open that year was won by Albert Costa, beating Juan Carlos Ferrero to win his only Grand Slam title. This was a time—tough to remember—when that tournament was won by Spaniards *other* than Rafa Nadal. And Wimbledon hadn't yet entered the era of Roger Federer's dominance. Instead, it was Lleyton Hewitt's year to win the title, beating David Nalban-dian in straight sets. "This is a real ripper," Lleyton memorably said to Sue Barker in the on-court post-match interview after lifting that trophy. Credit to the guy, though: Lleyton had won on the back of his US Open win the previous year. He'd also been world number one at the end of the year, so he totally deserved that victory. On the other hand, David Nalbandian, who went on to have a great career and reach world number three, had got to the Wimbledon final in his first ever grass-court senior tournament. As Sue Barker pointed out, he'd even managed to go one better than I had in 1977 when I'd reached the semis. That hadn't escaped my notice either, Sue. But as good as Nalbandian was as a player, he never got to another Slam final.

In contrast, the women's game was in an exciting place at

that time, with great players like Monica Seles, Jennifer Capriati and Martina Hingis—and that was even before Maria Sharapova came into the mix. But the biggest thing that was happening in women's tennis was the way the Williams sisters, Venus and Serena, were totally shaking it up. From Paris, to Wimbledon, to the US Open finals of 2002, they had an amazing run of facing each other in three consecutive Grand Slam finals. That was a crazy situation. Many people wondered what or who the hell was going to stop these two sisters from completely dominating the sport for years to come—an awesome and yet very real prospect.

Personally, I had mixed views on that. On the one hand, what they had achieved was amazing. They had fought their way into what is still basically a white person's sport, they had the most incredible physiques, and they had the most unbelievable determination and focus, so I thought, "Good luck to them." On the other hand—and this may surprise you because you might think I don't give a damn about that sort of thing—for the sake of the game I prefer it when the prizes are spread out amongst more players, rather than have the same people winning all the titles. So I wasn't too keen on utter domination by Serena, Venus, or anyone else for that matter.

The Williams sisters' father, Richard, obviously saw things differently. It's not like I know Richard well, but in person he is somewhat likable and seems incredibly smart, and at the previous year's French Open we'd had a funny dinner together where he was giving me advice on which new avenues I should explore. First he told me I should get my own perfume, because there was a lot of money in perfumes. Then he told me he owned some big ship—like a navy battleship or something, only three in the world like it, apparently—and I should think about that too. If I'd been able to get a word in edgewise, my first question would have been, "Why?" God knows. I never got to ask.

You had to admire the guy, he was certainly thinking outside a pretty big box, making my own thoughts of doing some dumb-ass game show feel lame. But I swear he talked all evening. I was left dumbstruck by so much of what he said, incredulous, in fact. I figured that some of it was probably true, it was just impossible to tell which part. Richard is one of the great characters of the game, and what his two daughters have achieved is truly extraordinary, so I'm in awe of him. But I still don't think the world is a poorer place because it lacks a Johnny Mac perfume, even though Eau de McEnroe does have a certain ring to it.

Straight after Wimbledon of 2002, I came back to New York to play Team Tennis for a week, something I'd been doing for a few years. Some of you diehard tennis fans out there might remember that Team Tennis was big for a while in the 1970s, when players like Borg, Connors, Nastase and Chris Evert signed up to play for various teams around America, competing in matches staged at major venues like Madison Square Garden. For a while it was so big that it threatened to damage the main tour and even the Grand Slam tournaments, which would suffer through their absence.

It was championed (and still is) by Billie Jean King, and the format remains unchanged today: five sets of tennis—one of men's singles, one of women's, one of men's doubles, one of women's and one set of mixed. The idea is to have a different take on tennis, to make it more of a showcase, to inject more razzmatazz. There are no ad-scores; lets are played on serves. Playing as a team can be fun, with guys and girls together—something that hardly ever happens on the pro tour—so I think it can still have its place, even though the venues tend to be small these days and it's down to a three-week season starting at the end of Wimbledon.

As the summer of 2002 came to an end, I found myself back at Flushing Meadow calling the US Open for CBS and USA Network for the eleventh consecutive year. This was a special tournament, because it was the first US Open since 9/11, which happened two days after the end of the 2001 event. To mark this, during the opening ceremony before the first night session, a huge US flag was unfurled onto the main Arthur Ashe Stadium court by New York police officers, firemen and women, plus armed forces personnel, reminding us of the role they played on that indescribably terrible day almost a year before, one that had changed the world forever. It was also a way to show everyone that, despite what had happened, New York and the USA were still very much there, still proud of who we were and what we stood for. New York City Mayor, Michael Bloomberg, gave a speech and I was honored—choked up actually—to be asked to say a few words, along with Billie Jean. Other American champions such as Chris Evert and Jimmy Connors were also there and it felt like there was a kind of karma to the fact that all four singles finalists that year—Venus and Serena, Agassi and Sampras—were American.

So there I was on Super Saturday, the day at the US Open when the two men's semis were played, followed by the women's final in the evening. For the US networks, it was the biggest tennis day of the year, and having an all-American women's final with the two biggest names in the sport was definitely an added ratings boost. As one of CBS's key commentators, I was supposed to do an on-camera intro piece before the match and had been told I'd be filming at 8.10. All the networks I work for know that I come in at the last minute. For a while they would get very nervous and uptight, wondering where the hell I was. Now they're all used to me cutting it fine, because they know I always show up.

Except this time. I was in the food area with Paul McNamee, former Aussie doubles great and at that time tournament director of the Australian Open. Paul and I were discussing whether I could come and do some commentating for Channel 7 in Australia the next January. It was the only Slam that I hadn't done any commentating on, because ESPN had the rights and at the time I wasn't working for them. So there we were, deep in discussion about whether I could do the second week at the tournament and what my role might be. We were getting close to finalizing the deal and at that point it was about 8:02, 8:03—plenty of time—when I happened to look up at a television monitor nearby and saw that the on-camera coverage had begun. Jesus, I was nowhere near. I'd totally blown the network off and missed the build-up to the year's biggest night of American tennis. To say that this was embarrassing would be an understatement. I left Paul standing, mouth open, mid-sentence, and ran. I made it back to the booth just in time for the start of the final, but someone had had to cover for me in my absence. Nothing was said, but it was not my finest moment. Oh, and Serena beat Venus in straight sets.

On reflection, my mind had been distracted, not by my conversation with Paul—which did eventually result in me cutting a deal to do the following year's Aussie Open—but because my ego had taken a hit earlier in the day when I'd played Boris Becker in an exhibition match. The year before, Boris had pulled out at the last minute, and I hadn't been too pleased. He'd claimed that he had sore feet and bad ankles, but I'd said that it had been more a case of having cold feet. This year, he'd honored his commitment, and we played in the main stadium, the 23,000 Arthur Ashe venue. Boris, who was hardly playing at the time, had tried to get into shape by warming up with a couple of seniors tournaments beforehand. My preparation had consisted mainly of sitting in a commentary booth for thirteen days. Not the best way to get in shape and not easy, after calling both of the men's semis earlier that day for several hours, to leap up and say, "OK, here we go, fifteen thousand people, let's kick ass."

Before the game, both of us were concerned about our ability to perform and to put on a good show for the crowd. We didn't want one of us to come out 6–1 6–0 winner in forty-five minutes—that's never the goal in an exhibition. So Boris said, "OK, let's win one set each, and then we can play out the tie-breaker in the third." Seniors tennis usually has the format where you play two sets, followed by what they call a "Champions' tie-breaker" where it's first person to 10. That way the matches don't go on forever, the public doesn't have a chance to get bored, even if it's a terrible level of tennis—which believe me sometimes happens at our age—and everyone goes home happy, having seen two and a bit more sets of hopefully decent sports, mixed in with some on-court banter between a couple of old rivals.

I'd never played in the stadium named after my old Davis Cup captain before—it didn't exist when I was on the circuit—and when I first came out onto the court, I thought, "This is OK, I've still got some pop in my body." But it soon became apparent that Boris had considerably more pop than me. After all, he was only thirty-four, whereas I was fully nine years older at forty-three, so although I was reasonably confident, he ended up being the one doing all the leaping around.

If Boris had read the seniors script, he'd forgotten it by the time we got out on court. Before the match he'd seemed more worried than I was about potentially laying an egg, but it turned out it was me who ended up looking bad, as Boris over-compensated for his performance anxiety by beating me in straight sets, 6–4, 7–5. This was annoying, but if I'd asked him what happened, Boris would probably have said, "John, I tried to make it one set all so we could play the tie-break, but you were just too terrible." The worst part of it was, I couldn't have disagreed with him.

Losing to Boris in that way made me mad, no doubt about it. I decided I had to be in better shape, go for that extra push. The days when I could rely on being the old Johnny Mac who'd worked out in a casual way, relying on his tennis skills to get through matches, were long gone. Time was starting to catch up with me, the younger oldies were starting to beat me, and I sure as hell didn't want to wake up one day unable to get close to the sort of level of tennis I was used to, simply because I hadn't taken care of myself. I'd seen other past champions slide down that path, and it didn't appeal to me.

So I called up a trainer I knew named Pat Manocchia. He owns the gym I use in New York, not too far from where I live. Pat created a great program that pushed me to my limits. Ever since then he's somehow managed to keep me on the road, in as close to peak condition as the passing of time will allow. Because, let's face it, there's a limit to the number of miracles that can be performed on an old guy like me.

5

*"I'm standing in the middle of life
with my plans behind me"*

The Pretenders, "Middle of the Road"

After that relative low point, the highlight of the fall of 2002 was undoubtedly joining Chrissie Hynde onstage at Madison Square Garden when the Pretenders opened for the Rolling Stones. No two ways about it, that was one cool gig.

In the early years of being on the tour, I'd never realized how good it could be to *play* music as well as listening to it. When you're on the road, there's a lot of time to kill in those hotel rooms and playing the guitar helped relieve the boredom. My first guitar was a very heavy electric Les Paul. I didn't know there were others out there that were quite a bit lighter. So I struggled on with that for a while. Even though I found it difficult and fatiguing to play because it weighed so much, I continued to take it everywhere with me on my travels. Then one day, about ten years ago, Paul Simon, who used to work out at Pat Manocchia's gym, gave me a guitar. Or rather, we traded: he was looking to work on his arms, so I gave him a heavy-duty piece of cardio equipment I had, and he gave me a beautiful light acoustic guitar, specially made for me, with marble inlays and my name on it. Something tells me I got the better deal.

In any event, I've been playing and making music—well, that's what I call it—for some years now, though I've long since accepted that I'm never going to be Grand Slam standard when it comes to rock 'n' roll. Patty once memorably said that I "wrestled the guitar into submission," which sums up my relationship with the instrument. As a matter of fact, I've wrestled—or should I say smashed?—a few into submission over the years in frustration, after seeing real musicians like Buddy Guy play, or listening to live tapes of one of my own shows

Much as I love playing, the guitar doesn't love me back. The same goes with singing. In fact, I'm no longer allowed to sing at home when Patty's around, which I understand, given that she's the singer in the family and has built a whole career from writing and singing great music, whereas I can just about sing in key. She put her foot down one day, not too long after we were married, making a couple of things crystal clear. First, if I was still harboring any hopes of getting to play with her onstage regularly, I'd better let them go, because she'd never worked with anyone she was involved with and never would. Second—and this was the killer blow—"The Lord doesn't let you be one of the greatest tennis players that ever lived and then be Keith Richards. It just doesn't work that way." As so often, Patty was right, advising me—no, telling me—to stick to jamming with friends, something that I still enjoy doing to this day.

Occasionally though, a friend will be generous enough to invite me to join them onstage during one of their gigs. Which is how I came to play with Chrissie Hynde. Actually, it wasn't the first time I'd played a song with her on stage, but in front of a sold-out crowd, at the Garden? That was amazing and definitely one of my top ten rock 'n' roll experiences.

She told me which song I would be doing—"Middle of the Road"—and I practiced and practiced to make sure I got it right. When I arrived, I was told it would be the second to last song, so I sat backstage, trying to enjoy the evening, but understandably a touch nervous as I waited to be called.

Inevitably, the moment came. "Ladies and gentlemen," Chrissie announced, "I've got a friend of mine, a special guest, who's gonna come out and play with me: John McEnroe!" That's when you hope you don't walk out to "Boooo" from half the Garden crowd—which luckily I didn't. That would have been somewhat deflating, especially as it's my home city, my home stadium, and I've lost count of the number of concerts, tennis matches or sports events I've been to (or played in) there.

Anyway, we started the song, although I was too worried about messing up to be able to enjoy the moment. Then, halfway through, I broke a string. I'm not going to pretend that the whole show fell apart, but it was a pain. I had wanted to feel I was adding something, and Chrissie knew I had the chords down. Even though I wasn't going to be playing an intricate guitar solo, I wanted her to feel I was hitting the right chords and doing something to justify being on stage with her. So losing that string put me out of tune a bit but, as they say in rock 'n' roll, "The show must go on." It was scary, because I'm not as good at adapting when I break a string on my guitar as when I break a string on my racket. But I got through it, to sympathetic cheers at the end, and I'd certainly made progress since Joe Walsh invited me to play with him onstage at the LA Forum, shortly after I'd beaten Borg at Wimbledon, and I'd had to turn him down because I knew I wasn't good enough (though the fact that he changed the words of "Rocky Mountain Way" in honor of my victory still meant a lot).

The other problem is that I'm a lefty. Unless you're Jimi

Hendrix and enough of a genius to play a right-handed guitar upside down, then the only way you can play is if you bring your own guitar, which is good in a way, but in another way bad, because if you do bring it, it's like, "Oh, I happen to have my guitar with me."

I've never had any illusions about my level of musical ability. On the rare occasion when anyone is kind enough to give me a compliment in that area, I'll usually reply to their somewhat over-generous "You're a good guitar player," with: "Yeah, for a tennis player, really good. But for a musician, er . . ."

Being lucky enough to watch very talented people play up close is one way of keeping your feet on the ground about your own abilities. One time in the 1990s I went with Chrissie to see Jeff Buckley play at this tiny place, when he was just starting out. It wasn't my cup of tea musically, because I didn't know his stuff at the time and he was singing in this bizarre voice, but there was no question the guy was a hell of a musician. Chrissie asked him if he wanted to come along and jam at her rehearsal afterward, and he did. So then he stepped up and it turned out he knew every song the Pretenders had ever written, and every note the original guitar players had ever played. He even seemed to be playing better than them—"Oh my God, this guy should be in the band." What a great night that was. But sadly Jeff died—drowning in the Mississippi—not long afterward. The mortality rates in rock 'n' roll are no joke.

I can't deny that the time when I suddenly found myself hanging out with the rock musicians I'd admired from afar was one of the most exciting experiences of my life. One minute I was playing air guitar in Rob Ellis's basement with my high school fraternity friends, and going to see Led Zeppelin at Madison Square Garden as a fan and complaining 'cos the gig didn't sound exactly like the records. The next thing I knew I was hanging out with Robert Plant and he was telling me what *I* did was cool. There's a quote by the film director Richard Linklater—I was reading an article recently about him in *Men's Journal*—where he says "If someone says to me the best years of your life are in high school, I'd say that's fucking pitiful." Well, that's me in a nutshell. If I didn't ever talk again about the first eighteen years of my life, I'd be perfectly fine. Because to me it all changed in a dramatic way when I went to Wimbledon in 1977. Before that I don't remember much anyway—which pisses Patty off. She'll say, "Not one Christmas? Not a birthday?" But that's the way it is.

I guess there was a fair amount of tennis practice involved, plenty of tournaments, a lot of traveling. The tennis wasn't full-time until I was eighteen, but it was always enough to make me feel separated from the other kids at school, because most kids didn't play tennis. Unlike football or baseball, tennis wasn't considered cool—everyone thought it was a sissy sport, so I felt out of the loop.

What made it worse was that, apart from me and one other person in Douglaston Manor—which was where I lived—all the other kids went to high school in Queens. That one other boy who went to the same school as me—Trinity, in Manhattan— got expelled for cheating in the tenth grade, so from that point on I was the only one. It wasn't that I didn't have any friends, but when I'd be with them I felt that they were always a little closer-knit with each other than they were with me.

Commuting was a major factor. Because I was the only kid at school who came from Queens, a lot of the parties—especially early on—I wasn't invited to, or if I was, I'd have to be home and not stay out too late. I couldn't learn to drive until I was seventeen, which was halfway through eleventh grade. So that was one reason I didn't enjoy high school—not that it was terrible, the whole thing just seemed a bit off to me. I remember praying that these wouldn't be the best days of my life, and as it turned out, they weren't.

As a teenager, I remember sitting up and taking notice when the girls started screaming for Björn Borg in his first year at Wimbledon. It was like something out of Beatlemania. I began to take the sport I was playing a bit more seriously.

Once I started going to Europe to play Wimbledon every year, I went from being the kid who played the sissy sport to someone who was cool enough to hang out with the British rock stars who'd been my heroes. That was one of my greatest perks when it came to success on the tennis court. I'd never have imagined rock guys like Robert Plant being into Wimbledon—that was the opposite of what I would've expected. But the Stones, Zeppelin, all these bands I'd grown up loving—even Tony Iommi of Black Sabbath—were telling me, "You're great," or, "Wow, I really respect what you're doing." I was still only a kid at the time, and I remember thinking, "Holy shit! This is amazing!"

I met the rest of the Pretenders before I met Chrissie. They turned up at the flat I was staying in on the night I won Wimbledon for the first time, in 1981. In fact, they were the reason I got in trouble for not going to the Champions Dinner. My father called me and said, "Look, these guys, they want you to go to this dinner." I asked him, "Do you think it's important to go?" And he said, "I don't know. I'm not going to say yes or no."

At that point I remember thinking, "Look, I'm hanging out with these rock guys—why the hell would I want to leave all this behind to waste my time with some bunch of old farts?" So I said, "Forget that, I'm not going."

I might've been the Wimbledon champion, but I knew I wasn't in the same league as these rock guys when it came to partying.

At one point the Pretenders' guitarist James Honeyman-Scott asked me, "Do you know where I can get an eight-ball?" I wasn't even entirely sure what that was—I guessed it was a mix of heroin and speed or cocaine or whatever, but either way, it was a long way out of my comfort zone—which was probably just as well; less than a year later, James sadly died of a drug overdose. Within another year or so the Pretenders' original bass player, Pete Farndon, was dead too. Chrissie and the drummer—my old buddy Martin Chambers—were the only survivors.

The Rolling Stones were also people who took it to another level. The first time I met them was in 1981, on the *Tattoo You* tour at the Meadowlands in New Jersey. As usual, it was Vitas who took me backstage. After making our way through all the different areas you have to go through, we eventually got back to a room where only Keith Richards, Ronnie Wood and the guitar tech were hanging out, and they said, "Come on in." They were warming up before the show, having a drink and party-ing pretty hard. I was thinking, "How the hell are these guys going to play?" I'm not sure what the exact time was. I think they'd announced to the crowd they'd be going on at 9.30, but the crew knew the real time would be well after 10. As they were hustling us out so they could finally go on stage, someone said, "Mick Jagger wants to say hello," so the next thing we know Vitas and I are smoking a joint with Mick Jagger. He's talking away and seems reasonably happy to see us, but all the people running things were totally freaking out because by now they were well past the time that even the Rolling Stones knew they were meant to be on at—heading for what would later become Axl Rose territory. That was a memorable night.

The next time I saw them was not long afterward, when Ronnie and Keith came to the ATP Finals at Madison Square Garden—the big end-of-year tournament which is now held at the O2 Arena in London. I was playing Vilas in the semis. Of course they showed up late. I was at the changeover and someone started tapping me on my shoulder. I'm trying to ignore it, because that's how you are in a match, but this guy's going, "John, John." I'm about to tell him to get lost, but when I turn round, it's Ronnie! I had this incredible jolt of adrenaline, I've got to say, to see Ronnie Wood and Keith Richards sitting in their leather pants at a tennis match.

Athletes tend to be lean, but these guys have absolutely no extra bodyweight on them. It's amazing how skinny they are—they make Iggy Pop look fat! Patty and I went to Ronnie's house in London once, where he lived for twenty-five years. He and his then wife Jo were the nicest people in the world, Keith and his wife came over too, and the two Rolling Stones' wives cooked us this huge elaborate dinner and served it, buffet-style. Now both of these guys load huge amounts of turkey-meat onto their plates—it felt like Thanksgiving to me—but they don't eat any of it. I'm thinking, "I'm the only guy eating, this is amazing!"

A few years later, Ronnie invited me to his place again. He told me, "John, I haven't had a drink in nine days," and I said, "God, that's great, Ronnie." Apparently he'd gone to the hospital and the doctors told him, "Your liver's so shot, you're going to die if you keep drinking the way you have been." But then Ronnie asked me, "You want a bump? You want a hit of weed?" I remember thinking, "Are coke and weed OK now?" That was pretty unconventional medical advice, but I guess desperate times call for desperate measures. What do I know?

Somehow he managed to stop drinking—I think he's still sober at the time of this writing. You can tell how long ago this was because it was back in the days of fax machines. Apparently Ronnie sent a fax to Keith, who was at his place in Connecticut, saying, "Look, I haven't had a drink for nine days." Now Ronnie loves Keith like he's his older brother—basically looks up to him more than any human being on earth—so he adds something like, "Aren't you proud of me?" And Keith sends him a fax back saying, "You're a fucking pussy, call me when you're drinking again." I remember Ronnie started laughing hysterically—he thought that was the funniest thing ever—and that made me start laughing too.

They're two very different disciplines—rock 'n' roll and sports. People ask me: "If you had the choice, would you rather have been a tennis player or the guitarist in a rock band?" And even though there's something unbelievably intoxicating about the idea of being in a band, ultimately I'd always pick sports.

First because I love sports—not just tennis, but basketball, football, athletics, boxing, whatever—but also because, for me, there's always a certain time of night where I'll get jittery and start to think, "I've got to go to sleep." That time might have been four in the morning when I was younger. But now if there's a gig someone wants me to go to that doesn't start until eleven or twelve, I'll say, "Isn't it a little late?" Maybe age has turned me into a lightweight, but I couldn't handle the world Keith and Ronnie live in (although I did try). Those guys are night owls.

6

*"Ever tried. Ever failed. No matter.
Try again. Fail again. Fail better."*

Samuel Beckett

If I tried to convince you I'd got that quote from my close reading of the work of the Nobel Prize-winning Irish writer, you'd probably think I was bullshitting. And you'd be right. I got it from a tattoo on Stan Wawrinka's arm. No one bats an eye when a tennis player gets a tattoo these days, but imagine the kind of British tabloid shitstorm there would've been if I'd turned up to Wimbledon with one in the late seventies! Going back to Samuel Beckett, though, he definitely had the right idea when it came to my career hosting TV shows.

One afternoon in 2003 I was on my way to play tennis in New York when I got a call from the producers of the David Letterman show. The host of the huge, daily, prime-time *Late Show* had come down with shingles and could I stand in for him that afternoon? "What, now?" "Yeah, now. Come down to the studios, we tape in a few hours. Can you do it?" "Er, yeah, I guess, sure!" I mean, what else could I have said? "Sorry, I've got to go practice?" So I literally did a U-turn in the street and headed downtown to the studios, like Superman saving the day, only minus the tights with the underpants outside.

I thought they'd be all over me as soon as I got shown into the studio—thanking me profusely, briefing me on what to do. But it was like "no big deal." I waited around for a while, but no one even approached me, so I went to find someone who looked like they were working on the show. "Maybe we should try to decide what we're doing here . . . do we do a monologue or not?" I asked. "Do you wanna do one?" "I don't know . . . er . . . maybe?"

To me, this seemed the kind of basic question anyone would want answered if they were being asked to step into Letterman's shoes *for the first time* at such short notice. But could I get an answer? Everyone was so casual, no one seemed to care about what I should or shouldn't be doing. I like to think I'm good under pressure, but this was somewhat outside my comfort zone. Nowadays, I'd probably be more relaxed, but at the time, I needed to know what was going to happen. After all, this was a show that a lot of people would be watching, and I didn't want to be known as the guy who replaced Letterman and totally sucked.

Not long before we started taping the show—which was to air later that evening—somebody did finally run through a couple of last-minute jokes they'd written for me. The material wasn't too bad and I delivered it with as much conviction as I could. But throughout the monologue I heard myself blurting out, "Hey, pretty good for a sports guy!" which was kind of lame, although it was probably an accurate reflection of how I was feeling.

You might be wondering why I got the call-up in the first place. Don't think I didn't ask myself that same question. It's possible they'd asked half of Manhattan and everyone said no, so that's why they'd wound up at my door less than two hours before the show. Or they might have been waiting until the last minute to see if David would pull through. He must have been really sick because he missed a month of shows. Bruce Willis did one the day after me, so there were some bigger names than me in the frame. Presumably my name came up because I'd been on Letterman regularly for the last I-dunno-how-many years, I'd had meetings over the last two or three with David and his producers, and they were saying positive things about me and how I should do more TV. But I was still surprised to get that call.

The guests that evening were actor and comedian Tom Arnold (who used to be married to Roseanne Barr), New York comedian Todd Barry, and Éric Ripert, the chef of Le Bernardin, the three-Michelin-star restaurant here in Manhattan. It all went well with the American guests. But when it came to Mr. Ripert, a proud Frenchman, I admit I may have mentioned somewhere during the interview—because let's not forget, this was not long after 9/11—that the French weren't exactly supporting the Americans in the war on terror. I'd hardly called them cheese-eating surrender monkeys, but as far as Mr. Ripert was concerned the atmosphere deflated as fast as a soufflé in an ice-box. During the taping, I didn't particularly notice and thought the show went well, but Éric Ripert never forgot. Over the years he seemed to get more and more pissed about it, until it reached a point where he was asked in an interview, "Who is the one person you wouldn't serve in your restaurant?" And he named me. Can't say I didn't feel like shit about that. (Luckily this feud was laid to rest after Patty found herself sitting next to his wife at a charity lunch and they overcame some initial awkwardness to discover that they got on really well.)

After taping the show, it was still early evening, so I was able to go on to a benefit evening for an autism charity that Adam Sandler supported. There, riding high from my supposed success, and still running on adrenaline, I bumped into Jon Stewart, who had not long before started his *Daily Show*—which went on to (deservedly) become an incredible success, until he stepped down in February 2015. But when I told Jon what I'd just done, and bearing in mind how big *The Late Show* was, he couldn't help himself: "You mean you actually *hosted The Late Show*?" Did I detect a note of sheer incredulity in his voice? Jealousy even? "Yeah, I agree, Jon, how the hell *did* I get the gig?" I nearly replied. It was a legitimate question, and no, I didn't have a good answer.

In November 2003, Andy Roddick—also known as A-Rod—was at the peak of his Hall of Fame career, ranked number one in the world, having won what turned out to be his only Grand Slam title by beating that year's French Open champion Juan Carlos Ferrero in the US Open. This qualified him for an honor that I have never been able to attain: hosting *Saturday Night Live*, the late-night satirical sketch and comedy show. That show had incredible ratings, it's been running for forty years, and it's always hosted by someone—an actor, comedian, athlete, whoever—who is riding high in popular culture at the time.

I'd long wanted to do it, but whenever I'd been asked back in the 1980s, when I was the top player in the world and had a certain, let's say, notoriety, I'd always said no, either because I was too busy or because my dad—who handled my financial affairs in those days—thought they weren't offering enough money. No, actually it was me who thought they weren't offering enough, but in retrospect I realize that wasn't the point—dumb-ass! It was a bad call on both our parts, because once I was no longer so hot, I wasn't getting asked anymore. And the show went on to have all sorts of athletes like Michael Jordan and Chris Evert as hosts, so I would have been in good company.

From the start, *Saturday Night Live* has mostly been produced by a good friend of mine, Lorne Michaels. Lorne and I were at a Yankees baseball game together when he told me that Andy Roddick was going to be hosting the show. "What? Wait a second now!" "Yeah, but he's going to need a bit of help and it would be great if you could be, like, his sidekick." "Thanks a lot!" I felt like saying. But I figured it might be the nearest I got to the gig, so I told him, "Sure," trying to sound pleased.

At the start of the show, the host always does a monologue to camera, so Andy had to say, "Good evening, I'm Andy Roddick, you may know me from winning the US Open this year," or words to that effect. I was sitting in the audience and had to interrupt him with, "Wait a minute, why are *you* hosting it? I've won seven Grand Slams, you've won one!" "Ah, McEnroe it's you," Andy replied. "What are you doing here?" And so on. OK, so I didn't get to host it properly, but I was still involved in several of the sketches and it was a fun thing to do. Maybe TV might have something for me after all.

I'd been having meetings on and off for a couple of years with various people about the possibility of hosting a talk show of my own. Patty has always described me as a loquacious athlete—meaning, I guess, that I like to talk—so I thought it could potentially be an interesting option. Sometimes it was with the Letterman people, sometimes I was talking to David Hill, the legendary Aussie producer from Fox, who was talking me up and offering me a once- or twice-weekly sports show, though it was not clear to either of us in exactly what format. Then a producer named Douglas Warshaw approached me at a party thrown by a mutual friend and said he was putting together a talk show for CNBC, a cable network belonging to NBC.

They were looking to get some new viewers in an evening slot where the station had traditionally performed poorly (CNBC's well-heeled viewers almost always switched off when the stock market closed). They were opening the door to people and he had these grandiose ideas: "Wow, it would be great if we did this together, it's gonna be incredible, we can do anything, come on in with us, John"—that sort of thing.

I'd been in the game long enough to know that this kind of talk was meaningless until a contract was on the table. But all the same I was seduced by the idea of a talk show—different guests, music, comedians and a chance to go broader than just sports, just tennis. This was something I thought could be new and exciting for me. So I sat tight and waited, hoping the offer would turn into a reality. And it did. In January 2004, the contracts were signed for a commitment of forty-two weeks of shows, 168 episodes, starting in July, right after Wimbledon. In theory, the show was to run indefinitely, like Letterman or Leno. Jay Leno was kind enough to call me, welcoming me to the talk show hosting club and wishing me luck. As it turned out, I was going to need it.

During the next few months, we got down to planning the show. Who knew there were so many things to think about? Should there be a desk? Should there be a backdrop? A sofa? An armchair? Should it be straight talk, even political? Funny, reverent, irreverent? All of these things? None of these things? The discussions rumbled on endlessly. Should we have a co-host? Should the co-host be a woman? Should it be an athlete? Should it be an unknown? A comedian?

We met with a number of people before Doug suggested John Fugelsang, a guy who'd hosted a late-night political talk show, *Politically Incorrect*. He did seem the best of the bunch, but I wasn't convinced, and strongly felt we should meet with some more people before deciding. But Doug was telling me again and again that this was gonna work, no problem. Meanwhile, we were getting nearer and nearer to the first show and we still weren't agreeing on a whole lot. Plus I had to go off to work the French Open and Wimbledon for two weeks each, so time was running out.

The first show was scheduled for July 7, 2004, because CNBC was trying to capitalize on me being in the public eye during Wimbledon. The problem was I arrived completely burnt out after two weeks of long hours in the commentary booth. Nonetheless we started taping the creatively named *McEnroe.* There were to be four shows a week, Monday to Thursday. These would be filmed in front of a live audience, even though it soon became clear that it wasn't easy to get people out to where we were taping in New Jersey, so the logistics weren't working.

Despite me managing to get Will Ferrell as my first guest, and Patty writing a great theme song, things didn't start out too well. It was obvious to me that my co-host John Fugelsang and I had no chemistry. Early on, he ended up missing a show because something unfortunate had happened—an unexpected death or something—and then the plane he was on had engine trouble. At the start of the next show, I got on him a bit, just kidding—"Hey, you didn't even turn up for the show. Nice!" It was meant to be tongue in cheek, but he took it personally and, in retrospect, I don't blame him.

Then there was the station itself. This was a business cable network that was all about talking stock markets, so we were hidden away upstairs in a separate office, far from the main action. We stuck out like sore thumbs. One time, for example, the reggae band Toots and the Maytals came in and Toots was smoking so much weed you could smell it from a mile away. There were all these buttoned-up business people running around and then all of a sudden here was this reggae legend who was preparing in a different way than the suits were used to, which I thought was sort of funny. Judging from their faces, the CNBC executives absolutely did not see the humor in it.

Being McEnroe on *McEnroe* wasn't as straightforward as it sounds. For a start, there was the problem of who came on the show. CNBC was not exactly a natural stop-off for celebrities, actors, musicians or those strutting their stuff. The studio being in New Jersey didn't help either. So I had to work extra hard to get the guests. It may have been naive of me to think that part would be easy, but as I said, this was a business cable network and it soon became apparent that it was extremely difficult to get the right kind of people, because if you looked down the list of talk shows, the pecking order of the ratings decided whether a publicist brought an A-lister on. George Clooney? Brad Pitt? Are you kidding? I didn't want to be constantly calling in favors from famous friends—"Hey, come on my show"—but that was what I ended up doing. How else would I have managed to get Elton John and Tom Hanks, even if I had to interview Tom in a hotel room in between *Good Morning America* and the other big shows he was doing. And boy, did we milk that interview, cutting it into segments and making it into the entire show.

Jeff Koons came on, who as I mentioned earlier is one of the biggest artists in the world. I loved the idea of having guys like him on the show. "Artists suck," I was told. Terrible for ratings. Plus, Jeff wanted to bring in this contraption—one of his pieces— but it cost money, and that pissed off the producers. I was given seven minutes with him—seven minutes!—because apparently no one knew who Jeff Koons was, even though I thought (and still do think) he's a much more interesting interviewee than most of the people I ended up talking to. I should've put my foot down and done what I wanted. I didn't know what the hell Jeff was talking about that day, but I loved it, and I should've had him on for half an hour—hell, why not? No one was watching anyway.

I have a special appreciation for artists—and stand-up comedians—because, like tennis players, they're out there by themselves. That's part of the reason I love art, because I realize artists have to expose themselves to criticism, just like we do on a court. There's always the potential to embarrass ourselves, and we have to learn how to deal with that. For tennis players, it's not about who hits the tennis ball better, because a lot of people can do that. It's about getting over jet lag, getting over the nerves, getting over fear of failure—and actual failure—among other things, because very rarely do things go the way you want them to.

For artists, there's this constant process of appraisal and rejection, especially with abstract or conceptual art—"What the hell is that? It sucks. My kid could do better." That sort of stuff. So I respect them for putting themselves through that, I admire them for having the guts to put themselves and their work on the line, and as a result I'm interested in them as characters. But the producers on the show saw things differently.

Most of the time I felt the guests were people the network needed to promote. The interviewing wasn't easy, either. I didn't want to dump on guests who were, let's face it, doing us a favor coming on the show by putting them in an awkward position or prying into their lives. But I did want to ask more than the standard superficial questions. For me, Letterman was a great example of how it should be done. If you were doing well, he'd let you go on, but if you were doing badly, he'd try to pick you up or help you out. That's the key, but often it wasn't easy to do.

For one thing, guys like Letterman have fifteen or twenty writers helping them, whereas *McEnroe* was quite a low-budget show, so I didn't have any writers in the beginning. Yeah, I had segment producers, and they were talented, but they were already trying to do too much with too little. And despite the best efforts of everyone who worked on the show, it was an uphill battle.

All too often, the conversation I'd script in my mind—the one I wanted to happen—didn't materialize. I remember one guy who came on to promote his new show and as I interviewed him, I thought, "This guy's giving me nothing. It's like getting blood out of a stone." He didn't care. If the audience could have heard the conversation I was having with myself during that dull-as-hell interview, there would have been a very different vibe in that studio. "Hey, you're fifty pounds overweight—have you ever thought of working out? If you had the energy to work out, you might have some energy to answer my goddam questions!" Better it stayed all in my mind, right?

Because it was my show and I was the one coming up with the questions, I could ask anything I wanted. Well, that was the theory anyway. When I asked Amy Poehler and Will Arnett—both of whom I'm still friendly with, by the way—about how tough it was to be married while one of them was living in LA and the other in New York, I didn't think I was doing anything horrible. They're professionals so they answered the question—or questions, because I threw in a few follow-ups—but I heard they were pissed afterward and Patty told me I'd gone too far. As it happened, they got divorced five or so years later, citing those east-west problems, so I'd obviously gotten too close to the bone. But it wasn't like I was trying to break them up or anything.

Who knew being a talk show host was so hard? I guess TV is the same as sports—the professionals make it look easy. I have to admit, most of the time I was bored listening to people's answers. I wasn't a natural at the interviewing, but I was getting better, and with a bit of guidance maybe I could've at least learned to *seem* interested in the stuff my guests were telling me. But that kind of firm but gentle hand to push me along the right road was exactly what the show lacked.

I should have seen the warnings. I'd run into trouble early on. Laird Hamilton—who's also a good friend of mine—was on. He's one of the greatest surfers of all time (his mother gave birth to him in an experimental salt-water sphere, and he's been in the water ever since) and one of the few people I know who's as competitive as I am. My good friend Marshall Coben tells a story about the time he got caught in the crossfire of a fitness duel between the two of us and barely made it out alive.

Laird's whole thing is to ride the biggest waves in the world— if there's a hundred-foot wave, he'll be on it; this guy is nuts!— and he was promoting his latest documentary. So it was all set up to be a really good segment. Unfortunately, right before the show started, I'd had a fight with the producer about wearing an earpiece. I hadn't wanted one in the first place—I told them "Letterman doesn't wear one, Leno doesn't wear one"—but they insisted it was necessary, because they wanted to use it to feed me questions or tell me to cut guests off who they thought were boring. So I'd be sitting there, trying to get a conversation going, while a voice shouted in my ear: "Get these people *off*!" I knew that wasn't going to happen with Laird, but to make it even more of a party I'd decided to bring Patty out—she's also a good friend of his. She'd come on the show a couple of times already, and because she's got a good sense of humor, she'd been more help to me than my co-host. Patty was waiting in the wings as I turned to the audience and said, "Hey, I'm going to bring on my wife here," but right as I said it, I heard them say into my earpiece, "Don't do that. Don't bring her on!"

Later, they claimed it was because she wasn't miked up, but I was seriously pissed. At the end of the show I went up to Doug Warshaw and told him, "If you ever say that to me again, I'm going to punch you in the mouth." I was as angry as I've ever been—and that's saying something. I was so angry, I asked the men in suits to get rid of Doug, but the guy in charge said, "Listen, John, Doug is going to be here, we're not going to fire him." So I went home, calmed down, and returned the next day. As soon as we finished filming, the head of CNBC brought me into his office: "I just fired Doug." "Are you fucking serious?" I thought. "You told me yesterday you were keeping him."

Was I right to have behaved in the way I did? Maybe not, but if there's one thing I've always done it's speak my mind. It's got me into trouble in the past, as everyone knows, but at least people know what I'm thinking. I've always been like that because it's how I was brought up. We were a noisy family—three brothers, parents who had opinions—we argued, we were straight to the point, and everyone learned to speak up. I know I'll always be like that, even though, believe it or not, nowadays I do sometimes try to count to ten.

Anyway, to replace Doug Warshaw they hired Woody Fraser, who I was told was an experienced talk show producer. Yes, he was, but that was in the seventies, and now he was a hundred years old. He seemed like a nice guy, but I sure wasn't convinced by his ideas to turn the show around. "Throw it against the wall and see what sticks. Do dumb-ass tricks," he told me (or words to that effect). "Put yourself in idiotic positions." We still had guests, but now I'd have to go outside the studio and do stunts, throwing baseballs with a pitcher to see how fast I could throw them, or get in a car and do some stupid thing with the driver. Some people found this funny, but to me it felt lame. Obviously, I've been wrong a few times in my life and subsequent events suggest I was wrong about this, too. Hey, Jimmy Fallon, thanks for stealing the act I didn't want!

The whole thing came to a head in early December. By then the ratings were shockingly low. And the rest of my life was still going on around the show. I had to make a decision about the Australian Open, because if I didn't commit to commentating on the next one, they were going to get someone else. That someone else turned out to be Jim Courier, who I have to admit has done a good job. So I lost that gig and then, guess what? A couple of weeks later, I was at London's Royal Albert Hall playing the ATP Champions Tour when I got a call from Jeff Zucker, head of NBC. "We're canceling the show," he told me. It was two in the morning, my time, so you can imagine how well that went. He gave me an option to do the last two weeks or "it can end right here and now."

As it was coming up to Christmas I did the last two weeks so that the crew would get paid. Those turned out to be some of our best shows—or at least the most fun—because we were winging it, and we actually had a couple of writers by then. The one with actor Ryan Reynolds where we had tequila during the show really pissed the producers off. They threatened to pull us the next day, so we calmed down and finished as rowdily as we could but without the alcohol. It wasn't pretty, but funnily enough, given that we had a death sentence hanging over us, there was real life in those final shows.

The cancellation of *McEnroe* was a blow. We all want to be successful at what we do, but though I was upset, I was also relieved. The reason I'd taken the show was because I thought I'd be able to pay my dues for a couple of years and learn my trade. If I'd got the hang of being a talk show host and enjoyed doing it, then I might've been ready for the next step. Kind of like Jimmy Fallon. Don't get me wrong, he's way more talented than I am, with his impressions and his natural wit, but even he took some time to figure it all out. Now he's at the top of his game. He's like the Federer who won his first Wimbledon and then all of a sudden he's *Roger Federer*.

If I'm honest, the talk show was a full-time job that I wasn't doing totally full-time—either in reality or in my mind. I tried to work nine to five, whereas the production people lived and breathed it. They would look at me, like "What's wrong with you? You've got to be here from eight in the morning until nine at night." But as far as I was concerned, I was already doing more than enough—I always seemed to be reading some book or checking out some movie that had to do with the next person on, and by the time the show ended I was completely drained and needed a break.

Alongside the chance for some much-needed time with my family, one of the big upsides of the end of *McEnroe* was being able to go back to having a level of variety in my life that a forty-two-weeks-a-year talk show was never going to allow me. Maybe I wasn't cut out for the talk show game. I felt I'd done the best I could, and if that wasn't good enough, well, so be it. Better to try and fail than not try at all. I'd just have to find a different way to bounce back.

7

"Champions keep playing until they get it right"

Billie Jean King

In the summer of 2003, I'd been back in the commentary booth at Wimbledon. No one knew it at the time—least of all me—but as I watched Roger Federer win the first of his seven Wimbledon titles, I was watching the dawn of a new era. What's incredible—with hindsight, and given who he has become—is that back then no one was totally convinced about Federer. Sure, people had been talking about him for a while as the next big thing, especially after he'd beaten Pete Sampras at Wimbledon in 2001. But by this time he was almost twenty-two, and in the Slams he hadn't gotten further than the quarters, so there was a question mark over whether he was ever going to get it together enough to win one Grand Slam title, let alone eighteen (at the time of this writing!). No one was jumping up and down shouting, "This guy is going to be the greatest player, just you watch!" Even so, I believe the expectation of what he might be capable of was getting to him. Yes, I know, *Roger Federer*!

I remember watching the match he played in the round of sixteen, against Feliciano López, a solid, talented Spaniard. It was out on the old court number 2, which used to be called "the graveyard of champions" because it had been the scene of so many upsets. Roger seemed to be having back problems during the match, and it looked like he may even quit. I think part of it was the stress, but to me he definitely had that look in his eye as if he might throw in the towel. At the time some people thought he was a bit soft, both physically and emotionally. But then, he suddenly seemed to decide that he wanted to hang in there: he found another gear mentally, and he somehow gritted his teeth and got himself through that match. I could see him digging deeper, finding that something within himself, a way to want it more, and he ended up winning in straight sets and racing through the rest of the tournament without dropping a set, beating Mark Philippoussis in the final. For me, that was the turning point in his career. It was after that match that he started becoming the Roger Federer we all know, perhaps the greatest player that has ever lived. If he hadn't won? Who knows.

Winning your first Slam is always a game-changer for a player—both in your own head and in the way other people see you. Suddenly you're on another level from the other pros, a potential title contender wherever you go. My own first Grand Slam title win was at the US Open in 1979. I was twenty years old, and up against my fellow New Yorker Vitas Gerulaitis, who was four years older than me. This was the guy who had taken me under his wing and become my friend and mentor, and I was feeling uncomfortable about having to play him now in what was the biggest match of either of our careers. The crazy thing was, here we were, two guys from Queens, and we actually got booed by the New York crowd. Why? They'd wanted a Connors–Borg final and we'd gone and spoiled it for them. Too bad. I didn't care. I'd had a great run in the tournament, I'd beaten Connors easily to get to the final, so I felt like it was my year.

On the day, I was able to put my relationship with Vitas aside and ended up beating him in straight sets. Now I had taken my place at the top along with Connors and Borg. Vitas could've held that against me, but he never did. In fact, he even took me out with him on the night I beat him. Straight after the final he asked me, "What are you doing later?" I replied, "What are *you* doing?" Because I knew whatever he was doing was going to be a hell of a lot better than what I might have planned! I guess there's more than one way to be a winner.

Pete Sampras, one of the great American champions, had gone out of tennis in a way few athletes in any sport do—right at the top. In what turned out to be his last match on the main tour, he beat his great rival Andre Agassi to win the 2002 US Open. Even Pete knew it was special to have won that one, his fourteenth Grand Slam title, saying it "might take the cake," which was about the most emotional thing he'd ever done on court. Until the next year's US Open, that is, when there was an on-court ceremony on the first evening to commemorate his retirement. Pete is the best fast-court player ever, in my opinion, and ranks alongside my all-time idol Rod Laver as one of the true greats of the game. So I was honored to take part in the ceremony, along with Jim Courier and Boris Becker, and to say a few words about him in front of a full house at the Arthur Ashe Stadium. I even got a laugh out of Pete by thanking him for "kicking my ass every time we played and taking away all my records," and he displayed some very un-Sampras-like emotion by shedding tears as he was given a standing ovation.

Champions come and champions go, but the game goes on forever. It's hard to put your finger on exactly what the qualities are that make a great one, but you almost always know them when you see them. The next few years after Federer won that first Wimbledon would see the emergence of three more.

In October 2004, I flew to London for the inauguration of Superset tennis, an eight-man knockout event played over one set or eight games, winner takes all. The organizers encouraged crowd participation, the coaches (for those who had one—I didn't) were allowed courtside for thirty seconds at the change of ends, wired up so the crowd could hear them give their advice, and the players were encouraged to call for Hawk-Eye on close line calls, which would then be played in slow motion on large plasma screens. Perfect for me, right?

Pretty much, as it turned out. Tim Henman was injured, so the seventeen-year-old Andy Murray was put in his place. And in front of a noisy crowd of ten thousand fans at Wembley Arena, I found myself—age forty-five—playing this youngster on whom so many British hopes were pinned. God knows, every time I used to set foot in Britain, I'd get asked if I thought Tim could win Wimbledon. I was too diplomatic to say so at the time, but if I'm honest, I didn't think he'd ever lift that trophy. Yes, he was a very good player—you can't reach the Wimbledon semis four times without being that. But Andy? I could tell straightaway that he was going to be a champion: he had a lot of natural skills, all he needed was a little seasoning. It's impossible to say how far a player is going to go because you don't know what's going to happen with the mental or the physical side, and Andy wasn't as strong then on either of those as he is now. But I'd started to hear good things about him, so that day I wanted to see what he had to offer.

Those teenage years are all about learning, and I'd like to think my 6–1, twenty-four-minute win did Andy a favor by showing him there was still work to do. Or maybe I'm kidding myself and he was being kind to the old American guy. According to the British press, I served up my volleys with "cold eyes," but what I did to Andy was the same thing I keep expecting people to do to this day: attack the second serve, which was much weaker then than it is now. Since that time, he's improved his defense and also added a bigger variety of shots. He's in great shape, he's strong, and his game is still improving—particularly his offense—which is how he got to be number one in the world at the end of 2016. In any event, that was the only time I've ever played Andy, and hey, I've got a 1–0 winning record against him, which I can't say I'm unhappy about.

The next spring, Rafael Nadal played his first ever French Open at Roland-Garros. And won it. He was a few days over nineteen years old. You could see right away that he was the best clay-courter around. It was that obvious. He'd been injured in 2004 with a stress fracture to his left ankle, so he hadn't been able to play. Otherwise, he probably would have won that year too.

I'd heard about Rafa but I hadn't really seen him play, and not on clay, but as soon as I saw him, I was like, "Whoa!" His build was amazing for a teenager because he already looked like a grown man. The last player I'd seen like that had been Boris Becker when he took Wimbledon by storm in 1985—only seventeen but with those great tree-trunk legs. But Rafa was different—he was so upper-body developed as well. We were advised not to have too much muscle up there (this was easy advice for me to take, because I never had any muscles), but he was the opposite. And the clothes he wore made that even more evident, with his sleeveless shirts that showed off those bulging biceps, and the pirate-style shorts. What with the sweat pouring off him, the fist-pumping, the cries of *"Vamos!"* Rafa had this unique warrior look about him.

So now tennis had Roger Federer, with his effortless, quiet, graceful game that was dominating grass-court tennis and looking pretty unbeatable elsewhere too. The arrival of a guy whose grunting, physical, sweat-drenched style was clearly going to dominate clay-court tennis for a while initiated what will be looked back upon as a golden age of men's tennis. Over the past dozen or so years, I've been lucky enough to witness, commentate and give my opinion on some of the most incredible matches ever to be played by two of the greatest players ever to pick up a racquet. It was like the Beatles and the Stones—take your pick. It's a win-win.

These two monumental talents could not have had more contrasting styles. In the space of a couple of years, we'd gone from having no particular player dominating the sport since Pete Sampras in the 1990s, to having two guys who would take the game up to another level, who were going to dominate it and represent it in an impressive way for another ten years. Here were two totally contrasting class acts and it was exactly what tennis needed. Novak Djokovic and, to some extent, Andy Murray caught up with them eventually, but the influence of Roger and Rafa on the world sports stage, especially because they came along at more or less the same time and were so different from each other, would be a blessing for the sport.

When I was growing up, tennis was not the coolest sport to play—some people say it became cooler because I played it! To be fair, it was already changing as I came through—Connors and Nastase and most of all Björn Borg were laying the groundwork. Before long, more clubs were popping up, more public courts were being built, and most importantly more people seemed to be playing. The sport was exploding, and I was a part of that. It was amazing, to the extent that we'd be on the front page of the sports section all the time, which tennis rarely is now, even though the greatest player that ever lived is playing—possibly the two greatest, Nadal and Federer.

If people ask me who I think edges it out of those two, I

usually say that there have been times when Nadal was better, but overall I think Roger is the better player. Of course there's an argument the other way, because Nadal's record against Federer is so much better. I think Roger's probably been more consistent over time, but then Rafa's been injured more often . . . In the end, playing on anything medium to slow, I'd pick Nadal, but on a fast court, I'd pick Federer.

Djokovic has now given them both something to think about, and for a long time watching him struggling to break through reminded me of how it felt for me, trying to get up there with Connors and Borg. But Djokovic has taken it past what I did— he's really shaken it up. The irony is that, even though he's probably become a better player than I was, and than Roger and Rafa are now, they're still way bigger than him.

In their own world, all three of these guys are giants—Mount Rushmore guys—but that's not reflected in the sports pages, at least in America. These days the coverage has been reduced to a few lines, "Nadal beats so-and-so," or "Federer loses." The lack of American contenders definitely hurts on the home front. When Murray won Wimbledon for the first time, all of a sudden the BBC ratings were double what they had been when Nadal played Federer in the greatest match ever. That hometown (or home country) player thing makes a huge difference. Thank God for Serena and Venus, and hopefully there are some new American champions just around the corner in the men's game.

8

*"I don't want to belong to any club that
would have me as a member"*

Groucho Marx

As I'm lucky enough to have been friends with a few musicians over the years, I've attended a number of ceremonies when they were inducted into the Rock and Roll Hall of Fame. Although the actual Hall of Fame is located in Cleveland, Ohio, these events generally took place at the Waldorf-Astoria hotel in New York, because I guess it's more convenient for a lot of people to get to (me included).

In March 2005, it was the turn of Chrissie Hynde and the Pretenders, so I went along to support her—not that she needed it. What I found interesting was that Chrissie wasn't too happy about the Hall of Fame thing. She thought it was bullshit, and I'm sure she still thinks that. At the time I told her to try to enjoy the ceremony and celebrate the fact that she was now a Hall of Famer, but I think she disagreed with the whole concept of what it said about people as musicians: that one was supposedly better than another—who the hell were these people to decide? Although she did still show up, so it can't have been totally meaningless to her, right?

Chrissie's not alone in feeling ambivalent about these events. I subsequently went to Rock and Roll inductions where the people they were honoring weren't even there. One of those was the great rock band Van Halen in 2007. I'd known Eddie Van Halen since the mid eighties. He had coincidentally—because I wasn't yet with her—asked Patty to join the band as the singer after David Lee Roth left (she turned him down—luckily for me, or we might not be together). To me, Eddie is the greatest living guitar player, so I thought it was a no-brainer that the band was being inducted. The problem was that Eddie and his brother Alex, the band's drummer, were locked in a bitter dispute with Sammy Hagar, the singer they'd gotten in instead of Patty—so they didn't show up. They were also still feuding with David Lee Roth, so the only people who ended up being there were Sammy Hagar and the bass player, Michael Anthony. It was too bad neither of the guys who gave the band its name showed up. In fact, it was ludicrous, but that's rock 'n' roll for you.

It's not that unusual to have no-shows in Rock and Roll inductions, and that probably says a lot about the difference between creative people and sports people. With sports, you can measure success. You know if one person is better at something than someone else, because they run faster, win more, or whatever. You can then decide to put them into their sport's Hall of Fame in a fairly objective way. As a result, people in sports tend to appreciate when that happens to them and to at least look like they're pleased. With creative careers—whether it's the movies, art or music—to some extent it's a matter of judgment. What does an Academy Award or a Grammy really say about you? Does it mean you're superior to the guy who didn't even get nominated? It's hard to argue against an Olympic gold or a Wimbledon trophy and say it's all meaningless bullshit. But if you disagree with the whole concept of handing out awards for something that you can't measure, and which therefore feels arbitrary, then why show up to the ceremony?

Also, the Hall of Fame concept for sports has been going for a long time and it's more fixed in our collective minds as something to be proud of than the rock 'n' roll version. The International Tennis Hall of Fame, for example, was established back in 1954 at Newport, Rhode Island—incidentally by the founder of the tie-break, Jimmy Van Alen—and it's officially sanctioned by the sport's governing body, the International Tennis Federation.

So it feels like it's a legitimate way to honor those who have done something for the sport, as happened when a feisty old lady named Dodo Cheney was inducted in the summer of 2005. For those of you who might have missed her career, Dodo was the first American to win the Australian Open, back in 1938. She reached the semis in six major singles tournaments, including the French Open and Wimbledon in 1946, and that same year had been number six in the world. An amazing competitor, always beautifully dressed, she was still winning tournaments at eighty-seven years old, which I loved. She'd once told Bud Collins, the veteran tennis journalist, "The more I played, the more I loved to win." Sounded a bit like me. Is it any wonder that I'd long championed her induction?

It was good of the Hall of Fame committee to ask me to induct her. Though as I stepped up, I could see them thinking, "For God's sake, don't let him take hold of the mic." At my own induction, five years earlier, I'd been asked to speak for four or five minutes and was still going forty-five minutes later. But I kept my introduction for Dodo short and sweet. I told those present how she'd won 250 gold balls—they're awarded by the USTA to winners of national events, and she was still winning them well into her eighties, eventually winning a total of 391 by the time she finally stopped competing in 2012, aged ninety-five! I also spoke of her contribution to the game and then I walked her to the court where we hit a few balls back and forth. For once, I wasn't the oldest player on the court! Dodo died in 2014, aged ninety-eight. Her attitude and style made her an inspirational figure in tennis. And she's one of the reasons that I think the Hall of Fame is a good thing in sports, and that tennis is truly a game for your whole life.

One of the challenges of getting older as an athlete is that while it's nice to still get recognition for what you achieved in the past, you don't want your life to become one long lap of honor. Unlike most former athletes who don't have the option of continuing to play and are often too crippled by injury to do it, I was incredibly lucky: I continued to turn out for legends tournaments and exhibitions throughout the year and people were still willing to watch an old fart like me hit the odd decent volley or lefty serve. I still love competition, the energy I get from it, and yes, I'll be honest, the applause. Because let me tell you, there's no better way to get my juices flowing (and give me the incentive to keep training) than seeing if I can still cut it with guys who are ten, twenty years younger than me.

Every Grand Slam has a seniors doubles event for the allegedly golden oldies that runs alongside the main tournament. The French event, called the Trophée des Légendes, is the best of them. There's usually a maximum of three matches to play—two in the round-robin group, then the final if you're the top team from your group—with matches on the big show courts, usually the Suzanne Lenglen, their second biggest stadium, which seats 10,000.

The fact that the stands are even close to being full is a testament to the big personality of the organizer, Mansour Bahrami—the Iranian walking mustache, and a legend in his own right—who always puts on a good show. Not only is his facial hair right up there with Ion Tiriac's as one of the all-time great tennis mustaches, but there aren't many other crowd-pleasing trick-shot merchants who can claim to have fled to France in the aftermath of the 1979 Iranian revolution with their life savings in their pockets.

The French really know their tennis, partly because so many of them play, and the sport doesn't have the elitist image that it does in America and Britain, which is why the all-round vibe at Roland-Garros is so great. Mansour's event has a real energy about it, and I have a pretty good record in that tournament, so while Rafa was busy sweating and grunting his way to his first title on Court Philippe Chatrier, I was teaming up with my good friend Yannick Noah to seal our first seniors title together. I've won it many times over the years with different partners, but I know that no one cares about that except me.

For other seniors events that take place the rest of the year, it's a whole different ball game because of the way they're organized and financed. Which is to say, they're set up on a purely commercial basis. The first seniors tour was started back in 1993 by Jimmy Connors. In the mid 1990s, after I'd stopped playing the main tour, I played a few seniors events but without too much commitment on my part, largely because of the stage I was at in my life. I was newly married to Patty, we were creating a new family together. But once I started taking the whole seniors thing seriously in the late 1990s—after Patty told me, "If you're going to do it, do it right," because she could see how bad I felt getting whipped when I hadn't practiced enough—I started beating Jimmy and winning more tournaments than him, which he hated.

Jimmy and I have a lot of history, dating back to him beating me in that Wimbledon semi-final in 1977, and our relationship has always been ... complicated, although we get along way better nowadays than we used to. When I demolished him 6–1, 6–0 at Royal Albert Hall in 2001, during one of those times when we weren't exactly on each other's Christmas card lists, Jimmy stopped playing seniors shortly after, and even I felt bad about it. Not least because Jimmy and I had been the tour's two biggest draws, and without him there to provide me with stiff competition, the tour started to struggle. That's not to take away from the other guys, but the fact was that Jimmy brought a unique brand of competitiveness and showmanship that the crowd loved, and which (much as I didn't realize it at the time) I loved too. Connors had always been a fantastic opponent for me. I got off on his intensity—no one I played against ever tried harder. And his antics, wow—they even topped mine; the way he'd grab his balls, tell everyone to go fuck themselves, then turn around later and put his arm around them. It was amazing.

Ever the hustler, Jimmy sold the tour to IMG, who ended up going into joint partnership with the ATP (which organizes the regular men's circuit) to organize a "Champions Tour" seniors circuit of tournaments around the world. The year-ending event is at Royal Albert Hall. But without Jimmy around for me to bounce off, crowds were starting to decline in the early years of the new decade, until four-time Grand Slam singles winner Jim Courier set up a rival tour as part of his InsideOut Sports & Entertainment company—and breathed new life into the whole seniors circuit.

Jim's franchise had more American players on it, with guys like Andre Agassi, Pete Sampras, Michael Chang and Andy Roddick, whereas the ATP Champions Tour had a much more international feel, with Stefan Edberg, Boris Becker, Goran Ivanisevic and Pat Cash amongst the big-name draws in 2005.

We weren't—and still aren't—selling millions of tickets but, depending on the market, our wheelhouse would be 2,500–5,000 people, which isn't bad in my book.

I can't deny that there is a hit-and-giggle element sometimes. The doubles scene is generally a contrast to the singles matches because it's usually—though not always—less serious. Old foes getting back together to put on a show, we know we're there to compete but also to entertain.

At the pre-Australian Open exhibition event in Adelaide a few years later, I found myself taking part in some extreme episodes of craziness. Each time, Frenchman Michaël Llodra was heavily involved. You could say he was to blame for pretty much the worst parts of it, and I've heard he likes to have a bit of fun in the locker room, but others, such as Mansour Bahrami (class clown leader), Henri Leconte (deputy class clown), and Pat Cash (always a willing accomplice), were all trying to outdo each other.

Michaël, or Mika, as the French call him, only retired in 2014, so back then he was still a fully-fit member of the regular tour (and one of the smartest and best lefty doubles players in the world, as it happens). In one of our matches, he, Leconte and Cash ganged up on me and started going through my tennis bag at the side of the court, trying to find something to embarrass me with. There's always a bunch of stuff in there—most of which doesn't smell too good—so the next thing I knew, they were pulling out anything and everything, displaying it to the crowds and trying it on for size. That included Cash putting my tight-fitting red underpants on top of his shorts (in case you're wondering, he somehow managed not to look obscene), while Llodra found my swimming goggles and put them on (teamed up with his baseball cap, he looked like a World War I flying ace), and Leconte found an elasticated back support which he put on his head and which made him look like a Smurf (or an idiot, depending on your point of view). It all got pretty chaotic because the guys playing on the adjacent court, including Mansour Bahrami, didn't need too much of an excuse to stop playing and join in the fun. Good thing I've gotten better at not taking myself too seriously.

Things could have turned out even more humiliating in the other doubles match I played against Llodra and Leconte. I was partnering with Ryan Harrison, a young American player who was only nineteen at the time and who was clearly not prepared for what the match turned into. At one stage, Leconte, for reasons best known to himself, but probably because he was about to lose, took his shorts off. The crowd loved it. As I said, class clown. Before long, and I swear to God I don't know why, except that we were all having fun and the crowd seemed to be enjoying what they were seeing, I'd taken my shirt off, in a sort of "anyone can play that game" kind of way. Who said I can't enjoy a good laugh? It did cross my mind that it might not be such a hot idea but, you know what, I figured I wasn't too embarrassed at what I'd be revealing, so off went the shirt. Llodra meanwhile had matched Leconte and taken his shorts off too. Next to come off were all our shoes and socks. Ryan Harrison, probably wisely, decided not to compete with us and remained fully clothed. Perhaps he didn't want to humiliate us by reminding us what a teenage athlete's body looked like.

Leconte was—*quelle surprise*—loving all the attention and milking things as much as he could. As usual. What I hadn't expected was that Llodra would decide to go one step further and take his shirt off. Suddenly he was down to just his tight underpants. At that point I became a little concerned because he looked like he was planning to keep going. When you're on court in front of a few thousand people, that could be a lot trickier to pull off, as it were. For once, Leconte, who doesn't usually have much of an edit button, realized what his own limits were: he figured that, as much as Llodra looked good enough in his underwear to carry off his stunt, it would be a smart move for everyone's sake if he, Henri, kept his shirt on.

With guys like this, doubles becomes a sort of circus, but once in a while it's liberating for me to get involved, and believe it or not, I'm happy to take part. Though call me a chicken, but I'd prefer not to play strip-tennis every time.

For me, if the seniors circuit keeps us guys out there, competing, kidding ourselves we've still got what it takes to serve up some good tennis while providing entertainment for people who are still willing to pay to see us, then it's a good thing. I always say I want to be the Rolling Stones of the seniors tour. Like the Stones, we're on a nostalgia trip. And even if we sometimes feel like those caged rats on a treadmill, running and not getting anywhere, that's still a lot better than nothing, because after all, what's the alternative?

Actually, I know what the alternative is—it's being forced to retire for real, like my father had to at sixty-five—and that rarely works out well. At first, my dad didn't sit around. He tried to think of things to do. But some of them were so crazy that we had to laugh. Like the time he called me up and said, "John, I think I could do some commentating. What do you reckon?" "What? Are you out of your mind?" I replied, almost lost for words. I mean, don't get me wrong, my dad was highly articulate and smart, but I don't think too many TV producers would have had him down as their first choice in a commentary booth.

My dad's Irish roots always came through in his love of singing (as well as an accompanying beer or two), and he used to love belting out his favorite songs at the top of his powerful voice. Can you spot the family resemblance as far as musical enthusiasm was concerned? This gave rise to another of his post-retirement ideas. One day, he announced to me that he wanted to be a singer, and could I have a word with Tony Bennett, since I happened to know him. He thought he could open for him next time he was appearing at Radio City Music Hall or wherever. Apparently there was some bar downtown that had open-mic nights and could I ask Tony to come down and hear him sing, with a view to hiring him?

Not long after, I ran into Tony at the US Open. Now Tony is the nicest guy in the world, so when he said, "John, I saw your father, and he wants me to go hear him sing," he didn't seem to be dismissing the idea out of hand. I set him straight right there and then. "Do me a favor, Tony. Say you're busy—like, forever. OK?" I think he got the message.

But nothing topped the time my dad heard that Patty and I had become friends with the comedian Don Rickles and his wife Barbara, and Patty had opened for Don at one of his casino shows in Las Vegas. My dad said, "Hey, I could open for him too." Even for Dad, that was a bridge too far.

Both my parents turned seventy in 2005, and I was starting to be aware that their later years weren't panning out as might have been hoped. I'd try to see them on all the significant dates because when I'd been on the tour I was rarely around for birthdays, Thanksgiving, Father's Day, Mother's Day—all the dates that are important when you're a family. I was still away often, but if I wasn't, we'd try to make the effort to go out, with as many of my kids as were around, usually to one of my parents' favorite restaurants, or we'd have lunch or dinner with one or both of my brothers and their families.

To some extent, I struggled with the whole issue of how

to deal with my parents' later years. I was conscious I didn't always cope with it very well, but at least when Patty told me I "lack the empathy gene" I usually managed to resist the temptation to point to my mom and dad and ask her, "Well, whose fault is that?"

9

"It's not bad to be runner-up"

Larry David

On February 16, 2006, I turned forty-seven. OK, I wasn't quite geriatric yet, but I was still watching the big Five-O getting ever closer on the horizon. Three days later, I won a regular tour ATP doubles title in San Jose, California, beating a couple of guys who were about twenty years younger than I was. My own partner, the Swede Jonas Björkman, who had once been world number four, was a mere thirteen years younger than me, and with a combined age of eighty-one we were pretty old to be getting involved in a full-blown ATP tournament, my first since 1994 (even if it was doubles). I'll be honest and admit that I was a little bit concerned I'd be a liability for Jonas, but somehow I managed to raise my level so that I wasn't too far off his. At least, that's what he told me.

It was my first doubles title since 1992, when I'd won indoors in Paris with my brother, so it felt weird to be winning again on the main tour. It felt even weirder when someone told me that I had now won a doubles title in four different decades. How to make someone feel their age. "I'm going to enjoy this and then take a few months off—minimum," I announced to the media afterward. "Then I will go back to the seniors tour where I belong, and tell them I can still cut it with the younger guys."

Did I believe that? Was that what I wanted, to still play occasional doubles on the main tour? What was I trying to prove—and to who? The answers to those questions were not straightforward. Yes, I had proved to myself, and I hope to others, what I had long suspected, which was that I could still play doubles at tour level if I chose to do so. But what did that mean? Did I now want to keep doing that? Short answer: no.

It was still pretty cool to be the oldest guy ever to win an ATP tournament, though Martina Navratilova had pushed back the boundaries of what was possible for forty-somethings by winning her first-round singles match at Wimbledon in 2004 at the age of forty-seven, the oldest player in the modern era ever to do so. Later, in 2006, she then went on to win the mixed doubles at the US Open with Bob Bryan, one month short of her fiftieth birthday. Clearly, I wasn't the only player to think I could still keep up with the youngsters. Looking back, it's too bad Martina and I never played mixed doubles together in our prime, because boy we would've kicked some major ass.

Back in San Jose, the organizers thought they were doing a nice thing by presenting me with an enormous cake on my birthday, not that I wanted reminding of my increasing age. My dad had been excited to come along to the tournament now that he had time on his hands—after all, he hadn't been the parent of one of the competitors for many years—and although I can't say I shared his excitement at the idea of him being there, for old times' sake I took him along. Problem was, I soon found myself looking after him in a way which I'd never had to when I'd been playing the main tour.

Once upon a time, he or Mom would have been the ones to make sure I was OK at a tournament, checking that everything was organized, that I was happy with the arrangements. After all, my dad was my agent for the first ten years of my career. But times had moved on and now the shoe was firmly on the other foot.

On top of the initial depressing realization that he was no longer the autonomous, independent dad who used to cheer me on when I was younger, selfishly there were moments that week when I was asking myself, "Why did I bring him here?" because it was taking away from what should have been an enjoyable experience. It sounds harsh, but I know I'm not the only person who is shocked to discover their parent's presence somewhere is suddenly more of a hindrance than a help, and you feel like the father/son roles have reversed. It was a sad truth, but that's what had happened.

Fortunately, after a few days of feeling down, I was able to overcome all those negative feelings and win the tournament, so on balance, it did turn into a very positive experience. But it came with some mixed emotions. Here I was, trying to hold back the years on court, while off it I was being faced with an unequivocal example of advancing time. Who was I kidding?

One of the advantages of being part of the sandwich genera-tion—caring for your parents and bringing up kids at the same time—is that having your own family gives you a new perspec-tive on how much your mom and dad did for you. The scathing response I got from my kids when I tried to start a tradition of discussing a specific topic at family mealtimes certainly led me to view the tribulations of the older generation in a more sympathetic light, especially when they called me "Larry the Lecturer."

When I look back on what my parents achieved, they have definitely lived the American Dream. My dad was a real striver— the son of an Irish immigrant, he worked his way through night classes at law school and wound up as a partner of one of the biggest New York law firms. Dad was always an upbeat sort of guy, and once my career was up and running was often seen (and heard, *"Come on, John!"*) at Grand Slam tournaments, wearing his trademark white hat, watching from the stands as I played. He was always smiling and telling jokes, and loved to have people around.

My mom, Kay, is a quieter sort of person, but still a badass. She was an operating room nurse by profession—so there was a real edge of steel to her—who then devoted herself full-time to her family when she had me and my two younger brothers.

Here's a story that kind of sums up my parents. Soon after I was born (in Wiesbaden, Germany, where my dad was in the Air Force) my parents moved back to the US, to an apartment in Flushing, Queens, near LaGuardia airport. By day, my dad worked as an assistant office manager at an advertising agency. By night, he went to Fordham University School of Law. When he'd finished his first year there, he proudly told my mom that he'd come second in his class. "See," she said, "if you'd worked harder, you could have been first." The next year he was.

My brother Mark, who is three years younger than I am, is a corporate lawyer, and is now also my personal attorney, so he handles my legal business, as well as the administrative side of things. I trust him and he's smart as a whip, which is useful when you're working with someone like me and stuck between two tennis-playing brothers (never mind taking over running my business affairs from my dad, which it would've been very hard to get anyone outside of the family to do).

Patrick was born four years after Mark and had a successful tennis career, mainly as a doubles specialist, but he was also a US Open singles quarter-finalist and got to the semis at the Australian Open. (I didn't play in the tournament that year, and the other semi-finalists were Becker, Edberg and Lendl, so when Patrick was asked how he felt about getting that far, he said words to the effect of "What do you expect? The semi-finalists are Becker, Edberg, Lendl and McEnroe," which I still think is one of the best responses to a journalist's question in tennis history.) Patrick took over the US Davis Cup captaincy after me and, as well as being a regular commentator for ESPN, he would later become the head of the USTA's junior development program for seven years. Unlike me, Patrick's great at dealing with bullshit, which is why he was able to carry on in a set-up where I would have bailed out long before. On top of all that, Patrick and I regularly make up a fear-inducing doubles team on the seniors tour. Or at least, that's what we tell ourselves.

Both my brothers are married with kids, one living in New York, the other in Connecticut, and we see each other regularly, so that's a good thing. As with any group of siblings, there are the usual ups and downs, but looking at how we've turned out, I think you could say my mom and dad didn't do a bad job of raising us.

We were all brought up Catholic, because religion was something that had meaning for my parents. It still does—for them, but not for me. Maybe it's the whole guilt thing that the Catholic faith seems to be so good at, but religion had long been a turn-off for me, even before the strange conversation with my mom that I'm about to describe. She called me up one day out of the blue, and we got talking about this and that. Then she finally explained why she'd called.

Did I remember Father Byrns? she asked. Sure, I did. He was our parish priest for years at St. Anastasia's where we used to go to church every week and where I went to kindergarten and first grade. He was this good-looking guy—the girls in particular seemed to love him—and everyone thought he was a great example of what you'd want a priest to be. So much so that when Tatum and I got married, he was the priest my parents wanted to marry us, so I agreed.

"Well," my mom announced, "you should go online and have a look, because it seems he's been arrested and accused of pedophilia." I was totally shocked. He was one of the last people I'd have thought would be doing anything close to that sort of thing. We talked about it some more, but I guess it just goes to show that you never know. Anyway, my mom was about to hang up at the end of our conversation, when she suddenly came out with what had really been bugging her: "Did he ever do anything to you?"

No, thank God. I can't explain away my tantrums by blaming my unsuppressed rages on the crimes of Father Byrns. I was lucky enough to have no such grim excuse for having sometimes behaved like a jerk, though God knows what might have happened to me if tennis hadn't saved me from becoming an altar boy!

My parents' Catholicism has occasionally been a bone of contention in the McEnroe family, especially when it comes to Patty and me bringing their grandchildren up outside the church. My mom took our oldest son Kevin to be baptized in secret, to save him from burning in hell—or so she told me twenty years later! You càn imagine the heated discussion which took place when Patty and I found out about that, though we decided not to have her charged with religiously motivated kidnapping.

I must admit that as the years have gone on and my sons in particular have struggled to settle on a direction in life, I have at times wondered if I went too far in keeping religion completely out of their upbringing. Not because I think either of them would've been likely to embrace Catholicism—not with our genes—but at least the strictness of religion would've given them something else to push back against apart from Patty and me.

The notion that work was vital was instilled in my brothers and me from a very young age, and the fear of being short of cash was one that was deeply ingrained in my mom, in particular. For example, when I took the first half of 1986 off because I was burned out and I wanted to spend time with Tatum and my newborn son, Kevin, my mom's first words to me after I told her I would be rejoining the tour in early August were: "Thank God! Now you can buy some diapers for Kevin."

At the time I was mad at her—"How much is enough? Tell me. How much money do I have to make before you don't have to say things like that?!" But looking back I can see that part of the need I have to keep working, to keep earning, comes from the way my parents were about money, and believe it or not I am grateful for that. Their work ethic, along with the strength of their marriage and their faith in the value of education, was part of what gave my brothers and me such a secure foundation to build on.

My kids have been brought up in a more relaxed atmosphere in financial terms, but Patty and I have worked hard to prevent them from taking their family's good fortune for granted. The whole tough love thing is called that for a reason, though: it's tough. Not just for the kids, but for the parents too. Telling your kids "No, you can't have that," is something we've struggled with over the years, and I know we're not alone in that in today's affluent Western society. So many kids today seem to suffer from affluenza, and I don't know what the cure for that is. As parents, all we can do is our best and what feels right at the time.

From the moment I took that six months off from the tour when Kevin was born, right up to present times with our youngest, Ava, my role as a dad has been central to my life, and I've made it a priority to be at home as much as my crazy tennis life has allowed me. As difficult—even impossible—as it's sometimes been to figure out the juggling of different schedules, I hope all my kids feel like they've been able to count on me being there for them when they've needed me.

When my brothers and I were growing up, my parents were incredibly supportive and encouraging of us. They loved sports and loved playing tennis, so they'd come and watch us play the whole time. Too much, I sometimes thought, especially once I was on the tour, because I felt there was this additional pressure. My dad could be pretty demonstrative when he watched me play—I guess that's not surprising, given what I sometimes was up to—but my mom was always more reserved. Either way, their presence didn't necessarily help. Although I'll admit that, when I was younger, I used to like having my mom there because if I lost, I could put my arms around her and cry, something that was no longer an option once I started playing Grand Slams and was supposedly a grown-up.

At the other end of my career, I've had to balance my desire to keep on playing for as long as I can enjoy it with not wanting to overstay my welcome. When I played and won that doubles tournament in 2006, it wasn't a case of seriously believing I could keep up with the younger guys, but it was a good feeling to know that I could still compete with them as an equal, at least on the doubles court. I've said many times that the doubles game nowadays is for the guys who are too slow to make it in singles. Deep down, even the top doubles guys know that, whatever some of them might say to the contrary. After all, if a forty-seven-year-old and a thirty-four-year-old can win an ATP doubles event, what does that say about the rest of the field?

Another American former world number one was taking his final bows on the main tour in 2006. Where I'd kind of passed on the whole public farewell circus when I quit Grand Slam singles, Andre was very clear about the fact that he was retiring, and this gave him the opportunity to go out with the crowd behind him, supporting him, cheering him on. To be honest with you, I'm not sure which is the better way to do it.

In any event, at Wimbledon Andre made it safely through the first couple of rounds. It was then that he came up against Nadal. Rafa had just won his second consecutive French Open, so he was without a doubt the top clay-court player in the world. But it didn't seem like he had the game to dominate on grass. In the past, the Spanish contingent of clay-court specialists, guys like Carlos Moyá or Albert Costa, tended to give Wimbledon a miss, or if they played, they'd get mowed down in the early rounds. I remember wondering how the hell Rafa was going to play on grass. He'd gone out the previous year in the second round, he took those huge swings at the ball, so I figured he'd probably be lining up for another early exit, like so many of his countrymen. Just goes to show what I—and all those other so-called experts—know about the game.

Andre also seemed to think he had a good chance against Rafa. And guess what? He was wrong as well. Totally. In his own autobiography, *Open* (which is a very good read, by the way), Andre remembers Rafa being "a brute, a freak, a force of nature . . . he annihilates me. The match takes seventy minutes."

What was interesting for me was that afterward Andre said that playing Nadal on grass was a total nightmare. Although I'd called the match for the BBC, watching Rafa was clearly not the same as having to return his shots, and at that stage I'd never hit with or played against him—that pleasure was yet to come—so I'd never have imagined it would turn out to be as one-sided as it was. OK, so he had that huge amount of topspin, but on grass it doesn't have the same impact as on clay, it doesn't jump up quite as high. He also had that incredible forehand, which caused Andre major problems, his movement was great, and he was so competitive on every point, as if every point was a match point, which all added up to a really tough package to handle. But Andre was always very smart about tactics, he analyzed the game very carefully, sized people up well, and knew what to do on a court. So when he said that it was a total nightmare to play Rafa *on grass*, not just on clay, it made me sit up and think, "Maybe I'd better look at this guy more carefully, he's obviously not a one-surface player, and he is even better than we all realized." If Andre, with all his skill and experience, couldn't handle Rafa on grass, then this guy was the real deal. And he proved it by going right through the draw and straight into his first Wimbledon final, where it took all of Roger's formidable talent to beat him in four sets.

At that September's US Open, I watched Andre make his emotional goodbyes to the home crowd and shuffle off court for the last time with that pigeon-toed walk of his to join the ex-pros on the dark side of that dividing line, the one where you have to find your own path, where it's often unclear where you should be going, and where many former athletes stumble and fall. A month later I played what turned out to be my own very last main ATP tour doubles event—with Jonas Björkman at the Stockholm Open. I had one of those light-bulb moments—right in the middle of our match against third seeds Todd Perry and Simon Aspelin, as it happens—when I realized, "You know what? I'm bored by this." That's when I knew, "OK, enough is enough. Stop."

Unlike Agassi at his last match at the Open, I felt no emotion as I left the court for the last time as a regular tour player. I just had no desire to be out there anymore. I still loved to compete, but I'd done what I'd set out to prove, so now I could let it go. Actually it was a good feeling to quit in that way, because it involved a conscious decision on my part, and I knew that rather than masquerading as an occasional doubles player on the main tour, my future lay in competing in singles as well as I could, and for as long as I could, on the seniors circuit. So that's what I continued to do.

The best part of the whole year for me had nothing to do with tennis. It was filming an episode of *Curb Your Enthusiasm* with Larry David. If truth be told, I hadn't watched much of the show up until then. I like stand-up comedy; I really admire comedians who put their neck on the line each time they get up there on their own and hope for some laughs. When I was younger, I loved to go out to the comedy clubs and see all the greats of the time perform—David Letterman, Chris Rock, even Jerry Seinfeld, who I thought was great (he lives one floor below me in our New York building now, so he's not done too badly). I remember seeing Larry David then as well, but to be honest, he was terrible. At that point, he was what's known as "a comedian's comedian," which basically means his peers liked him more than the crowd did. To me, he just wasn't funny, and I don't think I was the only one who felt that way, because he would come off stage all bent out of shape and go, "They don't understand me, they're a bunch of assholes," in that typically Larry David kind of way.

Anyway, fast-forward thirty years and Larry's the toast of the town, the great comedy writer/performer who co-created *Seinfeld* and then came up with the semi-autobiographical HBO hit *Curb Your Enthusiasm*. My three oldest kids were huge fans, so when I got asked if I wanted to be in an episode in series five, they told me, "Dad, you've gotta do it!"

I'd met Larry a few times but I didn't really know him. When he called me up with the offer, it was already mid-December and I was finishing up a long year and was exhausted. Unlike other offers of film or TV work, where usually they say it'll be the following month or even later, Larry told me we'd be filming in a couple of days. And the shoot involved me flying out to LA. Now, most people would be dying to do a Larry David show, right? But my first reaction was, "Who pulled out?"

Larry never told me. "John, it's not bad to be runner-up," he shot back. "Hundreds of people would want this job." Which was true. But what was also true was that it meant filming Friday, Monday and Tuesday, so I figured I'd be stuck out in LA for a weekend with nothing specific planned only a few days before Christmas. I felt I needed to at least create the impression that I was helping Patty get ready for the holidays, so I tentatively tried asking if there was any way they could film my scenes on three consecutive days, say Monday to Wednesday, because I knew that going off for yet another trip, this time at the very last minute, would not go down well with Patty when it seemed like I'd only just got back from a trip. It turned out, though, that Larry had had to get permits for two of the places we were filming—LA airport and the Staples Center—and those permits allowed for filming at specific times only and they couldn't be changed.

So I agreed—slightly reluctantly—and flew out to LA the next day. In the end, thankfully, Patty came too, so at least we got to spend some time together in the days before Christmas. My episode was called "The Freak Book." There was no script, just an outline of what Larry wanted, so rather than me having to learn a ton of lines, we were sort of winging it the whole time, which I enjoyed. After reading the outline I found myself thinking, "How the hell does he even come up with these ideas?" It was unbelievable—hilarious.

At one stage, for example, I was in the back of a limo (playing myself—as usual; they never want me for Chekhov), with Larry as my driver, and he was questioning me about all these crazy things, which started to anger me, because I wasn't prepared for half of them. But it worked. Between takes—and we only did a couple for each scene—Larry was going, "Yeah, I think we're on to something." So he obviously knew what he wanted and what he didn't.

In the Staples Center scene, I'd supposedly been driven by Larry to a Paul McCartney concert where I'd been invited to a pre-show party, which Larry then invites himself to. I'm like, "You're the limo driver, you can't come and meet Paul McCartney." But eventually he talks me into it and I do invite him. Once inside, we're looking at this book about freaks together and I say something like, "Oh my God, what a freak!" At that point everyone goes quiet because this is the exact moment when Heather Mills—who has only one leg and was Paul McCartney's wife at the time—walks in. Of course Larry and I get thrown out of the arena and have to miss the show, and we're yelling at each other outside: "Fuck you!", "No, fuck *you!*" You get the picture.

It was a lot of fun, and the whole thing ended up being one of my most enjoyable experiences of filming and a great way to end the year. The funny thing is, along with Adam Sandler's *Mr. Deeds*, that episode of *Curb* remains one of the things that a lot of people most know me for. Not the tennis. Not the commentary. Just those two short moments on screen. Go figure.

10

"At first we couldn't be establishment,
because we didn't have any money"

Phil Knight, Nike CEO

At the start of 2007, I flew to Portland, Oregon, to do a tennis clinic with Pete Sampras at the Nike HQ. Nothing particularly unusual in that, you might think, and you'd be right. What made the day a little different was that Nike's founder and chairman, Phil Knight, was going to be on court with us. Phil had been a well-known tennis nut, but more recently golf had taken his fancy, and of course basketball was his company's bread and butter. So the chance to get Phil Knight thinking tennis again— even if only briefly—was one the Nike tennis team was eager to take.

My story with Phil goes back a long way, all the way back in fact to my first Wimbledon in 1977. Phil saw me play as a raw eighteen-year-old and got in touch with my dad just before I turned pro. Nike was a relatively new company at that stage and made only tennis and track shoes, but Phil—a graduate of Stanford Business School and a born entrepreneur—must have felt that I could potentially provide some useful exposure and credibility for his brand.

He liked that I was not a safe, "establishment" athlete, and I wasn't scared of saying what I thought, even if that got me into trouble. The fact that Ilie Nastase and Jimmy Connors had been the first tennis players to sign with Nike, back in the mid seventies, says a lot about the sort of athlete Phil was interested in doing business with, especially in those early days. I duly signed an endorsement deal to wear Nike shoes (the clothing deal would come later). The first slogan they proposed to me was "McEnroe's favorite four-letter word," but my dad vetoed that one. We settled on "McEnroe swears by them."

Phil's an unbelievably smart guy who developed a brand that everyone recognized and many wanted to wear. He's covered all the bases in tennis, with players ranging from the saint-like Roger Federer to current bad boy Nick Kyrgios paid to wear that well-known logo. As one of the early adopters of Nike's "Just Do It" attitude, I feel I have a particular bond with Phil, not least because a few years after we faced each other across the net at Nike HQ, he agreed to become the first sponsor of my tennis academy.

When Phil built the big Nike headquarters in the Portland suburb of Beaverton in 1990, each one of the eight original buildings was named after a Nike-endorsing athlete. I have to admit it was pretty cool to be one of those original eight, especially as Phil's own office was in the "John McEnroe Building." I guess it just shows, if you stick around long enough, you become part of the sports establishment, whether you want to or not. Nowadays, Pete Sampras also has a building in that headquarters so I'm no longer the lone tennis guy on the campus, but I have been under contract longer than any other athlete—even longer than Michael Jordan, although I wish I'd had his deal.

As for Pete, I didn't actually play him on that occasion in Portland. But I had to play him later that year in three exhibitions on three consecutive days across the US. Given that Pete is twelve years younger than I am, I was obviously somewhat concerned about these matches.

As it turned out, Pete was cool to me when we played those exhibitions. He's not one of those guys who has to win every single point. He doesn't have that kind of intensity about his every move. Even when he was playing at his best, as long as he won that final point, Pete never looked as if he cared too much if some of the others went to his opponent. Pete's the sort of player where you could lose to him 6–4 and not remember doing anything wrong, but he'd just have that one great return game, he'd pick it up on exactly the right points, and however well you'd played the rest of the time, that would be it. He did that to everyone, throughout his career.

As a pro on the regular tour, I lost to Pete all three times I played him, including once in the 1990 US Open semis, the year he won his first Grand Slam title. I hated playing Pete because nothing I ever did seemed to bother him, and that made me feel even older and even slower than I already was. On the seniors tour, I have probably played him fifteen times and beaten him maybe three, so not a very good record, but hey, it's better than zero. In the end, those exhibitions in 2007 went fine. Although I lost all three, I know it looked and felt OK, and I didn't even need to have the "don't make it look too bad" discussion because he's always been so relaxed about that sort of stuff.

I'm a great admirer of what Pete's achieved in the game. Even though we function in totally different ways, we get along very well. The same is true of my brother Patrick and me. As well as playing doubles together, we now both do quite a lot of commentating for ESPN, and in May of that year, we got asked to do a radio show together called *Mac and Mac in the Morning*.

There were two big morning radio shows in New York at that

time, and people tended to listen to one or the other: either Howard Stern, who had a whole range of guests on, from hookers to politicians, and whose shows got a little crazy; or cowboy-hat-wearing Don Imus, who while also a loose cannon is more conservative and politically oriented. Both still have a big cult following—particularly Howard—and have been going for years. My dad, for example, loved Imus's show, which is one reason why I would never listen to him—Imus that is, not my dad, though I didn't always do a whole lot of that either.

Patrick and I weren't aiming to break Don and Howard's airwaves duopoly right from the start, but when we were asked to fill in on WFAN for that 6–10 a.m. morning slot, we thought it would be worth a shot, and a potentially interesting thing to do down the road. The show itself was a good experience for both of us. I was still being talked about as someone who could maybe do something in that arena, possibly with a regular sports radio slot, but in the end we only did it a couple of times. Partly because Patrick was too busy with other commitments and partly because, if I'm honest, it was back to the eternal dilemma for me. The bottom line was, did I actually want this as much as I should—or would need to—in order to make this my main job? The short answer was no.

A while later, I was offered a drive-time slot in the afternoon, and it was close to happening at one stage. But the same kind of dilemma arose every time. If I did the morning drive time, it would mean getting up at four in the morning, five days a week, which would mean never having breakfast with my kids. If I did the drive-time 4–7 p.m. slot, that would mean bailing not only on dinner with them but also anything else they were involved in, like a basketball game or a school function. That's a lot to miss out on. Most working people don't have any choice about those kinds of time commitments, but given that I didn't *have* to take the gig in order to pay the bills, it felt a bit selfish. Plus, it would have gotten in the way of all the other things I enjoy doing.

Aside from taking on a five-day-a-week, all-encompassing job for far less money than I was currently earning, I'd also be reading commercials every few minutes—"Go to Goodyear for your tires! Eat at McDonald's! Go lose all your money in Atlantic City over the weekend at one of Donald Trump's casinos!" Not that I'm snobbish about commercials. They've paid the bills for me over the years, and I'm grateful that companies still feel they can use my image to market their products.

In 2007, I even shot a couple that, given the way most commercials you see totally suck, I thought were passably amusing. The first one was for an Australian cell phone company. The premise was that you could get a connection even in an elevator, which, in those days, was not only a novel idea but seemed like a good one. In this commercial, supposedly set in Australia, I get into an elevator while doing a deal on the phone, but as I'm about to close out the deal I get cut off. I immediately throw the phone down on the floor of the elevator, screaming (you guessed it) "You *cannot* be serious!" The guy who's in there already thinks he's recognized me from somewhere, and as I stride out angrily, he goes, "Wait a minute . . . Australia . . . tennis player . . . Pat Cash!"

It seemed to go down well, maybe because, as with all the commercial work I've done, I'd been involved in the script, seeing it in advance to make sure it not only sounded like me but also hopefully showed I didn't take myself too seriously. One of the best commercials I've ever done was shot in August of that year. I flew to London from LA to do a television commercial with Björn Borg for Tesco, a chain of British supermarkets. We filmed for a couple of days in an actual store but, because of opening times, we could only shoot from 11 p.m. to 6 a.m. That was perfect for me because it meant I kept on LA time with my body clock, so I never got jet-lagged. It was as if we were filming during the daytime for me and I then slept during the actual daylight. Very weird, but it worked.

The commercial itself involved us being in a store and competing up and down the aisles for the same things, trying to outrun each other to reach them and then get to the checkout first, the premise being that the supermarket chain wants to help us to do our shopping fast and efficiently. The final shot is of Björn beating me to the front of the counter, then smugly holding up a silver foil plate and waving it in my direction like he's holding up one of those Wimbledon trophies. I get it, Björn, so you won a few more than I did.

That commercial was right up there with *Mr. Deeds* or *Curb Your Enthusiasm* as a positive experience, because Björn turned in a really funny performance and the whole thing was great to shoot. I thought we'd do a few more together after that, but for some reason, other than one commercial in Sweden, we never did. Too bad, because it's always good to work with him.

Generally, nowadays, I try to do one decent commercial a year, rather than indiscriminately doing anything that comes my way. I don't want them to be totally lame—I've done a few of those in my time, believe me—and I want to be involved with a product that has enough credibility that I'm not embarrassed to be taking the money—ideally a product that I would actually use myself. I know that, with chain stores, for example, there are many ways to look at the whole subject: for example, you may be hurting the little corner grocery store, but you're also potentially helping busy people to find a way to shop that's convenient for their lifestyle.

I hope I haven't spread myself too thinly over the years when it comes to commercial endorsements. You've got to check yourself sometimes when commercial decisions start to take on their own logic. At the higher levels of business, there's a strange kind of crossover territory where show business, sports, charity and advertising all meet, and you're not quite sure which currency you're dealing in. A good example of that would be a trip I went on a few years later to Richard Branson's ultimate holiday resort, Necker Island.

I was invited along with a bunch of other players, including Tommy Haas and the Bryan brothers. Plus Novak Djokovic—somewhat incredibly in the latter case, considering he was winning Slams by then and he should've been in training for the Australian Open. It must have been the last thing he'd felt like doing. But Novak had had this event in downtown New York for his own charity right after that year's US Open, and he'd cut some sort of deal with Richard Branson where he would auction himself off to play with some people on Necker Island, and the money would go toward his foundation.

I'd gone along to the charity evening to support Novak and at one stage the bidding for Novak got stuck with two guys on a six-figure sum. So Novak—who as well as being one of the game's good guys, is also one of its smartest operators—started thinking fast on his feet, just like he does on court. "John," he yelled out to me at my table, "if you come along as well, you guys can both pay and you'll each get to play against the two of us. How about that?"

When you put it like that, Novak ... I've got to give him credit, though, because he returned the favor and came and played an exhibition match for free at Randall's Island in 2014 to raise money for my tennis academy. As I said, he's a good guy.

So we all arrived on Necker Island, which is a real pain to get to. I guess that's the point—it's not exactly somewhere that scheduled flights go in and out of, even if you have your own airline. You have to fly to the British Virgin Islands (which is funny when you think about it, as they're one of the few things around there that Richard Branson doesn't own), then take another plane, then take a boat or helicopter to this tiny island.

There were probably a hundred people at this event, plus fifteen pros. A few of us, like me, Novak and his now-wife, Jelena, were staying on the island, in one of Richard Branson's guest villas. Everyone else was coming in just for the day, because it was only a short boat-ride from another island nearby. Everyone had paid a lot of money to play with us pros and to go on a trip to Necker Island. The point is that the money goes to charity. The players, including me, also get a decent flat fee to show up, which I donated to my tennis foundation. So as far as I was concerned it was a win-win.

The tennis itself was unbelievable, but not in a good way. We were all in teams, pro-am, round-robin, and there were all these crazy rules. Like if you were aced, you had to have a shot of tequila. That meant guys got pretty drunk because some of them weren't too good with the racquet.

At one point some guy I'd never met before came up to me and said, "I've got four hookers. Are you interested?" "Hey man, I'm married. I'm good." He looked at me like, "Why would being married mean hookers were out of bounds?" It was that sort of day.

Even Novak was aced a few times, even though God knows he tried not to be. So he had to play along with the whole tequila shots thing. I think he was a little stressed by the end because the Australian Open was only a month away, and he needed to focus. This trip was not exactly ideal preparation but, credit to the guy, he was being pretty loose and friendly. He managed to down the odd shot and, even though he's famously gluten-free, he didn't demand everything be gluten-free. I believe he did actually have a french fry, but God forbid he should eat a piece of pasta. (And just for the record, Novak did go on to win that year's Australian Open.)

Richard Branson was there throughout. To me, he's totally nuts, but in a good way. He's got all these ideas, to the extent that he makes me feel quite boring in comparison. During that trip he was so full of energy and enthusiasm—"Hey, John, I've got this world expert coming in on Saturday to discuss coral-reef preservation, if you want to hear about that." "Well, I wasn't planning on it, but, OK, that sounds like a good idea." Next thing you know, you've signed up for it because he's such a convincing guy.

When it comes to tennis, let me tell you, Richard is pretty serious. He's very passionate about it and when he's on court—as at all other times, I suppose—he totally means business. I guess he and Phil Knight didn't get where they are today by having their service broken.

11

"It's tough, it's tough . . . it hurts"

Roger Federer

The French Open of 2008 ended with another Rafael Nadal win over Roger Federer, but this time the match was so incredibly one-sided—6–1, 6–3, 6–0—that it was almost embarrassing to watch. Rafa had also beaten Roger in the final the two previous years but each time he'd at least lost a set to him and both matches were competitive. This time, it was so bad that afterward Roger felt he had to apologize to the crowd for only managing to win four games.

When Wimbledon came around, you can bet that Roger wanted to send a loud and clear message to Rafa that, "OK, you're the king of clay, but hey, my reign on grass is still going strong." Trouble was, when they came up against each other in the final, Rafa wasn't in any mood to respect the plan. Björn Borg was watching in the royal box and whichever way the result fell, one of his incredible records was at stake that day: if Roger won, he'd be beating Björn's record of five straight Wimbledon wins. If Rafa won, he'd be the first guy since Björn in 1980 to win at Roland-Garros and Wimbledon back to back. And no, I can't for the life of me remember who Björn beat in that Wimbledon final.

With Nadal having lost to Roger the previous two years—in five sets in 2007—this final was lining up to be a fight to the death. Sometimes, as with the French Open that year, these finals don't live up to the hype, and it's difficult to know why. This one was the opposite—and then some.

Both guys had had smooth paths through to the final, including easy semi-final wins. Roger had cruised past Marat Safin—a former world number one and future Hall of Famer—while Rafa had done the same with the German, Rainer Schüttler. I was relieved to see Rafa going through, because I'd warmed him up on court before that match. The fact that I was a lefty and Schüttler was a righty didn't seem to bother Rafa, even though lefty and righty spins come at a player differently, so it's unusual to warm up against a "wrong"-handed player.

Remembering Agassi's verdict after he'd lost to Nadal on grass in 2006, and having watched Rafa a bunch of times through the commentator's window, I thought I knew what to expect as I walked onto court number 11 of the All England Club, but here's the thing: I had no idea that he comes out with guns blazing from the moment he hits that very first practice ball at what seems like a billion miles per hour. His intensity level is extremely high, his spin is unbelievable, he's rifling these shots all over the place. It's fun—as long as you're not his opponent! I practiced with him for forty-five minutes but it felt like two hours. I was a lot younger then than I am now, but I was sweating from the start.

Rafa's people had asked my agent, Gary, years before, when Nadal wasn't yet completely "Rafa," if I wanted to play doubles with him at the US Open, and, misguidedly, I'd said no, because I was too busy with TV and also I was a little, "Rafael Nadal can't play doubles" (and how much of a dumb-ass does this make me look in hindsight?). This time, I was happy to say, "Yes, let's hit," because I wanted to see what he did up close.

Our practice session happened late morning, not long before the Federer–Safin semi was due to start. That day I'd happened to go into the locker room at the same time as Rafa, so I'd dumped my bag near his. I guess the duty guard assumed I was part of the "entourage" and hadn't said anything. Wimbledon had recently changed the rules so that, unless you were in the seniors event (which I wasn't), you weren't allowed into the locker room. Apparently, being a three-time champion no longer cut it.

After the practice session, when I went back to shower and get changed, the guard on the door barred me from going in. "A security threat, Mr. McEnroe," I was told. You've gotta be kidding! I've had my issues with the people who run Wimbledon over the years, but I'd never been called that before. (I could see why they were jumpier than usual as this was the first Wimbledon after the 7/7 London bombings, but come on! This was me . . . if it was Jimmy Connors, I could understand.) I was due on camera shortly to commentate on the first semi, and as I was still sweating profusely after playing Rafa, the "on camera" wasn't shaping up too well, even if I managed to reclaim my suit. "Look, those are my clothes there, I can see them," I said, pointing through the open door. Eventually, after a bit of persuasion, I was allowed in, but that's Wimbledon for you. Rules are rules. You won here three times, you say? I don't care. You could still be a terrorist.

Truth be told, I didn't mind looking like Albert Brooks in *Broadcast News* on camera because I'd just hit with Rafael Nadal. My bigger worry was whether my practice with him had given him enough of a workout before his semi. I sat through the first match, a one-sided win by Federer, hoping that Rafa didn't have a bad start, because then it would feel like, "Jesus, why did I ever play with him? What was I thinking?" Then he won the first set 6–1 and I relaxed.

Clearly, I hadn't affected his chances. Nor in the final. Which turned out to be the best tennis match I had ever witnessed. When it finally ended, after nearly five hours and three rain delays, it was almost dark. With all the lights on around Centre Court, the atmosphere was electric as Rafa finally broke through to win the fifth set 9–7. Some people were ready to say it was a changing of the guard, and were already writing Roger off. I never believed that. For me, it was more a case of this guy Nadal being even better than any of us had thought. He proved that he was Roger's equal, he won the gold at the Olympics in Beijing later that summer, and he showed everyone that he could basically win on any surface. As for Roger, he went on to win the US Open a couple of months later and, at the time of this writing, he's just won his eighteenth major. Need I say more? So much for being written off in 2008!

Watching that final from the NBC commentary booth, I was in a situation where the less said in the fifth set, the better. I learned some time ago that less is often more behind the microphone, which is one reason I prefer not having three commentators in the booth, because it makes it more likely there'll be someone who doesn't know when to shut up. When the match is that good, you let it speak for itself. You don't have to blab on, because it's not about you, it's about the players—their heart and will, and the absolute intensity of this one-on-one encounter.

It was also getting dark out there toward the end—the third time they came off for rain at 2–2 in the fifth, it was already almost 8 p.m. This was crazy, everyone was thinking, are they even going to finish or are we all coming back tomorrow?

Incidentally, this was the last Wimbledon before the roof was installed, so that situation will never occur again. That's good, if you ask me, but in this particular case it would've been bad, because the gathering gloom added to the unbelievable atmosphere, something that only occurs at Wimbledon. For those of us calling the match, it felt like a privilege to be witnessing such a titanic battle.

I had to go speak to the two players for NBC as they came off, straight after Sue Barker had done her on-court interview with them. I couldn't help but start by thanking Roger for allowing us to be part of an amazing spectacle. I immediately saw that he was really emotional. His eyes were glistening. "It's tough, it's tough . . . it hurts," was all this normally highly articulate player could say, before stopping abruptly. I'd heard the unmistakable tremble in his voice. I'd also seen that Rafa was lurking, in camera shot, just behind, waiting for his turn. Class act that he is, he soon ducked out of view, aware of the emotions of the moment. I had to improvise, because there was nothing I could ask at a time like this without spoiling the mood, plus I understood what Roger must have been going through, so I went on: "I know you're feeling so much emotion right now, but come on, give me a hug." It happened totally spontaneously, but at that point, as I hugged Roger, I could feel the tears were about to start flowing. Somehow—God knows how—he'd avoided crying on court with Sue, so I wound things up there and then: "Thank you, man, thank you, thank you so much, OK?," I said, as Roger exited out of shot giving a brave thumbs-up. I too was emotional and almost lost for words. How would I have handled that losing finalist's interview if I'd had to do one when I was in the same situation twenty-eight years earlier?

*

It's weird how often in sports everything seems to come together at the right time, those kind of neat coincidences and
circular connections that would seem phony if you saw them
in a movie. In that 2008 final, Roger was aiming to break Björn
Borg's record five straight wins—and we'll never know how
Björn felt about that because he never had to find out. Back in
1980, when Björn himself achieved that incredible record fifth
win by beating yours truly, well, not to toot my own horn too
much, but that final wasn't a bad match either.

That day, Saturday, July 5 (finals were still played on a Saturday
back then), I'd blasted out of the starting blocks and wrapped
up the first set 6–1, but I'd then lost sets two and three without really playing any worse. I'd just tightened up very slightly
toward the end of the second because I'd felt like I was going
to win that one too. Subconsciously, maybe I wasn't ready for
the final to be that easy for me. Or maybe Björn had upped
his own intensity level. In any event, he served for the match
at 5–4 in the fourth. But by the time I broke him and forced a
tie-break, I could tell the crowd was clamoring for a fifth set. I
don't know whether they wanted me to win the whole thing or
not—I don't think they knew at that stage. They just wanted the
match to go on. That can happen in tennis: a crowd can turn
and switch their support from one player to the other—and
even back again—within a couple of games. It's scary, and it can
make for some intense scenes, but crowd support can definitely
be a factor in the outcome of a tennis match, and in this case the
packed Centre Court was cheering for me.

The fourth set tie-break is the number one thing people remember and talk about from that final—and my career as a
whole, for that matter—especially the fact that it went to 34 crazy
points, including me saving 5 match points. Even at the time, I
had a sort of out-of-body awareness that this was something

special, that this was no ordinary moment in a match. There was this incredible mix of the crowd's increasing hysteria as break points and set points came and went on alternate points, followed by the extreme quiet that came down when we were about to serve. Then there was a collective holding of breath before a huge explosion of noise at the end of each point, as the crowd's tension was released. However much I was focused on winning each point, I could feel and hear the silence as much as the noise coming from the crowd.

When I won that fourth set tie-break after being down two sets to one, the momentum was back with me. So much so that a lot of people who talk to me about that match nowadays have the mistaken idea that I ended up winning it, which is funny in some ways. When I won the tie-break 18–16, I too thought, "OK, that's it now, he's going to be totally destroyed at losing that set after all those match points, and I'm now going to win the match. Surely it's mine for the taking."

But I had no idea how strong Björn was, both mentally and physically. That's when I finally understood that he wasn't the same as the rest of us. This is a guy who says he's "never been tired" in a tennis match—and I believe him. We were both on serve throughout the set and the whole time I could see no sign at all that he was fading in any way. How was that even possible? "You've won this four times already," I kept thinking. "Come on, isn't enough *enough*?" Seeing him so resolute and unflappable just drained me—mentally and physically—until finally I got broken and lost 8–6. Game, set and match to Borg.

12

*"John McEnroe—bridging the worlds of
art collecting and yelling"*

Steve Martin in *30 Rock*

In October of 2008 I shot an episode of the hit NBC show *30 Rock*. Tina Fey and Alec Baldwin played producers on this big late-night comedy show that was based very loosely on *Saturday Night Live*, which Tina had previously worked on. I'd gotten to know Tina through a mutual friend—appropriately enough, *SNL* creator Lorne Michaels—and although I wouldn't say I knew her well, I did end up doing four episodes of the show, all of which I enjoyed. But this one was potentially lining up to be the most fun because Steve Martin was due to appear. I've known Steve for some years. As well as being a great comedian, writer and actor, and playing a mean banjo (damn, he's so multi-talented it makes me sick!) he's also a passionate and serious art collector, so it's that love of art which we have most in common whenever we meet. We've spent a fair amount of time together over the years, much of it spent in long discussions about which artists we're following and what he or I might have bought recently. Steve's got some incredible art—a Bacon, a great Edward Hopper, among many others. He's so smart.

I usually choose film or TV projects on the basis of whether I think they're going to be fun, not necessarily for career-advancing purposes, so I was never going to say no to this particular opportunity. I mean, doing a scene with Steve Martin, as well as Tina Fey and Alec Baldwin? Unbelievable.

On the day of the shoot, I got up early, drove an hour north to Upstate New York, and got to the house where they were filming. The routine was the same as usual: hurry up and wait. All day. I must have been there for six, seven hours—hanging around, waiting to do my one scene with Steve Martin, Tina and Alec.

The character Steve plays in that episode is an agoraphobic. Being afraid to leave his house means he has to have people come to him, so he's invited some interesting people over for a dinner party, including, he tells them—introducing me to the other guests—"John McEnroe—bridging the worlds of art collecting and yelling."

When the time finally arrived for us to shoot our big scene, Steve came up to me—"John, take care, gotta go." "Oh . . . really?" I was so taken aback and deflated, though I hope I didn't make it that obvious. "Yeah, had a long day." And off he went. Well, that sucked. But hey, the show must go on. Then Alec Baldwin came up to me. "Great to see you, John, but I gotta go." "Oh . . . really?" "Yeah, I have an early call-time tomorrow." And off he went too. That *really* sucked.

Still, at least Tina stayed. She probably felt so guilty or embarrassed that she had to. Or maybe not. In any case, I basically did the whole scene—and my usual four lines or so—with a couple of cardboard cut-outs as stand-ins for Steve and Alec. If it wasn't so sad it would be funny. I'd been so psyched up about doing this thing with Steve that I was pretty bummed, but I'd learned another lesson about this acting thing: it really is all about make-believe. On the upside, I won an Emmy for that performance . . . and if you believe that, I'll tell you another one.

Very different from tennis, you might think. Or maybe not. Newport, Rhode Island was the scene of a less stellar performance of mine a short time later. I was playing the first round-robin match in one of Jim Courier's seniors tournaments when I came up against MaliVai Washington, a former Wimbledon finalist back in 1996. I don't know why, but it seemed like we weren't on the same page from the start of the match. Everything I said or did seemed to annoy him. If I said "shit," he'd complain to the umpire. I felt like saying "Hey, sorry, that's part of the act. I actually get away with this now." Maybe MaliVai didn't like being the Washington Generals to my Harlem Globetrotters routine, but that wasn't my problem.

For some reason, on this one occasion, MaliVai was having none of it. Apparently, my behavior was outrageous and un-precedented—or so he kept telling the umpire. And the more he did that, the more I acted up—or down—to what he was saying. The more I wanted him to chill, the more agitated I got. I was stalling, cursing, the whole lot.

After winning the first set easily, I was 4–2 down in the second with Washington serving at ad-in. I was getting more and more irritable about the score, plus his complaining to the umpire, and on the next point I got seriously pissed about a bad line call. Suddenly, in the space of a couple of minutes, I got a warning, a point deducted, then a game. That gave the second set to my opponent. "What the fuck are you doing?" I screamed at the umpire. "You can't do this!" Next thing I knew—when I'd reacted to someone throwing insults out from the crowd—the umpire announced, "Game, set and match Washington." Defaulted. Just like that.

"Holy shit, one of the tournament's main draws is now out!

What do we do?" Luckily for Jim and the other tournament organizers, there was no rule to say that if you're defaulted in a round-robin match you couldn't compete in the other group matches, so they let me stay on—no surprises there. Hell, it was their rules in the first place! I thought it would be cool to be the first guy to get defaulted in a seniors tournament (and this was the first time that had ever happened on that circuit) but to go on and win it all the same. Unfortunately, Pat Cash had to ruin the party by beating me in the semi-final.

Some people may find this hard to believe, but I only got defaulted once on the main tour, too (though I think I'm still the only player ever to be thrown out of a Grand Slam). I got tossed out of the 1990 Australian Open during my fourth-round match against Mikael Pernfors for various "audible obscenities," as the ATP politely put it. The case for the defense on this occasion (this testimony may also be of interest to the prosecution) was that I hadn't realized that the rule for defaulting a player had been changed not long before from four steps to three. In short, I'd miscalculated. I thought the fact that I was on my third penalty warning only meant losing a game (the first two steps being the verbal warning and the penalty point deduction). I'd figured I could afford to make the sacrifice at that stage of the match and then I wouldn't let things get any crazier. Instead, the umpire simply defaulted me because—unbeknownst to me—the game deduction stage had been eliminated.

What does that tell you about my outbursts? It screams, loud and clear (almost as loudly and clearly as I did), that as a general rule I knew how far I could push that envelope. First, because I knew the tournament directors never had the nerve to default one of their star players. They weren't stupid. Second, because I wasn't stupid either. I wanted to win, and if I totally lost control, I knew it would be tough to recover.

In my early career, my problems with tennis officials were almost always to do with how bad I felt their decisions were. I'd always been brought up to tell the truth, so when a mistake affected me, I was going to say what I wanted to say, because why the hell should I let it go? The officiating standards in those days was often pathetically low. These people—who were all amateurs—made horrible mistakes. But that's only human—anyone can do that. The worst part of it was the way they looked at anyone who dared to challenge them as if they were total lowlifes, almost smirking in their superiority. That was what drove me nuts—"Admit you're wrong, man!" That was the loudest and most oft-repeated mantra of the voice in my head. But they never did that.

When I was young, I was lucky to have the ability to keep my concentration on court the whole time, even though it sometimes looked like I'd lost it because I was going crazy over some line call or other. The funny thing was—although I don't think I realized this back then—losing my cool initially helped me stay focused. As I got older, and life off the court started getting more complicated, that's when I began to find it harder to keep my mind on the match I was playing.

As a way of combatting this, I would sometimes try things—in a completely calculated way—to mix the game up and make it more interesting for me. If I was 40–0 up and pretty much knew I was going to win the game anyway, I'd try to hit a second serve ace, just to keep my opponent off balance. Or when I was 0–40 down I might go for broke more than I would otherwise, to see what happened.

It didn't mean I wasn't trying. Quite the reverse—it meant I was doing everything in my power to win. Sometimes, if I was 40–0 up, I'd also use that as an opportunity to wear the other guy down mentally and physically by extending a point on purpose, rather than ending it. I'd try to get it to a twenty-shot rally so that he'd be expending some energy, then he'd be breathing hard on the next point which, if I'd won the rally, would be the first of his service game. So he'd be at a disadvantage. Tennis is like a game of chess—a mind-game—and all these "games" were a way for me to avoid running on autopilot, to keep myself stimulated and engaged by throwing in something unusual.

Am I the first player in the history of the game to do this? No. In a long five-setter or three-setter, nobody is on fire the whole way through—although Rafael Nadal or Maria Sharapova give a pretty good impression of players whose intensity levels never drop below the maximum on the dial setting. This might bring a smile to the faces of Henri Leconte or Mansour Bahrami, but one of the reasons I never wanted to bring any humor to my matches on the main tour—and, don't laugh, but actually my first instinct would often have been to say something funny in response to some line call or situation on court—was because I never wanted to risk losing that intensity, that edge, which I needed in order to stay competitive. Maybe that's why I've sometimes gotten annoyed with the players that do clown around.

The most obvious way for me to keep engaged were the run-ins I had with tennis officials around the world. But as I got older, life problems started to get in the way of the tennis. I admit it, that's when I sometimes started to lose control of what I said or did, but by then I was too big a draw for anyone to really call me out on it. A few fines, a few penalty points, a few suspensions—on my terms, not theirs—but that was it. Until that day in Australia. Should the authorities have done more? Probably. But if I wasn't willing to take responsibility for my increasingly wayward actions, why should I expect anyone else to do that for me?

Nowadays, people ask me all the time how different the game would've been for me if the challenge system had been around when I was on the tour. Truth is, if I'd been able to challenge bad calls, I would probably have been a 20 percent better player but a 40 percent more boring one, because at the time I absolutely 100 percent sincerely believed that these people—the umpires, the line judges—were screwing me. That was part of what gave me my edge.

And by the way, did it ever occur to me that, by sheer probability, I sometimes got calls that worked in my favor and my opponent was getting screwed over? Yes, sure. But my view on that was always that if my opponent wasn't strong enough to stand up for himself, I sure as hell wasn't going to do that for him. I mean, it was tough enough out there without fighting *for* the other guy as well. Others—like my Davis Cup captain, the late, great Arthur Ashe—used to tell me that mistakes even out.

There's never been a full-on equivalent of me, or Connors, or Nastase in the women's game—a player who would give the finger—but Serena Williams certainly put a marker down in her semi-final with Kim Clijsters at the 2009 US Open. Serena had already gotten herself a penalty warning when she was foot-faulted on a second serve at a set down, 5–6, 15–30 which was unfortunate, to say the least, because that put her at 15–40 and gave Kim two match points. There's certainly a question of whether that sort of call should have been made at that key moment, given that it hadn't happened all match. But once it did, Serena went crazy at the line judge, dropping the f-bombs big time, not letting go. In the end, the umpire gave her a penalty point, which then gave Kim the match.

It's highly unusual to see one of the women behave like that, but it was certainly memorable. Given how big that match also was, that was the one time I consciously remember thinking, as

I sat in the booth commentating, "Jesus, did I ever do anything this bad?" The short answer is: "I don't think so, at least, never in a Grand Slam semi," although my overall body of work certainly eclipses Serena's in this area. Nice try, Serena—close, but no cigar.

13

*"I watched you on TV and I don't like what
I'm seeing. Your serve's off and your return,
you need to move into it . . ."*

Tony Palafox

In the summer of 2009, I got one step closer to achieving a long-held ambition when I sealed the deal to set up a tennis academy. I'd spent years searching for a way to set up a tennis program that would allow New York kids—and the idea was always to have kids from all kinds of backgrounds—to train regularly but still live at home and continue their education, like I did when I was growing up. It's important to me that kids have a choice in their tennis training. It shouldn't just be "go to Nick Bollettieri's or forget it," though I have to hand it to Nick, his academy has turned out quite a few champions over the years, so it must be doing something right.

It was shocking to me that not a single leading male player on the circuit had made it out of my home town since my brother, almost a quarter century before. I wanted to help change that, so I'd been talking to the USTA for years about setting up a tennis academy at the National Tennis Center at Flushing Meadow, but they looked at me like I was speaking a foreign language.

Former CEO Arlen Kantarian was very much in my corner, but he wasn't in a position to pull the trigger on the money and he needed the USTA board's approval, which perhaps had one too many ex-umpires or players that I'd had run-ins with over the years!

When they built this whole new $75 million indoor tennis facility which opened there in December 2008, I thought that would have been the ideal time to set up an academy with my name on it, considering I grew up in the borough, considering I won there four times, played and captained the Davis Cup, and now commentate there. Anyway, for whatever reason, it never happened. Maybe I wasn't enough of a politician for them, I don't know. Instead, in 2008, they appointed my more diplomatic brother Patrick as head of the USTA's junior development program, so at least they got one McEnroe on the payroll.

Patrick's new job meant that he had to resign as director of tennis from another tennis facility in New York. It was on Randall's Island, north of Harlem but about as close to Manhattan as you can be and still have that kind of space. It's also got very good facilities, which I'd say are arguably as good as the USTA's. The club itself is part of a group owned and operated by Claude Okin. Claude is one of those guys who is just crazy about tennis, and has the luxury of being able to finance what I call his addiction, to the extent that he even paid through the nose for years to have me and others turn out in empty stadiums for his New York TeamTennis team. Thank God there are people like him around, is all I can say!

That summer, we had several meetings about what my role might be at the club, how the finances would work if we had a John McEnroe Tennis Academy based there, and in the end, we were able to cut a deal pretty fast. I was fired up to be involved with a program that I felt could help New York kids. Not

Sydney, 1979: in the dressing room right after the first time I ever went onstage at a rock concert, with Vitas Gerulaitis, Eddie Money, Carlos Santana, and a couple of Carlos's bandmates.

I'll drink anything Tina Turner gives me! The late, great David Bowie also seems to be enjoying himself ... (Bob Gruen)

An early night at the Mudd Club – trying to fit in with the dark shades.
(Kate Simon)

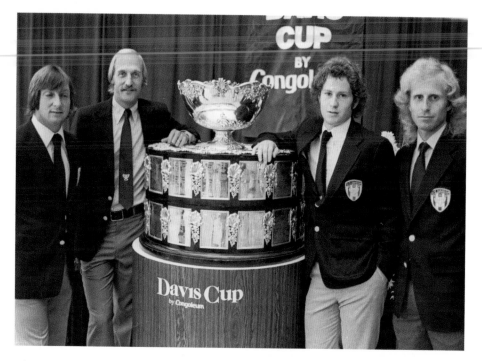

The winning 1979 USA Davis Cup team – Bob Lutz, Stan Smith, myself, and
Vitas.

At the year-end Masters back in the day, with Ivan Lendl, Mats Wilander, and, just behind me, Andrés Gómez. (Michael Scocozzo)

Basketball had its Dream Team in 1992, and this was the tennis equivalent. In Fort Worth, Texas, at the last Davis Cup match I ever played: Andre Agassi with hair (and plenty of it), Jim Courier, myself, Pete Sampras, and coach and captain Tom Gorman.

At my Hall of Fame induction at Newport, Rhode Island, in 1999 – my friend the wonderful artist Eric Fischl (on the right) painted this portrait of me serving especially for the occasion.

With Patty and Anna, cutting the ribbon at the opening of a neonatal nursing station at Lenox Hill Hospital, where my mom used to work and where Anna spent the first month of her life, having been born seven weeks prematurely.

At the first St. Patrick's Day parade after 9/11 – March 17, 2002 – I was proud just to be walking alongside these heroic firemen.

Me in front of the John McEnroe Building at the Nike HQ in the Portland, Oregon, suburb of Beaverton – just checking they still had my name on the building!

With Patty, meeting Nelson Mandela in the backyard of his Johannesburg home. He shook my hand and it was like being greeted by an angel.

Outside the Las Vegas theater where Patty opened for the great comedian Don Rickles in November 2001.

The only time I ever went camping – on the Futaleufú River in Chile. Sorry, Anna, your mom and dad love each other – what can I say?

All dads have to be Santa Claus, don't they?

Rocking out with my good friend Chrissie Hynde of the Pretenders.
Backward baseball caps are allowed when you're onstage.

only because I like working with young people and was excited about the idea of having some kind of legacy and giving something back to tennis, but the specific location of the academy was one I felt a real connection with.

Randall's Island was a place where I used to play high school soccer. It was really run down back then, the baseball fields became a place for drug addicts to leave their needles, and there seemed to be broken glass all over the place. Most adults and a lot of the schools stopped going there. Fortunately, Mayor Bloomberg—who, by the way, is one of the richest men in the world—saw the potential to expand his own legacy and set up a foundation—now called the Randall's Island Park Alliance—whose mission was to redevelop the site. He put a lot of his own money in, and with the help of other private investors, including Claude Okin, the new tennis facility was built alongside all the baseball and other fields.

The John McEnroe Tennis Academy now has twenty courts—ten clay, ten hard—most of which can be indoors or outdoors, depending on the season, and there's a public–private ownership set up whereby we lease the land from New York City and a percentage of our profits go back to them. My personal charitable foundation then tries to raise money, either through some of the exhibitions or clinics or fundraisers that I do, or by having some of the tour's good guys like Djokovic or Nadal play an exhibition at the academy itself. That then allows us to offer subsidized lessons and even free training for as many kids as possible who couldn't otherwise afford to play.

There's no doubt that tennis is still too expensive. It's a hard problem to tackle and one that applies to a lot of sports, but in tennis it seems that privilege is built into the very infrastructure of the game. One example is the way ranking points are given in the junior game; the system favors rich kids whose parents can pay for them to travel round the country over the local and minority kids who don't have that backing. We're doing our best to help them, but there's a long way to go, and those are the kids we most need to encourage.

It's a numbers game. For every ten kids you provide help for, nine won't make it, for whatever reason. So you need a bigger pool to choose from in the first place. For that to happen, the game has to be not only more affordable but sexier, more inclusive, and even possibly have a team element, like in TeamTennis, so that kids aren't out there all alone, playing in isolation.

We've had some success. One of our prize pupils, Noah Rubin, won Junior Wimbledon in 2014, and is now successfully working his way up the rankings; another student, Jamie Loeb, won the NCAA college singles title in 2015 and turned pro; and we've had numerous others—boys and girls—who've received full tennis scholarships into division one colleges, so that's really exciting.

In the meantime, I try to show kids at my academy a way of playing the game that I hope will help them get the best out of tennis, at whatever level they end up playing. So right from the start, I came up with a wish-list, called the John McEnroe Ten Commandments, which I would repeat to them in training sessions (these kids, unlike my own, were forced to listen to me—Larry the Lecturer rides again). The commandments are:

Thou shalt not beat thyself
Thou shalt never give up until the last point is played
Thou shalt not make excuses for poor performance
Thou shalt try to be mentally and physically fit to maximize
    performance
Thou shalt try to chase down every ball
Thou shalt respect every opponent but fear none

Thou shalt enjoy the game of tennis and try to stay positive
Thou shalt not throw thy racket
Thou shalt not curse

Hang on a minute, is this me talking? I'm so distracted I can't think of the tenth one.

One of the other things I really believe in, and which I try to emphasize not only to the kids at the academy but to their parents, is that they need to play other sports—ideally until the age of at least fifteen or so—and not just focus on tennis alone from the age of eight or ten years onward. Studies have now proven that it helps kids reduce the risk of injury if they do different sports at an age when their bodies are still developing and strengthening. Throughout my childhood, I was playing all the team sports going: basketball, football, soccer and baseball were my favorites, with basketball at the top of my list. My parents encouraged me, as well as my brothers, to keep them up. In fact, at age twelve, I probably wanted to be a pro basketball player more than a tennis player, and I continued on playing until I was sixteen years old, in the eleventh grade, when the Trinity school basketball coach at the time, Dudley Maxim, didn't think much of my abilities, so I decided not to try out for the team and end up collecting splinters on the bench. Thanks for not believing in me, Dudley. As a result of your shrewd judgment, basketball's loss ended up being tennis's gain. But I will say this: playing basketball and soccer not only improved my movement on court and my hand-eye coordination, they also helped me understand what it was to be part of a team, to enjoy the camaraderie, to have others there to share my victories and defeats. Plus, for someone like me who was shy—hard to believe, but true of me then—being on a team was a good way to develop friendships.

As well as playing a variety of sports, the other thing promising young tennis players should also do, if at all possible (though there have been some early-maturing exceptions like Becker and Nadal, and no doubt such freaks of nature will emerge again), is go to college. I would strongly advise all kids that get the chance to do that—whether for reasons of emotional or physical development—and I'm proud that my foundation's fundraising exhibitions and events have already helped quite a few kids get tennis scholarships to college which, whether or not they end up taking the sport any further, has helped their education and future life prospects.

The subject of tennis clubs brings up all sorts of potentially tricky issues to do with class, race, accessibility and money. Luckily for me, the club where I started playing tennis—in Douglaston, Queens—had no stuck-up members, and it was peopled with aspiring, young middle-class families just like mine. Back in the sixties, tennis still had that country-club image from the past, but the new professional middle classes such as my parents wanted a slice of the pie, and the Douglaston club was perfect for them. It was still all white, though, and I don't know how warm a welcome a New York version of the Williams sisters would've gotten.

I hate the idea that kids who are not white or rich might not feel that they belong in tennis. That elitist image—which is sometimes a reality—kills talent and stops those kids from choosing our sport over, say, basketball and football (American football), which is currently where our best athletes tend to go. I get a sense that it's still somewhat the same in England. A lot of those private clubs don't reach out in the way they should, in my opinion. And let's face it, unless I've missed something, Wimbledon itself is pretty much the ultimate white upper-middle-class enclave.

When I won there the first time in 1981, they were practically choking on their cucumber sandwiches at having someone like me, the mouthy kid from Queens (we're talking the New York Borough here, not the exclusive tennis club in West London), become a member. They were scared as hell at the thought of me propping up their bar. Don't worry, guys, I'd rather have chewed my headband than show up for a beer in SW19.

One thing I was happy to do was go back to our old family club in Douglaston in October 2009, especially because they'd finally decided to name their main court after me. I know what you're thinking—"about time," right? No, hang on, that's what I was thinking. It was a fun day because my band got to play after the ribbon-cutting ceremony and the dinner that followed. There were old childhood friends there, such as Doug Saputo and Andy Broderick, who I'd grown up with and known since we were kids, so almost half a century (did I really write that?). It was a great evening of music, tennis, friends and nostalgia. I don't go in for a whole lot of that, but I'm not averse to going down that road now and again. It's good to remember where you came from, even when you're constantly trying to move forward.

The opening of the John McEnroe Tennis Academy was finally announced in May 2010, and we formally opened our doors soon after that year's US Open. I'd actually been working there since the start of the year so that we could figure out what all the plans for the coaching would be and what exactly we were going to offer. I knew we'd have to hit the ground running if we wanted to give a new generation the kind of first-class coaching that I was lucky enough to receive when I first came into the game.

I started playing when I was eight, and soon I was beating kids who were a lot older than I was. I loved any sport that involved a ball but was always best at tennis—I had good hand-eye coordination and a feel for the ball on the strings of the racket. That also helped to make up for the fact that I was small for my age and would never win a point through my strength of shot. I was a touch player, I was fast, and by the time I was twelve, I was ranked number seven in the country in my age-bracket.

By then I'd moved on from the Douglaston club to the Port Washington Tennis Academy, about twenty-five minutes' drive from where we lived, which had been founded as a non-profit tennis facility and had a big junior development program. That was where I began to develop as a tennis player after coming to the attention of two major figures in my life—Antonio (Tony) Palafox and the great tennis captain from Australia, Harry Hopman.

Tony, who was head coach at Port Washington, had won doubles titles at Wimbledon and the US Open so had been a really good player. At first, I wasn't seen as one of the big prospects there, but things started to pick up once Tony encouraged me to take the ball on the rise, with hardly any backswing, to get up to the net as soon as I could and create angles wherever possible.

That's pretty much how I still play, even if my journey to the net is now a lot slower. The funny thing with Tony Palafox is that he hasn't lost his eye when it comes to my game. He called me up on the phone not too long ago. "I watched you on TV," he said. "I don't like what I'm seeing. Your serve's off and your return, you need to move into it—" "Hey, Tony," I interrupted him, "tell me something I don't know." Once a coach, always a coach, I guess.

Harry Hopman—who was the inspirational leader at Port Washington when I arrived—was a tennis legend (although I didn't know it at the time); an ex-Aussie player, he'd made his name as their Davis Cup coach, and inspired a whole genera-tion of great Australians, including Rod Laver, Roy Emerson, Ken Rosewall and Lew Hoad, all of them legends in their own right. Rod "the Rocket" Laver, the only guy ever to win two cal-endar Grand Slams, is still my absolute tennis hero: he was a lefty like me, and he had an incredible touch. I idolized him so much when I was young that I had a poster of him on the back of my bedroom door. I spent my time on court trying to play like him, and my time off court frantically exercising my left forearm in the hope of building up muscle to the Popeye level that Rod had.

When I opened my academy, what I wanted above all was to try to model myself, in some small way, on Harry Hopman. And if I ever manage to inspire a kid to anything approaching the same degree as he inspired me, I'll consider myself satisfied. "The Hop" was known to work his players hard, off court as well as on it, but he saw that I hated all the drills, the exercises and the stretching, so he was a bit softer on me. Maybe he realized that I already moved well on court and had an intensity about me that made up for the fact that I was small for my age and not as fit as some.

Either way, his approach worked for me, and so long as the John McEnroe Tennis Academy follows in the footsteps of Harry Hopman and Tony Palafox, it won't go far wrong. Today's young players need all the guidance they can get. The amount of money that's swimming around in the game now adds extra pressures, and kids don't always get the best advice from the people who are closest to them. I'd seen this first hand over the years leading up to the academy opening, when I worked in an unofficial capacity with a few young prospects who were coming up through the ranks that my agents, IMG, wanted me to have a look at.

For me it was fun to see who was out there and potentially interact with the stars of the future. And hopefully the kids were happy to get the chance to play with me before I totally deteriorated. I remember how thrilled I was to be on the same court as Laver and Rosewall when I was young, so hopefully it was a win-win situation. It was certainly an eye-opener. And talented youngsters like the American Donald Young or the Australian Bernard Tomic definitely faced a few extra pitfalls beyond the ones I had to avoid.

What was crazy was that some of the parents thought I was trying to steal their children from them. "Why would I want to do that?" I felt like asking. "I've got enough of my own." Plus, I didn't want to travel all the time, which I'd have to do if I was coaching full-time, nor would I want to sit there holding their hands 24/7, being positive, telling them how great they were all day long. Believe me, coaching is not an easy gig, especially with kids like Young and Tomic who have been previously coached by their parents (and still are). There's a whole dynamic you'd be getting into the middle of which I think would be tough to handle.

Donald Young in particular is a cautionary tale, as far as I'm concerned. He is someone who was picked out at a very young age for greatness. I'd hit with him when he was nine years old because he was a ballboy at one of my seniors events in Chicago. Even then, he had very natural hands, a great feel for the ball and was very fast. He won the Orange Bowl 16's in 2003 when he was only fourteen (the Orange Bowl is like an unofficial junior world championships), turned pro in 2004, and in 2005, he won the Australian Open junior title, at fifteen and a half.

For a while he was the number one junior in the world, which was an amazing achievement at that age, but I think the reason he's not yet produced on the big stage in the way that he could've is that he was put under too much pressure too young. He was given huge Nike and Head contracts when he was still a kid and lost his way a little in the glare of expectation. I think if he'd had Tony or the Hop to help him keep his eyes on the prize, he could have done a lot more by now. Throughout this time his mom was coaching him and whenever I hit with him, she'd want to know anything I told him. I didn't think that was the most productive dynamic.

Bernard Tomic is another player who clearly had a lot of potential right from the start. Coincidentally, it was Tomic who beat Donald Young's record as the youngest ever winner of the Australian Open junior title when he won it in 2008, at fifteen years and four months. But Bernard's father, John, would always be screaming at him. I didn't even know the guy then—not that I do now, although I did manage to play him at ping-pong at Queen's in 2016 without anyone sustaining serious injury (I won 21–16, which was fortunate as I'd never have heard the last of it if he'd whipped my ass)—and I remember thinking, "Jesus, what's he *doing* to this kid?"

The stories about John Tomic have been legendary ever since his son arrived on the junior circuit, and in 2013 he got barred from the ATP tour after being convicted of assaulting his son's training partner. We had a little run-in a couple of years later when I pointed out in a commentary that Bernard was tanking against Roddick in the US Open, but I'm glad to say it didn't get physical, as John is clearly someone you wouldn't want to mess with. Obviously there's no way I'd ever take on any kind of coaching role with a player whose father had an anger management problem. I mean, hey, I'm still dealing with my own issues there!

It's a difficult line to walk at the academy between doing

what we have to do to keep the most talented prospects under our roof, and not giving in to insanely inflated parental demands. When you've got a rival institution trying to poach one of your best fifteen-year-olds by offering them a personal coach to travel with them to eight tournaments a year—for free—it's tough to know the right response. Part of you thinks you don't really want to get into that, but then on the other hand it's the reality of today's tennis world, so there'd be no point in me bringing up the fact that when I went to Europe for the first time in 1977, I only got five hundred bucks to cover all my travel and expenses (and that included booking my own hotels) for six weeks. Never mind having my own coach.

When it comes to supporting my own kids' tennis efforts, I've been determined not to be the classic pushy tennis parent. My kids are all athletic, but thankfully none has wanted to compete in tennis at a high level, although they're all good players and several of them have played for their college or high school teams. Tennis is such a tough sport to enjoy, in a way, because you always feel there's so much more to improve on. Plus, God knows, they're endlessly compared to me. "Ava McEnroe?" someone will go. "Oh, *McEnroe*, I see . . ."

This college essay my daughter Anna wrote in 2013 gave me a much clearer idea of the kind of pressure my kids faced when they walked out on a tennis court. I asked her permission if I could reprint it here as I really like the way she described the pleasure she gets from the game as well as the burden of her family inheritance. We haven't negotiated payment yet, though.

Anna's Essay
I like the spring of the ball when it bounces onto the cement court. I like its almost penetrable skin that gives with just the slightest crunch of my knuckles. I like watching the ball

float through the air when I toss it; I like watching it glide up indefinitely until, just when I need it to, it plummets down to earth reaching my racquet at the perfect moment. I like that my tennis shoes make me an inch and a half taller and I like the way the racquet makes me feel so powerful. I like the feeling of satisfaction I get when my arm swings forward and slams my racquet against the perfectly flimsy neon tennis ball. It's a release. Any anger, resentment, sadness or anxiety that had previously been bottled up inside of me is gone, banished when the taut strings of my racquet reach the iridescent ball. I like all those things. I love tennis. Watching it, playing it, feeling my adrenalin pump just as I see the ball smash in my direction; it almost makes it worth the hours I put in. But this feeling doesn't usually last long. It lingers for a minute or two until I snap back into reality and remember where I am. The John McEnroe Tennis Academy.

So despite the exhilaration I feel while actually playing tennis, it's the underlying sense of insecurity, all the accompanying baggage, that truly defines my playing of the sport. I am Anna McEnroe, and to the eyes of a spectator, I was molded from the clay of Roland-Garros and run on the grass at Wimbledon. I am a McEnroe, a McEnroe who plays tennis well; a McEnroe who plays well, but not well enough.

This is not to say that my last name has caused me only troubles. The benefits of it are almost embarrassingly clear. My father is respected by almost everyone he meets; therefore, we are treated differently; mostly we are treated better. It also comes with attention, sometimes bad, usually good, always unwanted. It comes with big houses and beautiful paintings and trophies that line our living room. It comes with pride . . . but also with stares and glares and jealousy. Jealousy of something I was born into, something I cannot control;

145

something that makes me different from the average person. It comes with lies and rumors and almost forgotten headlines that one day, fifteen years later, I stumble upon and find out truths about my father that I never knew before. It's a mixed bag, is what I mean; a blessing with built-in curses.

What probably bothers me the most is that people assume being a tennis prodigy is genetic. As if I being the daughter of John McEnroe would somehow mean that I was exactly the same person as he is. So when I do step onto the tennis court, it's the stares ripping into my back that I feel. It's the giggles and the sniggers I hear—a McEnroe who can't play tennis?! That gives me the passion I have for the sport. It's not the passion to play that keeps me going, but instead the passion to improve. To me, what is worse than the stares and judgment I receive is the incomprehensible idea that I would not be able to prove them wrong. I can play tennis. I am a McEnroe. I will not allow these outside forces to taint the trust I have in myself. I believe in myself. So, I play to prove them wrong, to prove myself right, and to make my name my own.

I just wanted my kids to be able to enjoy the sport I love—that's why I discouraged them from playing in tournaments. I know how tough that road is, and I've consciously tried to shield them from it, because it gets even uglier out there once you start traveling around trying to make it, even as a junior. It's a totally insane scene, with a lot of pressure and a lot of crazy parents, and there's no way I'd want to encourage my kids to seek out that life, unless they were exceptionally gifted and really wanted it.

Whenever I've come along to support them playing tennis—which I'll admit isn't too often because of the obvious difficulties that brings for them and for me—it seems, whatever I do, I get it wrong. If I sit on my hands and have a blank face, they say I'm not supportive. If I start encouraging them vocally, they think I'm being pushy and embarrassing. I guess that's what being a parent is all about: your kids will always reproach you for something, right? And if I ever try to give them advice, they say, "Dad, you're not my coach." Yeah, you're right.

14

"I thought I'd thought of everything"

David Gilmour, "Learning to Fly"

Negotiating my kids' feelings about how much I should or shouldn't get involved in their on-court activities over the years (or their lives in general, for that matter, as they've grown older) has been as much of a diplomatic minefield as running my own tennis academy. Diplomacy wouldn't be an attribute most people would put at the forefront of my skill-set, but I hope I've picked up a few of the basics. Over the years I've certainly had some eye-opening encounters with some of America's political leaders, not all of whom are the best role models in this (or, indeed, any) regard.

We used to own a nice home in Sun Valley, Idaho, which we'd go to when the kids were little. We all learned to ski there, and we liked it because it was a low-key resort—below the radar, not like Aspen, for example. We weren't bothered by the paparazzi, either, even though some well-known people had homes there, like our friends, Tom Hanks and his wife Rita, and Arnold Schwarzenegger and his then-wife Maria Shriver. Arnold and Maria would have this great party every New Year, and it was fun to hang out and ski and socialize a bit and sometimes even play ice-hockey together, along with Democratic Senator John Kerry (later President Obama's Secretary of State), who being Colorado-born is a pretty good athlete among his many other accomplishments.

One of the great things about skiing is that everyone is in disguise because of the clothes you have to wear, so it's easy for well-known people to enjoy doing it with family and friends as they don't tend to get recognized as much, and that makes for a relaxing holiday. I'd sometimes go skiing with Arnold because we had the same instructor, Adi Erber. As it happens, Arnold's a far better skier than I am—being Austrian, he obviously learned on the Alps when he was young. And me, I'm a bit of a "girlie-man" on the slopes.

One morning, we were going up on the chairlift together. It was soon after it had come out in the media that he'd groped all these women. At that stage, Arnold was running for Governor of California for the first time. This was years before the news broke that he'd had a child with a woman who worked for Maria and him. Even so, those initial allegations weren't exactly something to be proud of.

We were making our way up the mountain, and we'd had a hit of the peppermint schnapps that Arnold kept in his hip-flask—sure beats coffee for loosening you up for the slopes, let me tell you. "So, Arnold, what did you say to Maria that morning?" I asked, kind of in a concerned way. I was expecting him to tell me that he'd gone, "Oh, baby, I'm so sorry," and that he'd had to beg for forgiveness. He turned to me, looked me straight in the eye, and boomed out, in his strongly accented English, "I told her, 'Maria, you must have wiener schnitzel on the table at six o'clock!'" I nearly fell off the chairlift. It was so shocking, it was funny.

"Get the hell out of here, you didn't say that!" "Yes, yes, John.

I told her that she had to have everything ready!" The guy was unbelievable. And lucky. Because Maria stood by him that time and in my book that was absolutely the reason why he got to be governor.

Another leading politician I got to spend some time with who was no stranger to scandalous allegations was Bill Clinton. It was at the US Open in 2000, and President Clinton was sitting in a sky box while I was in the CBS commentary booth alongside Dick Enberg and my old friend and former mixed-doubles partner, Mary Carillo. While Pete Sampras and Lleyton Hewitt were fighting it out in their semi-final, Clinton sent a note saying he'd like to talk to me. I dropped everything, and for once was happy there were three people in the booth, as it allowed me to head straight over to meet him, along with Patty, Kevin, Sean and Anna. The next forty-five minutes or so were spent listening to Bill Clinton talking about every subject on earth, from golf and tennis—which, as it happens, he knew far more about than I ever imagined—to geopolitics and the future of the planet. At one point, the cameras picked us out, set the timer and calculated that I did not say a word for eight solid minutes. A McEnroe record! Clinton seemed to know everything about everything so I was happy to do the listening for once.

I got a more detailed look at how our political machinery works around the time of the 2004 election, when I started to get invited to more fundraising and lobbying events for the aforementioned fast-skating Senator John Kerry. He was seeking the Democratic presidential nomination at the time (which he won, though unfortunately the actual election was a step too far). Having known (and liked) him socially, I was impressed by John as a candidate and found him to be a genuine guy who had done some admirable things, including his military service in

Vietnam. He'd volunteered and served there with honor for a whole year, which was not a distinction everyone in US politics could claim. To me, the fact that George W. Bush of all people started trying to cast doubt on his war record, even though it turned out he had only been a reservist and hadn't seen action himself, summed up what politics should *not* be about but all too often sadly is—at least in America: cheap point-scoring where candidates forget what the final goal is, which is surely to safeguard and improve the lives of the people who elect them.

At one stage when I was casting around for a new direction outside tennis, people began telling me I should think about going into politics. One friend even suggested I should run for Mayor of New York, which happens to be the toughest job in the country apart from being President. But the more I was around people like John Kerry, the less I wanted to do it. Here was someone I believed to be very much one of the good guys, still having to live his life as a constant back-slapping charade, and I don't know how he stood it.

Later, toward the end of the campaign, at another fundraiser up on 5th Avenue, across the park from our place, Kerry looked so tired he could hardly stand up. It was one of the few times where you could see how much of a toll this was taking on him. There were only about twenty people there, all presumably wealthy donors, and when this one guy came up to him, I saw Kerry had that look in his eye as if he was thinking, "Nearly there, one more hand to shake, then I can finally sit down, have something to eat and drink and relax." All of a sudden, this guy is right in his face asking, "Hey, John, how are you? Remember me?" Kerry did a good job of summoning up all his politician's charm to utter the reply, "Yeah, sure, great to see you!"

These politicians are so good at that, I'm always amazed by

them. But instead of taking John's reply at face value, the guy started pressing him, "Yeah? Really? You remember me? What's my name?" And so on. He would not let it go. Kerry was trying to get out of it, and still this asshole wouldn't drop it. I wanted to tell him, "Come on, cut the guy a little slack," but I thought that would only make the situation worse.

What would I have done if I'd been Kerry? Sure, I've matured enough that initially I would probably have done exactly what he did. "Yeah, great to see you ... sorry, remind me of your name again," and tried to be all nice about it. But eventually, I would have lost it. "Come on, give me a break, will ya? Back off!" All of which is a long way of saying that politics is probably not for me.

I was a late starter in that field anyway, and am somewhat ashamed to admit that I didn't vote for the first time in a US presidential election until 2000, when I put my cross on the ballot for Ralph Nader. I'd tried to vote in 1984 when, believe it or not, I was going to vote for Reagan, largely because my dad—who was still very much running the show at that point, as far as my finances were concerned—had said it would be good for tax reasons for me to vote as a Long Island resident (which I still was, then) rather than a city resident. As for which candidate I was going to choose, I wasn't going to vote for Mondale because he was hopeless, so that left me no other choice but Ronnie.

Anyway, I was coming back from London on the Concorde on the day of the election when the plane got diverted to Washington, and I couldn't get back to New York that night. So because you're registered to vote in a certain area—which I think is wrong, personally, but that's another story—I couldn't vote. I ended up getting to a friend's Washington apartment in the early evening, before the polls had even closed, and the TV was already announcing that Reagan had 550 electoral college votes and Mondale had like 3. I remember thinking "Why was I even trying to vote? This whole thing is total bullshit."

So that's why my conscience doesn't have to carry the burden of a vote for Reagan, although looking back I do actually think that not voting was no less shameful. I only really started to consider that—what a lousy example you're setting if you don't even care—after I'd had kids. But even though I began thinking about voting as my family started to grow, I still didn't do it. With Bush versus Dukakis, the Democratic candidate was kind of hopeless again, and I'd met George H. W. Bush and didn't think he was too bad a guy (in fact, I liked him). So that election couldn't draw me into the polling booth.

Once Clinton came along, I could see that he was super-smart and he seemed cool, but—and maybe this was my Catholic up-bringing—I didn't like the way the scandals came down, and this was way before Monica Lewinsky. If I had voted in 1996, I would've probably voted for Bill against Dole, but then by the time I finally felt guilty enough to make my debut at the polling station, in 2000, at the grand old age of forty-one, Al Gore was so pompous in his manner that I voted for Nader, the green guy, because I liked what he stood for. Obviously it didn't mean anything, because in New York Gore won by like a billion votes anyway, even though he somehow managed to lose to George W. Bush overall—who in my view he should have destroyed—despite actually receiving more votes than Bush.

A few years later, I had Ralph Nader as a guest on the second day of my talk show. When I said I'd voted for him, his response wasn't "Wow," he just looked at me like, "You did?" which for some reason I found disappointing. He didn't know it had been my first time and I wanted it to be special. I guess a million people have said that to him. It's like when someone tells me,

"Hey, I was at your match at the 1980 Wimbledon Finals," and I'm thinking, "At least 30,000 people have told me that. The only problem is there were only 15,000 seats."

I suppose it was a bit like the Jimmy Carter thing, in a way. If you're expecting something, you're in trouble—ask not what America can do for McEnroe, ask what McEnroe can do for America.

If I was going to sum up what my politics are these days, I suppose I'd say that I'm fiscally conservative but socially liberal. I'm pro-choice—I mean, I don't think it's a great thing that someone has to have an abortion, but if a woman's in that situation then it's not my place to stop her. When it comes to gay marriage, I love the country musician Kinky Friedman's line when he ran for Governor of Texas: "Gay marriage should be allowed: they have the right to be as miserable as everyone else." That's so true—why were we keeping it from them? It does seem sort of messed up, though obviously I did have that Catholic upbringing, so there's a bit of tension there, but I feel that people should be allowed to do what they want . . . and then feel guilty about it afterward.

Probably the political gesture that I'm most proud of was my refusal to go to South Africa at the height of the apartheid era. I'd been offered $1 million to play an exhibition against Björn Borg out there, and although a bunch of athletes were regularly defying the sports boycott and making a lot of money by doing it, I decided not to go, even though I was at the start of my career and could easily have been tempted to take what was an insane amount of money back then for a single match. I just couldn't condone a regime that stank. And saying no to that offer turned out to be a great decision, which led to a lot of positive karma over the years that I'm still reaping today.

Even now I get people from the black community coming up to me and saying how much they appreciated me deciding not to play in South Africa, which makes me proud. When I met Nelson Mandela he said it was an honor to meet *me.* Crazy, right?

It was also pretty awesome for me to meet President Obama, when Patty and I were invited to attend the Kennedy Center Honors in December 2010. Every year, the Kennedy Center in Washington DC honors those from the performing arts around the world who have contributed to American culture. The ceremony lasts a whole weekend for the recipients and it includes different events, including a big reception at the White House hosted by the President and the First Lady.

That year Paul McCartney was being honored, as well as Oprah Winfrey, among others. I ended up having to try not to do too much rubber-necking because there were so many well-known faces there, many of whom I happen to admire. Paul McCartney himself is a living legend, and being a lefty guitarist, is someone I'm particularly in awe of. When musicians are being honored, they get a selection of their peers to play their best-known songs, so that year, Gwen Stefani, Steven Tyler from Aerosmith and others got up on stage to sing "Hey Jude," and the whole audience, including the First Couple, were soon joining in. Quite a sight. Quite a night.

The next day, we went to the White House for a small reception of about a hundred people. That's where everyone got to stand in line and meet the President himself. I'd never spoken to him before, though I'd met Michelle three or four times, including at Flushing Meadow, because she's involved in various initiatives to get kids into sports. But as I stood waiting in line to meet President Obama himself, I was wondering what I'd say to him. I could see he was exchanging a few words with everyone, but I figured I'd better have something ready in case he didn't know who the hell I was and couldn't think of what to say to me.

I didn't want to be like the past president of the USTA who, on meeting President Reagan, said, "Did you see me at the US Open? I was sitting in the front row." He was actually asking the President of the United States if he remembered seeing him watching the US Open? No kidding. Luckily, I didn't have to try out my small-talk because President Obama told me right-away, in the very quick twenty seconds or so that I spoke to him, that he used to play tennis in high school. He came across as an amazing and engaging person, and—better still—seemed to know who I was. As soon as we were done, I joined a few musicians, including Kid Rock and Jamey Johnson, who were huddled outside. I detected an aroma that you wouldn't normally associate with the White House. "Yeah, we were just smoking dope on the White House lawn," Kid Rock told me. And no, in case you're wondering, I didn't inhale.

I guess the UK equivalent of an audience with the US President would be to meet a member of the royal family. I've spoken to Prince Charles and his wife Camilla, but never the Queen herself. Camilla seemed relaxed when I met her. She'd come to Wimbledon and there was a line-up of the usual dignitaries ready to meet her on the players' balcony. Tim Henman, Virginia Wade and I suddenly decided we should join them. Hey, why not, right? We were at the end of the line, and she stopped for a quick Obama-esque twenty seconds. Virginia had a few words with her, as did Tim. Then it was my turn.

"Do you play tennis?" I asked her. No points for originality, but it seemed a decent opening gambit. "Oh, very badly . . . I would love to start again, but maybe I'm too old." As we'd all three of us run from the commentary booth, our conversation with her—if you can even call it that—was aired live.

That was where the problems started. I swear to God, the reaction to what turned out to be a breach of protocol was absolutely crazy. The UK tabloids really went to town. You'd think I'd asked Camilla if she liked her whiskey neat or on the rocks rather than a bland question about whether she played tennis. I didn't know it was almost a capital offense to say publicly what a royal person says to you in private. I'd say we were lucky not to have our membership of the All England Club taken away that day—if lucky is the right word.

To be honest, I don't really care if I offended anyone. They're not my royal family, and I'm not sure how many people relate to these customs of deference anyway. Some of the so-called Wimbledon traditions I'm OK with, even though I remember the first few years I played there, I thought they were a bunch of stiffs. I found England strange, full of quaint notions that I didn't get. And Wimbledon was so full of itself in terms of how condescendingly it treated the lesser players, like they should be grateful to be even allowed into the grounds, never mind onto the court. They had trouble enough getting over Jimmy Connors and the way he thumbed his nose at them on a regular basis in his usual "fuck you" way. When I came along, they completely freaked. The two of us sort of fueled each other, and I think in the end it was good for them.

As for all the bowing and curtsying—and we're not just talking the Queen here, we're talking some pretty minor royals— what was all that about? This was the class system gone mad, the opposite of a meritocracy where hard work is rewarded, and people are respected because they've actually done something, not because they've been born on the right side of the tracks.

Thank God they've abolished the bowing-to-royals rule at Wimbledon, because it was totally perplexing to me. I did notice Andy Murray bowing to the Queen when she turned up to the tournament one year. That's fair enough, but why were players who weren't even British expected to bow to some minor member of the royal family? Who were the performers here? The players, right? So why were they bowing to someone else when they were about to provide the entertainment? Those people in the royal box should think about bowing to them.

15

"Listen to what your body tells you"

Jenny Holzer

The quote above comes from a piece by the conceptual artist Jenny Holzer which I'm lucky enough to own. I keep it at our house in the Hamptons. It's basically a series of bits of good advice: "Don't talk about religion," that kind of thing (one of many sensible rules I have already broken in this book). Learning to cope with the impact the advancing years have on you is one of the biggest challenges a professional athlete has to face— as everyone else does, but we get to do it in public.

Anyone who saw me show up in Paris for the French Open in 2010 with what can only be described as "Horror Hair" could be forgiven for thinking I was in the grip of a full-blown mid-life crisis. Over the years, the main problem with my hair has been working out how to hang on to it. I've just about managed to keep a decent head-covering, although I know that ultimately I'm fighting a losing battle. It's also been going gray for years— something which, truth be told, didn't bother me a whole lot. But in the early part of 2010, Patty and my manager Gary seemed to think that I could touch up the increasing gray with a bit of subtle color. I wasn't too hot on the idea, but supposedly the hair colorist was the best in the world so eventually I gave in. "Listen," I said to her, "maybe just pepper it up a little bit, OK?"

The result, however, was a total insult to the hair-coloring industry. I can't even describe my new color. It wasn't blond, it was some kind of crazy orange. I looked like the old wrestler, Gorgeous George. "Take it out!" I yelled, totally freaking out, because I knew in a few days I'd have to commentate at Roland-Garros and later walk out on court in front of a packed house of stylish Parisians. "I can't," the colorist said, explaining that this wasn't a wash-out hair dye. So there was no point in washing it a hundred times in the next two days, I'd have to wait for it to grow out. Patty didn't know whether to laugh or cry (in the end she opted—sensibly—for the former). I was so desperate not to look like turning fifty the previous year had (quite literally) gone to my head, that I ended up going to a local store to get some of that silver stuff people put in their hair at Halloween—anything to tone that color down a bit. We all like to poke fun at Donald Trump and his orange hair, right? I know I do. But when I arrived in Paris, I'd say I looked almost embarrassingly pathetic enough to put him to shame. By the time I got to Wimbledon, it had faded to a weird mid-brown color which was slightly more acceptable, but did the British tabloids decide to go easy and let this one pass, just for old times' sake? What is it that bears do in the woods again?

The most painful aspect of the tabloid mockery was knowing that I deserved it. My vanity had gotten the better of me. Or was this one more desperate attempt to try to halt the march of time? It's kind of the same thing, I guess. As it happened, after that I decided that being a silver fox wasn't such a bad deal after all, so since then I've embraced the graying hair. I also realized that it's one thing to keep my body together for health and professional reasons, but trying to change the way I looked? Forget it.

The fact was that turning fifty in 2009 had been a bigger deal to me than I liked to admit—even to myself. I hadn't found it easy dealing with my thirtieth birthday, because that was an age that seemed ancient for someone who was still a professional tennis player. Maybe it's a bit less of a landmark these days, but all the same, you're going the wrong way in your career, for sure (unless you're Roger Federer). Strangely, I had no trouble with turning forty—I hardly noticed it. But that was because I was excited that Ava was about to be born, and I had my hands full with five other kids. But fifty was shaping up to be a bad birthday for me—it just felt really old. At that age there's no kidding yourself: you're more than halfway through (unless you're planning to live to a hundred, and even then the later years won't exactly be non-stop sex, drugs and rock 'n' roll).

I'm very grateful that Patty somehow managed to turn what could've been a dark time into a very happy memory. The day itself was a Monday, and all I had planned was my regular workout with my trainer in the morning, then one of my monthly jamming sessions with my band in the evening. In other words, business as usual.

Patty, by the way, was off gigging in LA. She still loves to perform and probably does about ten gigs a year, and this just happened to be one of them—she hadn't organized it deliberately to get away from me moaning about being fifty (or had she? We'll never know). Anna and Ava were around, but it was a school day. I didn't mind that, though—I was quite happy having a low-key day (well, I thought I was, but when I said this to Patty, she called me a liar). The way I remember it, I just wanted to do a couple of things—exercise and music—that would make me feel good and perhaps reinforce the idea that I might not be

Jumpin' Jack Flash, but at least I was some way short of being totally washed up.

The discipline of exercise is important to me, and when I'm in New York I like to work out with my personal trainer at least two to three times a week. Pat pushes me that extra 10 percent, and we do a mix of aerobic and weights, stretching, the usual, but once I'm done—which is usually by mid-morning—I'm energized for the day and feel better about myself. This is something Patty and I have in common, and we like to work out together whenever possible.

Playing music with my friends matters to me too, even though I don't get to do it as often as I'd like. It's kind of my boys' night out. No one's taking it too seriously, we have a few beers, play a lot of loud music for a couple of hours, and are just happy that we're doing something we all enjoy. We used to jam at the apartment, but now it's usually at my gallery down in Soho—we can make as much noise as we want down there because no one can hear us. Well, not usually—the police have been called a couple of times. That happened once when my son Kevin was with us, and there was a funny reversal of traditional father/son relationships where he showed the police up the stairs very politely, and I was, like, "What are you doing?" Not that there was anything we needed to hide from them, as the scene was all very tame compared to what the Rolling Stones or the Pretenders used to do, but I just didn't think we should be making life too easy for them.

Anyway, there were no visits from New York's finest on the night of my birthday, and the whole day passed without too much soul-searching on my part. It was quiet, though, and in the days that followed I did start to feel a bit neglected. I'm so dense—friends had stopped calling me a few days before my birthday, and on the day itself, I'd complained to Patty that almost no one was getting in touch. I couldn't figure out why and got pretty pissed. Afterward I realized they were just afraid of ruining the surprise.

One of my friends (OK, it was the actor John Cusack—too late to stop name-dropping now) almost blew it. On what turned out to be the day of the party, he sent over a bottle of wine for me with a card attached. "You're the best," it said. "Sorry I can't be with you on your fiftieth." "What the hell is he talking about? He's a week late!" I said, slightly annoyed. Patty had to do some fast tap-dancing to gloss that one over, let me tell you.

Ten days after the actual day, Patty asked me to accompany her to a dinner someplace downtown with a few people who were going to help her with her career. She said it would be good if I could come and support her. We showed up at this burlesque place, and it was like the Crazy Horse in Paris where they do those naked cabaret shows. "Where's the restaurant?" I asked her. Then we walked into this room, and there—I swear to God I hadn't suspected a thing—were all these people that Patty had invited, friends from the past, friends from various parts of my life—tennis, media, music, art, high school, just a great group of people.

The way Patty managed to keep that surprise party from me was incredible, especially as she had to make sure all six kids, plus a load of friends and family, didn't give the game away. She told me later that it would have been easier to have an affair than to pull that one off, so I'm glad she didn't pursue the alternative option. And it turned out to be a great evening. I didn't make a speech because I was completely unprepared, but Patty did, and she sang too.

Had I wanted something special on my birthday? Secretly, yes. It's nice to be acknowledged, isn't it? Patty knows birthdays mean a lot to me—well, especially my birthday, because if I'm honest I've not done a great job of organizing hers over the years, which has been a bone of contention in the past. My lame excuse is that, at least until 2015 when the tournament dates were moved, her birthday always fell during Wimbledon. And I know that's no excuse, because it shouldn't have been too tough to arrange a dinner with some friends while we were in London, right?

This old warrior's misguided hair-dye experiment at the 2010 Grand Slams coincided with another changing of the guard at the very top in men's tennis. Novak Djokovic had been knocking on the door for a while, and I thought the US Open of 2010 was as big a turning point for him as Wimbledon in 2003 had been for Roger Federer. Novak always seemed to be in the mix in Slams, but up until that point, he'd only won one—the Australian Open in 2008 against Jo-Wilfried Tsonga. He'd not quite made the final breakthrough yet against Rafa and Roger, who still had this incredible stranglehold on the sport.

There had been a question mark over Novak's ability to tough it out, both mentally and physically, and he'd pulled out of a couple of big matches for various reasons. He seemed to find heat a particular problem and some people thought he was a bit of a hypochondriac.

He didn't win the US Open that year—he lost to Nadal in four sets in the final. But I felt his real breakthrough was in his first-round match against his fellow countryman, Victor Troicki, which I was calling. It was a very humid day and Djokovic was once again having problems with the heat. He was down two sets to one and a break with a break point to go 4–1 down, and I thought he was done. This is going to sound strange, but watching him play that day I also thought he was too thin.

Somehow he turned it around and ended up winning in five. Even though he fell short of winning the whole tournament, this match was one of the first times I remember seeing Djokovic find a way through that kind of situation. Seven years later, Novak is still skinny, but he's obviously worked on his strength and conditioning an insane amount—to the point where I think he's possibly the fittest guy on the tour.

Djokovic improved his game in so many ways to become the number one player in the world. He made himself unbelievably mentally resilient, compared to how he was, and he also became a much better attacker. He and Murray were born within a week of each other, but what helped Djokovic pull ahead in the early years of their time in the top four was that Novak was more attuned to the need to close things out, his second serve was better, and he attacked more on key points. At that level, those tiny differences are all it takes. For me, the turning point in his career, the moment he figured out how to get himself out of even the toughest of situations, was that match against Troicki. Later that year, he and his fellow Serbian teammates won the Davis Cup for the first time, and Novak went on to win three out of the next four Slams and become the number one player in the world. But there's no way of knowing if that would still have happened if he'd lost that low-key first-round match against his less well-known fellow countryman.

The semi-final of the 2011 US Open, in which Novak took on Roger Federer at that critical stage of the tournament for the second year running, illustrated perfectly why tennis is such a mental boxing match, and also how big a part the crowd can play in deciding a match's outcome. In 2010 Djokovic had edged Federer in five close sets after saving two match points. This time around, it looked like Roger was going to get his revenge when he went two sets to love up. Novak, who was world number one by this time, clearly thought differently, and fought his way back to two sets all.

As usual, the crowd—all 23,000 of them—were rooting for Roger as they went into the fifth. At 4–3, he broke Novak to love. At 5–3, 40–15, with two match points? This was it, we all thought. He looks as good as home. Roger doesn't choke. Then came an insane forehand cross-court return winner from Djokovic, played almost casually, as if he was playing a game in the park. Some of the crowd applauded, but given what a totally crazy shot it was at that stage of the match, it should have brought the house down. What did Novak do? Instead of getting on with preparing for the next point, he put his arms up and gestured to the crowd as if to say, "Come on, guys, give me a bit of credit for that incredible shot—what do I have to do to get you on my side?" Best of all, he managed to smile while he did it.

That one gesture was all it took to turn the tide. He'd helped the crowd realize that he too deserved some admiration for what he was doing, and some of them started rooting for him. Suddenly, it was Roger's turn to look rattled, and before long Novak had won the next four games and, for the second year in a row, edged him 7–5 in the fifth.

I was calling the match for CBS, and I remember thinking, "Wow, Novak has learned something I never managed to do myself out there." He turned what was pretty much the end-game into a situation where some of the crowd got behind him—not all of them, because they still mostly wanted Roger to win, but enough to break the Federer spell. And I had to admire the way he'd changed the delicate balance that there is between a player, the opponent and the crowd.

After Novak made that big forehand, Roger lost the next match point when he hit his forehand out. We were back to deuce and it was like this calmness suddenly overcame Novak. That's when I realized he was going to pull it out of the bag, and it's that strength of mind that has subsequently made him not just a champion, but one of the all-time greats.

16

*"No, John, being number one is
the only thing that matters"*

Björn Borg

I was happy to be accompanied by Patty as we walked the red
carpet for the premiere of *Fire & Ice*, the sixty-minute documentary that HBO made about me and Björn Borg. The 2011
film turned out to be something I was very proud of, although I
admit I was apprehensive beforehand because you never know
how these things will pan out. I'd had to do a bit of persuading
to even get Björn to take part because he was—understandably—wary. "Look, it won't be a hatchet job as I'm somewhat
involved in the production," I'd reassured him. So I was relieved
that there were no nasty shocks in the final cut. It was a pity
Björn didn't make it over for the screening, which took place in
front of a couple of hundred people at the School of Visual Arts
Theater in Manhattan, but he felt it was a long way to come for
just one hour, even though I think he would have enjoyed it. I
knew Björn well enough to realize there was no point in trying
to persuade him to get on a plane, but I tried anyway, and he
still didn't come.

People think Björn and I are polar opposites—hence the title of the film—and in some ways we are. That's what made our rivalry so special. It was so intense that people often misremember and think that it carried on for years. But, sorry to correct you, we only played fourteen times, and all between 1978 and 1981 (to put this in perspective, Djokovic and Nadal have played more than forty times, and Evert and Navratilova met twice that many). There was something about our matches that sparked people's emotions, and created a special atmosphere. As with Roger and Rafa (and also with Novak Djokovic, who it has to be said is a very different player from those two as well), we were such contrasting characters, with totally opposite styles of play, and those differences made for good and at times great tennis. Everyone knew what side they were on: that was what drew the crowds. You were either a Borg or a McEnroe fan. A supporter of the Ice Man or of the Superbrat, as those London tabloids liked to call me, among other things!

Borg was the ultimate tennis player, fitter and faster than anyone else on the circuit. He also had this incredible aura about him, that Viking god look; his skin-tight Fila outfits were the equivalent of a Superman caped crusader costume—no giant S on the chest, just a little F—and with that armor on it was like he became this extraordinary player, one who never ever showed any emotion on court.

I was definitely in the opposite camp in all those respects. I wasn't insanely fit, I wasn't a practice fanatic, and I felt it was somewhat healthier—for me anyway—to let those emotions out on court. Don't laugh, but I remember several times in practice sessions trying to behave like Björn to see if it might help my game. Let me tell you, those were short-lived experiments!

But alongside the contrasts there was also a symmetry to our relationship that not everyone understood. We're a lot more alike than we initially appear. Our low-key, dry sense of humor is similar, and Björn wasn't always the ice-man that people thought he was. The film showed that well, because they found footage of him imploding during a junior match and throwing his racket into the net in frustration and anger. Yes, we're talking about Björn Borg. In fact, he was so bad when he was young that his father wouldn't let him play for six months. That's when, as Björn says, "I promised myself I'm not going to open my mouth on the tennis court as long as I live because I love it too much." So don't think he didn't feel what was going on out there on court really deeply. He did, he just didn't show it. Unlike me.

Björn also explains in the film how his mental and physical strength are what made him special. "I never got tired in a tennis match," he said (tell me about it!). Again, unlike me.

When Björn walked out of tennis at age twenty-five, pretty much forever, after losing against me at the US Open in 1981, I had no idea that he'd never be back. But I never won another Slam either after the age of twenty-five, so there's some more weird symmetry between us.

By the time we played in that 1981 US Open final, it felt like I'd finally got his number. I'd beaten him the last couple of times we'd met, including the previous year's final and the 1981 Wimbledon final. This time, though, Borg was up 4–2, with a break in the third set, after we'd split the first two sets, and he seemed to have an extra intensity about him. He'd never won this goddam tournament, even though this was his fourth time in the final. This was the one he really wanted, and it was now looking like it might actually happen. Trouble was, I badly wanted to win my third home title in a row too. Tennis matches do turn on single points—not always, but amazingly often—and after I'd sent a second winning topspin lob over his head in that game and broken back, he suddenly started to look totally deflated, like the air had gone out of a balloon.

That was (literally) the turning point. He lost his edge, he seemed to lose his desire, and by the time I'd won the fourth set 6–2 and with it the title, I felt Borg was doing something that I never imagined I would see him do: giving up. It wasn't so blatant that he could be accused of tanking, but to me, he hadn't seemed like he wanted to be there anymore. When the moment of defeat came for him, he walked up to the net, shook hands with me, and didn't look particularly devastated, considering how badly he'd previously wanted to win the title. It was like the lights went out. He then calmly picked up his bag, walked off court and got into a waiting car. I received the winner's trophy, and no mention was made of the fact that Björn had basically gone AWOL and not taken part in the ceremony.

No one else has ever done that at the end of a tournament—either before or since. I was later told that he'd had a death threat against him, but I've never been too sure about that. After all, who would want to make a death threat against Björn Borg? The only possible suspect I could think of was Jimmy Connors. And to me, it felt more like the whole thing had been planned—as if he knew this was the end.

A few years later, in 1985 to be precise, I was still on the tour, and Björn and I were playing some exhibitions (though he was still retired from tournament tennis). I'd just got bumped off the number one spot in the world by Lendl and at that point—anticipating what Larry David would tell me twenty years later—I suggested to Björn that being number two wasn't that bad a deal.

"No, John, number one is the only thing that matters," he said in that soft, Swedish accent of his. "If you're number two, you might as well be number three or one hundred—you're nobody." I was dumbstruck. I thought number two was pretty incredible. I still do. I mean, I'd take it any day over, say, number one hundred, or for that matter number six, right? But that was one of the big differences between him and me. He was like Roger Federer. The true greats, they don't ever think, "Oh it's boring for the spectators if I keep on winning." No way. For them, they don't care how boring it is, they want that victory. For Borg, if you can't be number one, don't even bother showing up.

What's incredible to me, though, was that even thirty years later, in *Fire & Ice*, Björn still couldn't explain his decision to quit in 1981, at that moment and in that way. "The motivation to win is not there," he said. "If someone could explain to me *why*, I would be very grateful."

You might think Björn's retirement would've been good news for me, as it left the way open for me to consolidate my position as the number one player in the world, but it actually worked out pretty badly. In a strange way I felt that something was taken away from me: an opponent strong enough to push me on to better things. Björn and I had been a perfect match-up: he generally played better against me, and I upped my level against him. I would attack him, but I also provided him with a target at the net so he could try to pass me. I could be wrong, but I believe that if he'd stuck around a few more years we would each have continued to get better and moved tennis up to another level.

Because of what he'd already achieved by the time I arrived on the circuit, I had great respect for Björn and for everything he stood for, so I never trash-talked him the way I did with Connors. And I rarely got annoyed at linesmen or umpires during our matches (not least because it would make me look even worse because he was so damn calm)—though God knows sometimes I wanted to. I just played. More than anything, I wanted to beat him, to show him that I belonged on the same court as him. He pushed me to achieve greater things, and when he walked away from the sport it left a hole in my life. I don't want to say it was like a bereavement, but looking back, I think it definitely came close to that feeling of emptiness, of missing someone's presence and their influence in your life. Plus it shook me up and made me question my own future in the game.

I won two more Wimbledons (in 1983 and '84) and another US Open in 1984—beating Ivan Lendl in straight sets and to some extent avenging my French Open loss of earlier that year. In results terms, 1984 was my best year ever. I won thirteen out of the fifteen tournaments I entered, and started 1985 as the number one player in the world for the fourth consecutive year. But I also ended the year no happier. In fact, I felt a whole lot emptier than I ever would've thought possible, given the incredible success I'd had.

Was this hollow feeling due to Björn quitting the tour? Or was it something about the pressure of being number one? Once you've reached the top, there's only one way to go—down. Everyone is after you, and you're suddenly caught in a paradox: you're in an incredibly privileged position, one you've been working toward all your life, but also one that can leave you feeling paranoid and trapped. The isolation was worse for me, because unlike today's top players who generally have a team of five or six people around them the whole time, I was totally on my own—I didn't even have a traveling coach.

Maybe Björn had understood that, back in 1981. He'd had to give up so much when he was young—he'd been on the tour since he was about fifteen—and he wasn't prepared to keep making the sacrifices. I had a way to go before I understood that.

At his peak, Björn was undoubtedly one of the most competitive people I've ever encountered. But the surprising thing is, whenever we play nowadays (and we've played about fifty times in exhibition matches and at senior level), I swear to God he doesn't give a shit if he wins or not.

Did he suddenly stop being competitive? Can that happen? Not to me, it hasn't. Björn might make it look like he's trying, but considering he's one of the greatest players who ever lived, he's got an abysmal record on the seniors tour. Here's the thing: I'm pretty sure he doesn't care. Go figure.

When I'd started out on the main tour in the late seventies, being three years younger than Björn, I'd never seen a player like him. Not only how he played the game, and how he looked on court, but how he was off-court too. I certainly wanted a piece of what he was having—namely a lot of interest and a lot of girls. All of a sudden, being a tennis player was cool. Björn had the same effortless worldliness as Vitas Gerulaitis, my idol from my Port Washington Academy days. They both had the long blond hair, they both had an indefinable charisma, but they also shared a real work ethic. I didn't feel I could compete, but it didn't stop me from wanting to be like them and being totally elated when I first got to hang out with them. They seemed to be able to burn the candle at both ends without diminishing their athletic prowess, where I was never able to do that. I learned fast, but although I eventually equaled Björn and overtook Vitas in terms of my tennis results, I was never in their league off-court.

My rivalry with Björn Borg was different from my rivalry with Lendl or Connors in one fundamental way: we actually liked each other. Sorry to disappoint any pop psychologists out there who believe that athletes have to hate their rivals. In fact, although I didn't realize it at the time, in later years I understood that we have a unique and special connection that a lot of people would define as love, pure and simple. At one point in *Fire & Ice*, Björn says he loves me. Patty then turns to me and goes, "Did you tell him you love him too?" It's not exactly something I find easy to say to another guy. But it's true: there's this feeling of love deep down, even though we've splintered off and have different lives now. We were so close in the nineties that he even came to Patty's and my wedding, at Donald Fagen's house in Maui, which was otherwise just family and a few friends.

These days Björn lives near Stockholm in a great house, which surprisingly enough has a tennis court, and nearby he's got a boat moored because there are a lot of small islands he can go out to and enjoy. He's got a quiet life compared to what he used to, and he's been happily married to Patricia since 2002. He's had some well-documented ups and downs, personally and financially—I've had some well-documented stuff happen in the last thirty years too—but all I know is that when we do meet up for various exhibitions, tournaments or commercial opportunities, he's still that cool guy I've always known, and we hit it off as if we see each other every day. He always brings me some of his Björn Borg-branded underwear when he comes to America as well. It is both comfortable and stylish and I wear it all the time (except in bed—that would be weird).

Beyond his contribution in terms of my intimate apparel, there was a further example of Björn's positive influence on my life a couple of months after the *Fire & Ice* screening. We were both in St. Tropez, playing an exhibition, as guests of Johan Eliasch, the owner of sports manufacturer Head, and a great friend of Björn's and now a good friend of mine. That evening, over dinner, my manager's phone rang, and it was my dad, wanting to know if he could come with me to a tournament in Knokke-Heist, Belgium, a few weeks later. I was about to say absolutely not—I could foresee the problems that would involve—when Björn said, "Let me speak to him." Björn had lost his own dad, Rune, three years before, and he'd been really upset because, like mine, his dad had been a huge influence in his life and a big factor in his success. After talking to my dad a bit, he ended the conversation by saying, "Don't worry, JP, if John doesn't bring you to Knokke-Heist, I will." Jesus, thanks a bunch, Björn! But that's when he turned to me and said solemnly, "He's your father, John, you've only got one. Make the most of it, because it goes by so quickly. If he wants to go, you should let him."

That caught my attention. He was right. So I agreed to take my dad off my mother's hands for a while. Unfortunately, I tore my hamstring badly the week before in a match against Michael Chang in Toronto. It was the most painful injury I'd ever had, and it took me months and months before I was fully back to normal. So in Knokke-Heist, because playing was out of the question, I spent the week limping around, doing the promotional stuff.

Soon after we arrived, I had to do a press conference to talk about the tournament and the charity it was supporting, linked to a children's hospital. To be honest, it was a typical, uninspiring press conference, but there was still a lot of media there. We were just winding it up when the organizers asked for one final question.

Suddenly, my dad, who'd been sitting at the back of the room, stood up and said, "I don't have a question but I have a comment." "Well, go ahead," I said, sarcastically, with a "be my guest" sweep of the hand. All the cameras swiveled around to my dad. "I've never said this to John before," he began ominously. I froze. I had no idea what he was going to come out with, but I knew from past experience that it could be just about anything. Hell, he might even break into song. "I think it's probably well known by everybody in this room that my son, John McEnroe, was born in Wiesbaden, Germany, in February 1959, when I was stationed there for my military service. But I'm here to tell you what you don't know: which is that John's mother, Kay, and I came here to Brussels in 1958 to see the World's Fair. We had a great time. Beer, chocolates, lots of fun. And well, John McEnroe might have been born in Wiesbaden . . . But he was made in Brussels!" News to me too, folks, John McEnroe is part Belgian!

Everyone thought that was really funny—or at least they laughed, which is not necessarily the same thing—while I sat there as embarrassed as a teenager whose parents have suddenly started making out in front of them. "It's going to be a long four days," I thought.

That's the thing, though. You hate yourself for feeling embarrassed or angry at having to take time out of your busy schedule to attend to your parents ("Hey, how about remembering that that's what they did for you when the tables were turned and you were young?" you tell yourself, feeling like an ungrateful jerk).

I'm very aware that most people my age have lost one, if not both their parents. So I am grateful for the fact that both of mine were around for so long, even though we didn't see each other as much as we should have.

Oh, and by the way, my dad somehow managed to have a great time in Knokke, despite his son's presence.

17

"You remember, we met once?"

Olga Korbut

Andy Murray's decision to appoint my old friend Ivan Lendl to be his coach was not one of my favorite surprises of 2012. At first I was thinking, "Ah, no way, he hired Lendl. It's not going to work." Then I realized, "Oh my God, it *is* going to work." That was even worse.

Andy had tried Brad Gilbert a few years before and that hadn't worked out. I wonder why! One time when Marat Safin was struggling for one reason or another, Gilbert was all over him, trying to coach him—understandably, because Safin is really talented—but I remember Marat saying to me, "I'd rather be one hundred in the world on my own than number one in the world with Gilbert!" That was exactly how I felt, too.

Brad was no different when he was still playing, in fact he was pretty much the most annoying opponent known to man (and part of me says that as a compliment). When I lost to him at the Masters in January 1986—the one time out of the fourteen times we played that he ever beat me—I was so disgusted with myself that I stopped playing for six months. What Gilbert lacked in talent ("And he lacked a lot in natural ability," Andy Roddick said a few years back), he made up for with his unbelievable tenacity. "Winning Ugly," Brad called it, and he later wrote a bestselling book with that title. But Brad became an undeniably great coach. He got Andre Agassi back up to number one in the world and was in Roddick's corner when he won the US Open. So credit to the guy, he knows what he's talking about.

In fact, you can certainly say that about him, because he's known as a world-class talker. And coming from me, that's saying something. If there's ever silence, he'll fill it and then never stop—I swear he talks in his sleep—which may be why he's never been hired by the BBC. He is one of ESPN's regulars, though, and a colleague of mine now that I work for them too. ESPN is the biggest sports broadcaster in the world, so I figure that if they didn't like what Brad was doing, they'd have told him. He knows the game inside out, so he brings something to the party, but he's got all these nicknames for the players which, to me, are unnecessary and distracting. Del Potro, for example, is "Delpo." Djokovic is "The Joker," Milos Raonic is "The Missile," and on, and on and on. Please, Brad, don't you think they'd like to be called by their *real* names once in a while? And why not try shutting up every now and again, so we can ride this gravy train together in peace for another ten years.

Andy Murray is always complaining about one thing or another on the court, but he doesn't say too much the rest of the time, so he could've just been driven totally nuts by Brad's constant chatter. Or maybe Brad was telling him stuff he didn't want to hear? Whatever the reason, after a period of not having a coach at all, Murray appointed Lendl and, although I hate to say it, Ivan made a big difference to him. The biggest change was that he got Andy believing in himself more. He'd lost his first three Grand Slam finals and I'm guessing the thought of losing a fourth straight one was pretty unappealing. In fact, only

Lendl would have known how that felt because he had been the only previous player to have lost his first four Slam finals (before beating guess who to finally nail down his first Grand Slam win in 1984).

Lendl is astute, so he would also have brought a few technical things into the mix. "Be more aggressive on the return," "Try to take the court over," and of course "Beef up that second serve." I think Lendl also got Murray to take his fitness to a higher level. But the mental side was probably the key, and by the time Murray got to the Wimbledon final—the first British player to do that since Bunny Austin, who lost to the American Don Budge in 1938—he was as ready as he'd ever been to carry the weight of an entire nation's expectation. No pressure, Andy.

Trouble was, he had Roger Federer on the other side of the net. And Roger was aiming to equal Pete Sampras's record of seven Wimbledon wins and to reclaim the world number one spot. What did he care about the British people's feelings?

I have to admit that there was a part of me that was pulling for Andy in that match, because of the absolute magnitude of what he was trying to achieve. I had to feel for the guy. Plus, as ever, I like the spoils to be divided up a bit.

Murray got a great start, won the first set and was playing with real positivity—something Lendl must have worked on with him—but if your name's Roger Federer, you're going to fight back, which is exactly what he did by winning the second set. Then the players had to go off to the locker room early in set three because of rain, and once they came back on, as so often when a match restarts, there was a definite shift in momentum. The added element was that the roof was now on. I was calling the match for ESPN and I remember watching Roger's now perfect timing, and experiencing this faint tingle of jealousy that a Wimbledon final was being played indoors. It had always been my dream to have a Grand slam played indoors because you would get this pristine spectacle—tennis in its purest form, free from any interference from the elements. Roger was now getting that opportunity. He's always so aesthetically beautiful in the way he plays that he makes his opponents look clumsy, no matter who they are, and there was an inevitability about the result once that roof went on.

By winning his seventh Wimbledon that day, Roger equaled Pete Sampras's record number of wins there. He'd also now won seventeen Grand Slam titles, three more than Pete, who was at that stage number two on the all-time list. That's an insane amount of titles. But he still shed some tears when he realized his name was going on the trophy again. God knows, Roger has cried more than any other top player, but they are genuine tears. No faking emotions there, it really means that much to him. I never cried when I won. I cried on other occasions on court—under a towel, no one ever saw me—when my first marriage was breaking up, when the outside stresses of life were taking over my mind and affecting my tennis so much I could hardly play, but I never cried from relief at winning. I guess that's one more reason why Roger is so special: after all these years, he's still insatiably hungry for more titles.

As for Andy Murray, he didn't win that day in 2012, but he did something that was perhaps even more appreciated by the British public: he cried, too. God knows the British love an underdog, but one who shows a human side when they lose with grace? Perfect.

Sue Barker had to do the usual post-match on-court interview with Andy, which is never easy when you're facing the losing finalist. I've been on both sides of the microphone for that one, and let me tell you, it sucks, whether you're asking or answering those questions. Sue is a real professional, she's a natural in front of the camera, she's funny, she's got empathy, and she's done an impressive job over the years. But this time around, she only needed to stand there because Andy did this incredibly emotional speech, most of it in tears, while the public suddenly discovered he *was* human after all. Crying that day was possibly the single best thing he's ever done for his image—and I'm including all the big titles he then went on to win. Maybe I should've taken the towel off my head once or twice so people could see I had a heart, too.

Losing that final definitely helped Murray win the Olympic gold medal a month later back in London. One of the great things about the tennis event was that it was played at Wimbledon, but the players weren't wearing white, and the vibe was totally different. The crowd wasn't the usual bunch who go and have their Pimm's or strawberries and cream, then watch a bit of tennis. In fact, I swear I didn't see a single blazer during the whole tournament. Instead, there seemed to be a whole lot of people who never normally go to Wimbledon because they can't get tickets. These people were there to support their players from whatever country they hailed from. So as well as the Brits, there were people from all over the world, with their flags, rooting for their players, and the place felt energized but relaxed and welcoming.

In the final—in which he basically killed Federer—Murray saw how much of a difference it can make to have the crowd on your side; plus, the power of those tears was still there. I think Federer was miffed not to have the majority of the crowd pulling for him; he's so used to everyone loving him, it was a weird experience for him. It's the Olympics and it's in London, Roger, come on!

I was working for NBC but I was also hired by the BBC to appear on their late-night show with Gabby Logan, along with various other guests. Michael Johnson was another regular, and one evening we had Olga Korbut on the show, the tiny Russian gymnast some of us are old enough to remember winning her gold medals back in 1972. When a former athlete is on, you assume they've kept up with their sport and can comment on it. But shortly before we went live on-air, Olga announced, "Don't ask me about gymnasts, I don't know anybody!" Excuse me, isn't that what you're here for?

Gabby's opening question was: "So, Olga, do you think it's a golden age in gymnastics now?" "Ah, no, this era is going down," Olga replied dismissively, in her broken English. "We need to find a new Olga to change to grace and more beautiful gymnastics, more passion, more smiles, more enjoy."

Are you kidding me? I swear to God, it was as if I was on there saying, "These guys, Federer, Nadal, they suck compared to me." She then turned to me and, without missing a beat, totally changed the subject. Like, end of discussion. "You remember, we met once?" "Yes, but only briefly, at an airport," I felt like saying. Talk about going off script. But Olga just went off on a tangent, and it all became this crazy evening. It's a sign of how good Gabby Logan is at her job that somehow she kept it all together. Afterward, though, as we were leaving the studio, even Michael Johnson, who is normally a pretty reserved guy, mouthed to her, "Well done!" We both had a good laugh about it both during and after the show, but only because we hadn't been the ones in Gabby's shoes!

My main job with NBC was to cover the tennis, but also to supposedly be a roving reporter. What happened in the end was that I did quite a lot of sitting around and not too much roving, which was frustrating for me because I like to be kept busy. I'd filmed a few pieces with various athletes before the Olympics, but during the actual events, although I did a couple of segments with the snowboarder Shaun White, and a fun *Downton Abbey* piece with one of the actors who plays a butler, I felt under-utilized. "You're doing fine," my producer Jackie Smith told me. Really? I'd been offered slots at previous Olympic Games but it never seemed worth doing. Like weightlifting at the 2004 Athens Olympics. Oh yeah, I know a lot about that. Or hockey, but not at the games, just hanging around interviewing people at a bar nearby. The London Olympics seemed a lot more appealing, because I love London—that was why I agreed to come over. But for most of the time, although it was a great experience being there, I was thinking, "Do they even need me?"

One day, Jackie had this idea that I should interview Usain Bolt. "Are you *sure*?" At last, an assignment I could get my teeth into! His people said yes, Bolt had won the 100 and 200 meters by then, he only had the relay to go, and I was told that he'd do an exclusive interview with me on the practice field. That in itself was interesting to me because, while I was waiting for Bolt to show, I was watching the dynamic of all these athletes warming up together, what they do, how it all works. Eventually the man himself arrived, all 6'5" of incredible muscle and speed. To give him his due, he was a cool guy, and respectful in the way he answered all my questions, even though they were somewhat lame, but he said all the right things and was extremely nice. There'd been a lot of waiting around to get the interview, and the whole segment got cut down to a few minutes on air, but it was sure fun to spend some time with the greatest track athlete in history.

That year's US Open final a month or so later brought Andy Murray up against Novak Djokovic. How many more times could Andy lose a Slam final? He was now equal with his coach in having lost his first four finals and I'm pretty sure he didn't want to become a record-breaker and be the only guy to lose five. I'd read somewhere that when Ivan had come in, he brought a sense of humor to Andy's life and that they had a lot of laughs. My God, can you imagine, Andy and Ivan having a blast? Maybe they laughed about all those losses.

The final was played in extremely difficult conditions because it was super windy. All week they'd had terrible weather, but Arthur Ashe Stadium is windier than any other stadium I know of so it's tough for the players to play their best (though they finally put a roof on in 2016, so that should make things easier). Mentally, they've got to be very focused, and it's almost impossible to do that straight through a long match, which explains why, at two sets to love up, Murray let Djokovic back in, and soon, they were tied at two sets all and going into the fifth with the momentum seemingly in Novak's favor.

At that stage, it reminded me a little of my own 1980 final at Flushing Meadows when I'd been two sets up to Borg, had blown the next two, and it was like, "Oh no, I've just lost Wimbledon to him, am I seriously about to lose this one too?" That was definitely a potential outcome because, at the time, my fitness levels when I got into a fifth set could be a factor. I was pretty fit, but not as fit as Björn. For Murray, I thought the deciding edge would go to Djokovic, even though both guys were super-fit.

Here's where winning the Olympics helped Murray (OK, perhaps Ivan helped a little, too). Finally, he now had absolute belief in himself. Plus, Novak faltered, just like Björn had with me. Maybe in both cases, it had taken them so much to get themselves back into the match that they relaxed that tiny bit and expected the other guy to fall apart. But here's the thing: neither I nor Murray did. In my case, losing another match I should have won was not an option. No way. In Murray's case,

I'm guessing he felt the same, because he went off for a bath-room break before the start of the fifth and apparently gave himself a lecture in front of the mirror while washing his hands. He came back out, took charge and showed that he wanted it more than Djokovic. As so often in sports, that margin between winning and being runner-up is tiny. Yet the consequences can be huge.

Winning that title was a major breakthrough for Murray, no doubt about it, and I was intrigued to know how much Ivan Lendl had contributed to it. Afterward, on the rare occasions that we'd see each other, I'd pepper Ivan with Murray questions, and from his replies I could tell he was on to everything, no stone was left unturned. He'd say stuff like, "There's no reason why he can't win eight majors." That's a good thing to have in your corner, someone with so much confidence, and Ivan helped Murray with that. Plus, they were a very similar age when they each won their first title, so Lendl could say to him, "Look, it took me five attempts, but I did it."

Their styles weren't dissimilar either, though by nature Murray is more of a "wait-and-see" player—a counter-puncher, like Mats Wilander was in my day—where Lendl was some-where in between. His approach was more offensive—he real-ized he didn't have to serve-volley, he could attack from the baseline, which is why he tried from the start to get Murray to play more like that too. Basically, there was a symmetry to their paths, Lendl had the credibility, and the timing was right; not only for Murray but for Lendl too. It was pure serendipity.

Ex-champions who come out of retirement to help current players have to feel they've got some connection beyond having some advice to contribute. That was obviously the case be-tween Stefan Edberg and Federer when they worked together, and between Boris Becker and Novak Djokovic. I think it's good that we're now seeing some of these ex-players coming back, making that 5 percent difference. I respect Ivan for what he accomplished on the court, and I now accept that we made each other better players. So for him to come back into tennis, after he'd been out of the game for a long time, and achieve what he did with Murray, I've got to hand it to him. Truth be told, Ivan did a great job. Watching Murray win three majors with him, having won none without, made me wonder if I might ever take on some sort of similar advisory/coaching role? It would obviously depend on the player, and it wasn't something that was at the forefront of my mind, but it could be something that would potentially be interesting, if the fit was right.

18

"Wish I didn't know now what I didn't know then"

Bob Seger

I finally won a long-running battle of my own in 2013—one that had nothing to do with tennis. I guess you could call this insanely complicated saga a cautionary tale for anyone who thinks they know their way around the art world. It certainly was for me, and it also taught me a few things about human nature that I'm probably better off knowing, but would rather I didn't.

Larry Salander, the man at the center of the story, was the high-profile art dealer I'd interned with back in the 1990s. I'd become so close to him and his wife that I was godfather to one of his kids, and I'd bought and sold paintings very successfully through him. Even though I like to think I'm pretty streetwise and I certainly don't trust people that easily, I trusted Larry. He had a crazy energy about him, but in a good way (or so I thought at the time) and he was totally passionate and knew a lot about art.

Back in 2004, I was going to Europe to play some exhibitions when Larry said, "Look, I'm in Europe, and there are these two Arshile Gorkys for sale at auction in Paris." So I agreed to go and have a look at them.

Now Gorky was probably as big as De Kooning in the 1940s, but subsequently he ending up becoming a bit of an artist's artist—more Larry David than Jerry Seinfeld—which in some ways I liked because it could make his work more affordable. These two paintings were named *Pirate I* and *Pirate II* and they look almost like little owls—abstract owls, but you can sort of make them out. I was told by Larry that these paintings were a turning point in art in the early 1940s—certain technical things about how they were painted made them historically important in terms of the evolution of abstract expressionism.

I agreed with Larry that we should go into partnership and try to bid for them, and we ended up getting both. It was a lot of money—more than I'd ever paid for a piece of art in my life. I was thinking the initial plan would be to take one each and put them away for a while—you can't just try and flip them right away, because that's not the way the art business works. And the art world was then and still is to a degree too small to get away with that type of move. Besides, I'd like to enjoy the painting—live with it for three to five years, then see what happens.

Larry agreed to that at first, but a couple of months later he decided he wanted to put them up for sale at the Armory Show—this was in February of 2005. I asked him why so soon and he said, "Oh, they're worth $10 million each." I said, "But people are going to know what we paid." He replied, "That's what they do all the time in business—rip people off." To a certain extent, obviously that's true—he was probably thinking about what they get away with on Wall Street, and thinking, "Why can't we do that too?"—but the reason I probably wasn't born to be an art dealer is that I don't like to do that to people.

Anyway, Larry put the paintings up for sale at some crazy price like $15 million each. Dealers liked the pieces but were pissed off at him about the mark-up, because what we'd paid for them was on public record. After the show ended, I said, "Hey, let's take a step back here," and Larry reluctantly agreed. So I kept one at my house and he kept the other, but the deal was that we both owned half of each.

Meanwhile, Larry suddenly seemed to be flying around in Gulfstream jets, trying to corner the market in Old Masters, throwing lavish parties for his wife Julie and generally living high on the hog. I asked him how the hell he could suddenly afford a private jet and he said, "I don't have to pay—I have this deal where I get it for nothing." I remember saying, "Hey, let me know what that deal is, I'd like that deal too." In retrospect, this should've been a warning sign, especially as around the same time Larry also leased a huge building on 71st Street—ironically it was the old IMG building where the people who represent me had their offices. But for some reason he was still staying in his old premises on 79th Street. So he had two galleries on Madison Avenue—with massive overheads. That should've been another red flag.

We kept it low key for a while, but every now and then Larry would try to persuade someone to buy one of the paintings without getting anywhere, and I was starting to get nervous. So since the auction market was very hot at that time, I said, "Why don't we put one of them up for what we paid for both? If they're worth God knows how much, then we can certainly get our money back, and then the other one's house money, so we could hang onto it and maybe make a killing in five years' time."

Larry said, "Give me until the end of the year to see if I can sell it, and if not you can call Sotheby's or Christie's." I said, "OK," and a couple more months passed. During that time he came to me a few times with strange ideas—"Look, I've just sold this Marsden Hartley painting for $600,000. I only paid $300,000, but the guy's not going to pay me for six months, so if you lend me $150,000, I'll double your money." I thought this sounded amazing, so I consulted with my accountant and money manager, who said, "Well, if all the paperwork's in order, I suppose it's OK." But we should've been thinking, "This is too good to be true."

Larry and I went out to look at this place in Long Island City, because he wanted to do something for kids—to give something back—and I was still trying to find a place for the tennis academy. It was an old abandoned factory and they were asking $15 million for it. Larry was going, "This'll be great—we can build a great sports facility with baseball fields, tennis courts, etc." But I'm saying, "Larry, it's $15 million! And it's going to be another five, minimum, to get it up and running—where the hell are we going to get that kind of money?" He said, "Oh, it's OK, you've only got to put 10 percent down," because that was the time when everyone in Wall Street was leveraging everything—and look how well that turned out!

It all sounded crazy to me, so in January 2007 I called him and said, "Larry, listen, people are coming over from Sotheby's and Christie's tomorrow, let me grab the painting to show them." At that point, out of nowhere, he said, "I've sold it." I asked him how much for and he said, "For the amount we paid for both of them—to a museum in Canada." That sounded pretty good, but then he added, "Listen, there's one formality that needs to be taken care of: it has to go through the museum's management committee to get their blessing, but they have to meet first." I said, "OK, when is that meeting?" and he said, "December fifteenth."

Bearing in mind that it's around January 5 at this point, I was a little surprised, so I just echoed back to him "December fifteenth?" I didn't actually say "you cannot be serious," but he could probably hear it in my voice. I'd seen Larry go nuts on people, but this was the only time he did it on me. He's shouting down the phone, "What the fuck? Are you questioning my integrity?" And I'm going, "Um, well, um . . . I don't know, maybe I was." At that point he hung up on me, and I was thinking, "Uh-oh."

The next day he called me, all apologetic—"Hey, I'm sorry about what happened, man, I over-reacted, I mean, we're friends. I've got the museum to agree to pay in installments." I was taken aback by this, too, so I said I'd think about it, and the next day a private art dealer by the name of Josh Baer called me. I guess you'd call him my art consultant, or one of them— Lord knows, you need expert advice when buying and selling art. He said, "I know where that painting is." I asked him what he meant, and he told me: "That painting—*Pirate II*—was sold in New York recently. I know who bought it, and it wasn't a museum in Canada."

Now I'm thinking, "I want to speak to this person." At that point an intermediary stepped in—a guy named Asher Edelman, who presents himself on his emails as "the Gordon Gecko of art," or words to that effect. He called me up and said, "I know who bought your painting," so I asked him to give me the guy's name and number, because I still owned 50 percent of the painting and I wanted answers. But he told me he couldn't do that. "Really, you can't tell me the person?" And he wouldn't.

A day or so later, I was at a Rangers ice-hockey game with one of my kids when I got a call from some guy who announced himself in a strangely formal way: "I'm the Honorable Joseph Carroll and I'm the person who owns this painting." I said, "Really? How much did you pay for it?" And he refused to tell me. At that point I was starting to get pissed—"You're not telling me? I don't know if you know this, but I own 50 percent of that painting, and you're definitely going to tell me how much you paid for it." His response? Words to the effect of, "Don't treat me like an umpire." Classic!

This guy was convinced he owned the painting free and clear, but I knew I could prove half of it was mine. Neither of us was backing down, but after a few weeks of thinking about it—and very expensive legal discussions—the best way forward seemed to be for me to sign over my half of the painting he had already bought from Larry, in return for Larry signing over to me the one I still had at my house. Obviously I was taking more of a risk because I was left with the one unsold painting, relying on what Larry had said about its value, but it was worth it not to have to deal with the Honorable Joseph Carroll—although I did end up having to sue him, but we won't go into that right now.

So in February 2007, I went over to Larry's with my lawyer, Chuck Googe (a great lawyer from my father's firm, Paul Weiss), to get him to sign a piece of paper confirming I owned 100 percent of *Pirate I*. He asked me, "What can I do to have this not happen?" And I said, "Well, pay me the money for half the sale, that's one thing you could do. Help me out here." But he couldn't or wouldn't do that, so I told him "OK, sign here," and he did (although that signature ultimately turned out not to be worth a whole lot). He said he was hoping we could still be friends, but I was shaking my head by then. "Larry, man, you need to get your shit together. I don't know what's going on, but this is fucked up." I walked out, disillusioned, but life goes on, and at least I got the painting.

Another year or so later, a gallery that was an offshoot of Christie's asked to borrow my painting for a big abstract expressionist show they were doing, and I thought that would help get it better known and easier to sell, so I let them have it. At the end of the show I got a call from Christie's refusing to return the painting to me because—you guessed it—someone else claimed they owned it.

I was like "Holy shit!" It turned out Larry had done a *The Producers* type of thing, where he'd gone 50/50 with another guy as well, who'd ended up paying twice as much as I did while Larry hadn't contributed a cent. No wonder he was flying around in his own private jet!

To cut a very long story slightly shorter, me and this other guy—who turned out to live in Washington DC and be the kind of very rich, grouchy eighty-year-old who loves suing people—had to become reluctant partners to sue Joseph Carroll and try to retrieve the painting he owned, at the same time as establishing that we owned *Pirate I* free and clear. The whole set-up was basically a Steve Martin film waiting to happen, because needless to say the two of us didn't hit it off. And as the investigation proceeded, it turned out Larry had embezzled something in the order of $125 million worth of art. Lots of other people were involved, including Robert De Niro and his father's estate—Robert and I have had many conversations where we try to laugh rather than cry about this—and also the great American artist Stuart Davis's estate, which Stuart's son had spent his life trying to protect.

By this time Larry's whole operation had been shut down—they put locks on his gallery, arrested him, he had to go to court. There was fraud, tax evasion, forged checks—it turned out he'd been making the whole thing up as he went along.

In 2009, I had to make my first appearance before the Grand Jury in New York (tough crowd!). But not before Larry's wife had come to plead with me that she'd known nothing of what he was up to and had no idea that their lavish lifestyle had been funded illegally. She suggested I should contact the press and tell them we were still friends and still doing business together! I believed her when she said she was busy looking after their four kids and the three from his previous marriage, so she was in over her head with her husband's business affairs. It was horrible to see her there in front of us, crying and saying, "John, you've gotta fix this." But there was nothing I could do.

The next year, Larry Salander was jailed for six to eighteen years for grand larceny and fraud after running an operation that the Assistant District Attorney said "would make Bernie Madoff proud." It's cost us God knows how much money, but I can tell you it's broken seven figures to get legal title for both paintings. After numerous court appearances (hey, I was a regular before the bench now) over the better part of a decade, the judges at Manhattan's civil court finally ruled that both the paintings were ours.

Of course there were a couple of appeals—heaven forbid that the legal profession should miss out on another payday—but when the last one was thrown out in 2016, the whole sad story was finally over. In financial terms, there was something of a happy ending, in that we came out ahead after selling one of the paintings to a foundation and doing well out of it, but I'd much rather not have lost a friendship. What happened made me question my judgment about people, which was an unpleasant feeling, as I thought I had a pretty good bullshit detector. And I take no satisfaction from my share of the remaining painting. To be honest, I can't stand to look at it, and even the fact that it's called *Pirate II* seems like a bad joke—"Hey, dumb-ass, turned out the clue was in the name."

19

*"I wrote a letter to my dear friend
John making him the offer"*

Donald Trump

Now that I have four grown-up daughters of my own, what happens in women's sports—and especially in tennis—matters much more to me than it did when I was winning my own Grand Slams. The French Open women's final of 2013 was won by Serena Williams against Maria Sharapova. Those two athletes have managed that very rare thing in female sports: they have crossed into mainstream public awareness. Their faces are known beyond their sport, something that doesn't happen too often. Thanks to my daughters in large part, I now realize how important it is for young girls to have the same opportunities as boys to take part in physical activity. One of my daughters, Anna, is always on me about equality and feminism, but all of them have changed my view of the world for the better. Yes, Anna, I am proud to be a feminist.

I'm often asked about equal prize money and whether women "deserve" it. These days my usual response is to make a comparison with movies: just because a film goes on for three and a half hours doesn't automatically mean it's better than the one that lasts ninety minutes. Just because the guys play best of five doesn't mean we should get 40 percent more money or whatever. Women's tennis is as close to being equal with the men's game as any sport, which I think sends out a good message. I see it with my own girls. They want to play sports and don't want to feel like it's a stigma, or that it'll give you big legs or that it means they're jocks or they have to act like boys. This is part of the challenge that women have long been faced with.

Serena Williams is an unbelievable athlete, first and foremost, as is her sister Venus. It's what they've achieved in terms of breaking into what remains a white, middle-class sport that is most impressive as far as I'm concerned. They had to cope with the murder of their sister, serious illnesses, as well as the fact that since childhood their dad went around telling the world to watch out because he had two daughters who were going to be number one tennis players. Richard used to say that Serena was going to be even better than Venus—which at the time was a potentially crazy thing to say because Venus was already an incredible player by then. So most people thought he was totally nuts and waited for those girls to bomb out. I'd be ready to bet that his daughters have fulfilled his expectations more than even he could possibly have imagined. Either that, or he really is smarter than anybody ever gave him credit for.

The fact that Richard Williams has backed off these days, that you don't see him at tournaments anymore, or only rarely, is something that I respect. Not all tennis parents do that. The temptation to remain a part of the tennis world that you've pushed your kids so hard to get into is too great for most of them. But he's allowed his daughters to mature and to fly free. And maybe the sisters' mom Oracene was the real power behind the throne, because she's the only one that seems to be around now.

My relationship with Venus and Serena is pretty decent, compared to a lot of people's. It's not like I ever had dinner with either of them, but generally speaking they've always been friendly to me, and maybe—not that I understand what they've been through—they appreciate the fact that I'm honest in my opinions and that, as a player, I had somewhat of a controversial anti-establishment image so I can sympathize with some of the situations they've been in (at least as far as a white male in America can, compared to two black women from Compton!).

One of the other reasons I've got a sort of connection with them is that I'm still being asked, usually on some talk show or other around the time of the US Open, if I would ever play either of the sisters (nowadays it's always Serena) in a "battle of the sexes" type match. I swear to God, I'll turn sixty (which is not far away) and they'll still be asking me.

The first year it happened was in 2000 when Donald Trump put $1 million on the table for a winner-takes-all match between me and Serena. Or failing that, her twenty-year-old sister, Venus. "I wrote a letter to my dear friend John making him the offer," claimed Trump. His "dear friend"? News to me. But hey, neither Serena nor Venus took him up on his offer—which was a smart move, if you ask me.

For some reason, never mind all the things that have happened in tennis in the intervening years, the subject of me playing Serena has never gone away. Do I think I could beat her? Don't tell anybody, but I may still be able to do it. OK, so my daughters no longer think I can. "Are you crazy, Dad?" being one of their more supportive responses. No, I'm not crazy. If you asked ten people, maybe five would say I'd win and five would say I'd lose (with the divide usually falling along gender lines). And as great as Serena is, I still think I may have it in me. It's safe to say we would both have a lot to lose if we agreed to that match-up. Let's put it this way: if I were ever to play Serena, I'd have to put aside months of my life to make sure I was as physically and mentally prepared as possible so that I didn't go out there and embarrass myself.

Serena is now, without a doubt, the greatest female player ever, and she still seems to have an incredible hunger for the game. Although she's won a lot less, and has a horrible head-to-head record against Serena, Maria Sharapova is the same way. Her competitiveness and intensity on court are her greatest strengths. That's why when she hired Jimmy Connors to coach her in July of 2013, there was a kind of logic to it—because of their similar mentality. But I was surprised all the same, because in the past Jimmy hadn't had any involvement with women's tennis—and had privately dumped on it.

I think that karma caught up with him, because when Maria lost in the first match of their first tournament together—in Cincinnati—she didn't waste any time in telling Jimmy it was over. I hate to say it, but if they'd stayed together for a year, it could have worked. As it was, God knows what she'd been looking for in him, but she certainly made up her mind pretty fast that she hadn't found it. Andy Roddick summed the situation up: "Who had the under odds on a match and a half for Connors/Sharapova? If you did, congratulations on your newfound wealth."

Maria doesn't care what other players think of her, because she's the highest-paid female athlete in the world. But when it comes to fist-pumping intensity, she's right on a par with Nadal. She keeps battling through even though she's got some weaknesses, like her movement and her serve. It says a lot about her that she's figured out a way to win so much despite having two potentially big areas of her game where she's vulnerable. I have to confess though that the one thing I can't stand is her grunting.

I can't watch her matches—well, sometimes I have to for professional reasons, but if it was up to me, I would never want to watch, or rather listen to her. Which is a shame. Same with Victoria Azarenka, who's also a great player. When they play, the noise takes away from your appreciation of what they're doing. Serena used to scream like that but she's backed off in the last few years, as has Venus, so it can be done. The problem is, the pitch of the grunting is so high it's incredibly annoying. The guys grunt, but their pitch is lower so I think it's less of a turnoff for the public (or maybe grunting is just considered more acceptable for guys, but that's a can of worms I don't want to open).

Should the authorities try to stop it? Yes, for sure. How would they do that? Easier said than done. People say the grunting would stop at once if the rules said you're going to lose the point if you grunt beyond a certain decibel, but how are you going to have a meter which can measure that? The question of how much the grunters can help themselves does come up, and you could say that it's a nervous thing—that when you're tense, you do it more—which would potentially make it more legitimate. There are some noisy guys out there on the men's tour too—a couple I'd want to strangle if I'd been playing them. But Djokovic has learned to make less noise, so it can be done, and Roger doesn't make a sound, which contributes to people's appreciation of him playing such a beautiful, effortless-seeming game.

The question of gamesmanship arises, because you don't hear the way the ball is being hit as well if the opponent is covering that sound with a grunt of some sort (hearing definitely comes behind sight and touch in the hierarchy of tennis senses, but it's still in the top three ahead of taste and smell!). Lord knows, there's enough of that going on elsewhere on the tennis tour, women's and men's alike. As a matter of fact, the whole thing has become a total joke—people calling trainers, taking medical timeouts, taking bathroom breaks, faking injuries, all the usual stuff. Most of it is allowed and any loophole in the rules—or more likely in the interpretation of the rules—is fully taken advantage of. I should know—I made an art of bending the rules in my day.

Bathroom breaks have gotten totally out of hand. Now, when you lose a set, you generally take a bathroom break whether or not you need one, just to interfere with your opponent's momentum. We weren't allowed to go to the bathroom at all when I was on the tour. End of story. Only if you were gonna drop dead. Like when Connors beat Lendl at the US Open final in 1982 and he badly needed to go—he had an upset stomach or something. He basically said, "I'm going to the bathroom, default me if you want." Which of course they didn't.

With the question of calling for the trainer, I would say that if you break someone down physically to the point where they start cramping, then that's one of your goals as a player, because who wins should partly be a question of who is fitter. Borg was fitter than me, Lendl too. If I broke down or started losing my edge as a result, then that was too bad for me. If a trainer suddenly comes on court to bail a player out, they're putting a brake on the momentum of their opponent, who could potentially lose their edge, while the "injured" one is being helped out of a tough situation.

Sometimes it's legitimate, but I don't think you should allow someone on to help with a cramp unless the player is in desperate agony. The trouble is, there is no black-and-white solution. The rules aren't clear, players stretch them anyway, and tournament directors and television networks don't want players, particularly highly ranked ones, defaulted because of injury. There's too much money at stake, so the spirit of the game gets totally abused. If the ITF or ATP/WTA don't like what's going on, they should stop complaining and change the rules. In the meantime, it's human nature for players to play all the angles, and from the spectator's point of view it can even be entertaining. But as an ex-player, it is also totally lame.

It's the same with the rule about how much time players take between points. People complain that Nadal takes too much time and that umpires never do anything about it. Why is it that in regular ATP tournaments players can take twenty-five seconds between points when they're playing best of three, and only twenty seconds in Slams when it's best of five? Change the goddam rule. In fact, put a twenty-five-second shot-clock on court, nice and big, so that it's clear who is taking too long, then impose penalties for slow play if you're that worried about it. If it's that obvious you're a slow player, and you risk losing a point or worse, you'll soon speed up, let me tell you. And by the way, Nadal's slow play is not the reason why so many people lose to him. That's just an excuse.

Wimbledon of 2013 has gone down in UK tennis history. It was the first time I was back playing on Centre Court since my ill-fated attempt to win mixed doubles with Steffi Graf in 1999. Oh, and I believe a British player also did pretty well in the men's singles.

Now that my brother Patrick who was 45 had qualified for the 45 or over Gentlemen's Senior Invitation Doubles, we had decided to enter the seniors tournament there. The trouble with Wimbledon is that you have to decide in March if you're going to play that summer and I can't always commit that early, which was the main reason—along with my busy TV schedule—why I hadn't played there for eight years.

To be honest, one of the main reasons I'd decided to play

there again was because otherwise I couldn't have gotten access to the locker room—a pretty pathetic reason to play, when you think about it, but that was something I felt I needed to help me do a better job with my commentating. As I'd discovered when I'd warmed up Rafa Nadal in 2008, security was security, and I wasn't going to get in there any other way.

I still had unfinished business out on the court, too. Even eight years later I was pissed at having lost the last senior doubles match I played there—with my old buddy and doubles partner Peter Fleming. What put me off playing again for all those years afterward wasn't getting beaten, but how we were beaten—badly—by the talkative Australian pairing McNamara and McNamee. Peter thought I was taking that match too seriously. "Do you realize we are about to get our asses kicked by these guys?" And I replied, "No shit, Sherlock. Maybe we should try a little harder." The worst part was that I had been asked to introduce the band Velvet Revolver at the Live Aid concert that evening—and it would've been exciting to participate in that great show where Pink Floyd got back together. How much more fun would that have been than getting beaten by McNamara and McNamee? Oh well, *c'est la vie*.

But playing with my brother was very different and we ended up having a great time. The funny thing was, we came up against the two Aussies again—the return of the Mc's—but I'd already decided: "You're not going to get away with it this time. I don't care if you want to be kidding around, I'm gonna pay you back and beat your ass." The score? 6–1, 6–2.

Our next match, believe it or not, was on Centre Court, late in the day against Jeremy Bates and Anders Jarryd, and although we lost in the third set tie-breaker, it was a good match. I admit it was pretty awesome to walk out and play on Centre Court one more time. It would have been even more awesome if we'd won, but it was still cool to play in front of a great crowd there again. They only put us old farts out there if the regular day's play has finished early. Luckily, the public seemed to appreciate the effort we put in, and we appreciated their enthusiasm right back. In that situation, whatever the result, we all realize we've got to give off a little bit of a "Hey, we're lucky we're even out here" type of vibe, instead of looking miserable. Smell the roses—or whatever those purple flowers are around the All England Club. Or at least that's what I'm telling you in this book.

There were a lot of people who thought 2013 would finally see a British victory at Wimbledon. The fact that Andy Murray had won both the Olympics and the US Open the previous year suggested a real likelihood that he could win this tournament that no British player had won for seventy-seven years (since Fred Perry in 1936). I picked him to do so at the start of the tournament, so I obviously felt that way too.

As it turned out, the draw totally opened up for him. Nadal, Federer and Tsonga were all in his half, and they all got dumped out early. Credit to Andy, he had to hang tough against Verdasco in the quarters—coming back from two sets to love down. But Verdasco can be brittle, and grass was his least favorite surface, so Murray was always the favorite against him. He then came up against the Polish player Jerzy Janowicz—the number 24 seed—in the semis, and although the guy is talented and I thought he could potentially be a top-ten player, he was never that likely to win. So as far as the draw was concerned, destiny seemed to be on Murray's side, especially as Djokovic had to get through a very long, very tight five-setter in his semi against Juan Martín del Potro. But you can only play who you're given, and Andy still had to beat Djokovic on the day, which would have been tough any time, never mind in a Wimbledon final.

I'm not sure the British public could have taken a tough

five-set final. I was calling the match for ESPN and could sense that the crowd was in a state of high anxiety. Although Murray won the first two sets, no one was taking anything for granted, especially when Djokovic got ahead 4–2 in the third. "Oh no, here we go," I could feel them thinking. That's where Murray showed that, this time, he believed he could win. That's where Ivan Lendl's influence must have been paying off. He broke back and served for the match at 5–4, though the final twelve-minute game where he let a 40–0 lead slip and had to fight off three break points pushed up everyone's pulse rates. Even I was getting edgy, because I was rooting for Murray to win. Novak had won Wimbledon before, and I thought it would be good for tennis if Andy came out on top on this particular occasion.

Thank God he finally managed it, and for once Murray did look like he was actually enjoying the moment when he won. When Sue Barker asked him how he felt in her post-match on-court interview, he got a lot of laughs for his dry reply: "It feels slightly different than last year."

"That last game was torturous," she went on. "Imagine playing it!" More laughs of relief from the crowd. And when he added, "This one's especially for Ivan," the camera panned over to my old rival, leaning against the balustrade up in that players' box, just above our commentary box, as it happens. It showed a minor miracle: a laughing Ivan Lendl. Murray was seen shaking his head in disbelief. Was it winning that had shocked him, or was it the sight of his coach looking happy?

Would Andy Murray's 2013 win at Wimbledon and later Davis Cup success in 2015 (which he won virtually single-handed, taking eleven matches out of twelve, just one less than my clean sweep in 1982—one record which can only ever be equaled, not broken) make a long-term difference to tennis in Britain? I guess the answer is: "Only time will tell." Results won't come at once, but I hope Murray's success leads to more kids wanting to take up the sport and then getting hungry enough to want to keep going, even if that's despite the British LTA rather than because of it. Andy's achievement in carrying the weight of a whole country's expectation on his shoulders deserves that kind of legacy.

20

"I'm just waiting on a friend"

Mick Jagger/Keith Richards

Even now, at fifty-eight years old, I love the challenge of playing against guys who are younger than me and seeing if I can still cut it. I'm never really satisfied with my level, but it keeps driving me to try to hold it together for a while longer. In December 2013, I won the "Legends" Over-50s tournament at Royal Albert Hall in London. The Royal Albert Hall event is kind of the *Cocoon* version of Wimbledon, and that venue is an absolutely spectacular place to play tennis. As I recently told my friend Paul McCartney at a New Year's Eve party in St. Barts (is this fancy enough for you? How d'you like me now?), I'm proud to have played Royal Albert Hall more times than the Beatles.

My first opponent, Sergi Bruguera, was hurt, apparently, but he almost beat me, because he is considerably younger than I am and is a great athlete who can still run around. In the final I beat my old friend Mats Wilander, who has been waiting a long time for a win over me as a senior. Isn't that right, Mats? Occasionally, he asks me for some tips on how he could improve his game because he seems deadly serious when he tells me one of his goals is to beat me in a match. That's when he'll be able to paraphrase Vitas Gerulaitis who, after he finally beat Jimmy Connors after sixteen straight losses, said, "Nobody beats Vitas Gerulaitis seventeen times in a row."

On the final day of the Royal Albert Hall tournament, I was being interviewed courtside by Andrew Castle, and I thought it would be cool to get everyone to sing "Happy Birthday." "It's for my friend, Keith," I said. "Keith who?" said Andrew, right on cue. "Well, you might have heard of him, he plays guitar for the Rolling Stones, his name's Keith Richards." Blatant name-dropping, I know, but I wanted to do it because he was turning seventy a few days later, and I'd been asked by his manager Jane Rose to videotape a birthday message, and this seemed a good way to do it. Not bad, eh, Jane?

It's not like we're always partying together, but we've had a lot of interesting discussions over the years. He'll send me little notes asking me unusual tennis questions, like: "What would have been the average height of a tennis player when they settled on the size and shape of a court?" Actually, Keith, the short answer is, "I have no idea." But it's still a good question. And it's a sign of the sort of low-key, easy guy Keith is that he can even be bothered to ask it.

Normally, I'd be wary of being so open about being friends with someone as famous as he is (except in the pages of this book, where all bets are off when it comes to keeping things on the down-low). But as public as the gesture was, I guess Keith was touched by it, because I got a note a few days later telling me how much it had meant to him. So I obviously got that one right. In fact, just to show what a great guy he is, he sent me a second note a few days after the first, because he wasn't sure he'd thanked me and he wanted to be polite—he must have forgotten, which is maybe what happens with the rock 'n' roll lifestyle he leads. What do I know? At this stage in my life, I tend to forget as much as I remember, if not more, so Keith, I understand perfectly.

Over the years, I've met a few of my heroes, and Keith Richards is one of the special ones who don't fall short of what you want them to be as people. The same goes for Chrissie Hynde; she gave me one of my top-ten rock 'n' roll moments when she generously laid the memory of that broken string at Madison Square Garden to rest by asking me to record a track on her new album. Obviously more because she's a friend and she knows how much I love to play my guitar than because I'd be adding any vital missing ingredient to the music.

It worked out well, because she was making the record in Stockholm at exactly the same time that I was there for an ATP Tour of Champions tournament. So on the day I arrived I went straight to the studio to lay the track down. I was playing the same old semi-lame blues part that I usually play, but they were fitting it in with the other guitar parts—it's not like I was the only guitarist. I didn't play for long, let me tell you. "Great! Great playing!" said the producer (whose name happened to be Björn—a good omen if ever there was one). "What? Are you *sure*?" I was a bit surprised Björn and Chrissie seemed so relaxed about my effort. "Yeah, we got it!" What I was thinking was, "Really? I don't think so, but OK, well, you know best."

Then, about three days later, they came over to play me a version of the song with me in it. "Holy shit! How did you make me sound like that? I actually sound all right!" "Do you think I was born yesterday?" Björn laughed. Somehow he'd taken lemons (me) and managed to make lemonade. Hopefully the song—which is called "A Plan Too Far"—didn't live up to its title in terms of my involvement, but I'll leave that for anyone interested enough to want to hear it to judge.

One of the best examples of pure and simple friendship I can remember goes back to 1992—and there's an indirect link to Keith Richards, as it happens. I was newly separated from my first wife, and I was in such a bad place that, if I'm honest, I was having trouble functioning. On New Year's Eve, I went to see Keith in concert. The opening act was Pearl Jam and afterward I went backstage and I somehow ended up telling Eddie Vedder—who I'd just met—what I was going through. Not that I'd planned to do that, but there was something genuinely sympathetic about Eddie. We stayed up until six in the morning, just the two of us talking, with him telling me, "It's gonna be OK." For me, it was a turning point—the first time that I actually believed that things might turn out all right. That was down to Eddie making me feel better and being what I would say is a real friend to me. I've never told him this until now, but it's something I've never forgotten.

I have to admit that I do sometimes get a bit overawed and star-struck when I meet people I admire or who are super well-known, but I figure that shows my feet haven't yet totally left the ground. It's better to have that response than be there thinking, "Hey, dude, I'll bet you're excited to meet me." There have been a few people I've met in the past where I could immediately feel the beads of sweat forming on my brow as I was being introduced.

One of the worst was Tom Brady, the great New England Patriots quarterback. It wasn't even a private situation when we met, there were about a billion people around us—but I immediately started sweating. Muhammad Ali was even worse. I met him once at the Forum in LA—where the Lakers used to play—and he told me I was "a crazy guy." Another time Patty and I were at a political event for Andrew Cuomo, who is now Governor of New York. Ali—who was also there in support—whispered to her, "You married him?" He said it as a joke—he still had his wits about him.

Over the years, people in general have gotten a lot more supportive in terms of the kinds of things they say to me, and I'm a sucker for a compliment as much as anyone else is. Paul McCartney at a Foo Fighters concert telling me he liked my commentary was pretty big for me, but nothing topped what Michael Jordan said to me. That's happened a couple of times, most recently at the induction of my friend the great defenseman Chris Chelios at the Ice Hockey Hall of Fame in Toronto in November 2013. At the party afterward we were all shooting the shit, remembering an event we'd taken part in where tennis, basketball and golfers all had to play each other's sports, when Michael Jordan, one of the greatest athletes of all time, said those four little words that meant so much. "I'd pay a million dollars to have that on tape," I said. Since no one took me up on my generous offer, I'm just going to have to note it down here formally for the record: Michael Jordan told me: "You're good at basketball."

All of this is a long way of saying that I understand what it is to be a fan, and I know how exciting it can be to suddenly find yourself in close proximity to someone who you've admired from afar. But that's not going to stop me from doing what no one who gets recognized in the street a lot should ever do in their autobiography—which is moan about how badly selfies suck. OK, I'll back up a yard or two. If people want to spend their own lives taking them, that's their choice. But why do they have to try and involve me?

Years ago, when I was at dinner it would just be, "Can I have your autograph?" Even then, sometimes I'd say, "Uh, not now, maybe later, I'm eating," and people didn't always respond too well to that. But with camera-phones it's even worse. It's like a secret law has been passed denying anyone the right to say no.

The selfie-hunter will say, "Why not?" And then you find your-self discussing it, so you have to ask yourself every time: OK, is it worth engaging with someone for a minute or two to explain why I don't want to pose for a photo? Or do I just say "No," and let the person think I'm an asshole?

Once you've started asking yourself these questions, every time someone comes up to you, the whole thing becomes a bigger issue than it needs to be. "I hate to bother you" is one that drives me crazy. Whenever someone used to tell me that I'd always say (though I've stopped doing this now because it causes too much conflict), "But if you hate to bother me, why *are* you bothering me?"

What people should say is, "I don't hate to bother you, I want to bother you." Just admit it—"I'm sorry, I'm going to bother you" is slightly better, but "I'm not sorry and I'm going to bother you anyway" would be more honest. I could live with that. What I don't like is when people ask, "Am I bothering you?" and then get pissed if you say, "Yes." If you don't want to hear the answer, don't ask the question. And some of them will turn dark imme-diately when they don't get what they want—"Really? That's the way you want it?" It's like they're going to fight you!

I remember this guy who was sitting next to me on a flight to Australia once. Those flights take a long time—an entire day—and he didn't say a word to me the whole way. Finally we arrived and were starting to get off the plane—obviously every-one's bleary-eyed and we're all feeling (and looking) like shit. Then he came out with it: "Hey, can I have your autograph and take a picture?" And when I said, "Sorry but I'm not sure if this is a good time," he came straight back with, "I always knew you were an asshole." OK, so you were a big fan a second ago, but now this?

Even as I'm putting this in the book, I can feel it's only going to cause me more trouble, so I'm going to call in Patty for a bit of back-up, as a witness for the defense, even. She hates "selfie culture"—if you can call it a culture—every bit as much as I do.

Patty's Perspective

People think John is this out-of-control rageaholic who goes around yelling at people all the time. I mean, don't get me wrong, he definitely yells, but it won't be for the first thing, it'll be for the sixth thing.

Maybe it would be better if he called you on the first five, rather than exploding on the sixth. People expect him to be stomping around angry all the time, but he's not like that at all. OK, he's never been an ass-kisser, and some people don't like that, but one thing they may not know is that he really cares about doing the right thing. In our building in New York, he knows every person's name that works here—and that's like fifty people. And that's more than I can say for anyone else who lives in the place. I don't think Jerry Seinfeld can say that, and I know I can't. He knows their names because it matters—it's a mark of respect.

Some of what people can mistake for being aloof or abrasive is that John gets nervous when he goes out into crowds. But honestly, if you saw how people behave toward him, you'd understand why he'd get nervous. He seems to inspire real love and real hate at the same time. People have a really strong attraction to him, but they can turn in a second! Someone will come up and they'll be like, "You're the greatest person in the world." But if he's busy doing something else—eating or just being with his family or friends—and he says to them, "Not right now," they'll come back immediately with "You fucking asshole!"

I've thought a lot about why this happens, and what I think is that there are a lot of people who don't have the balls to express their discontent and their anger at things they feel are wrong. When John used to have his moments on the tennis court it was like he was doing it for all of them. I'm not saying he's the Jesus of Anger—though that would've been a good title for this book. When John went into a crazed yelling rage on the court he stood up for himself and challenged authority. That's why people love him. But I think it also made people who couldn't do it themselves feel threatened, which might be why, when they don't get what they want from him, they'll go instantly to the other extreme.

OK, it's true, maybe sometimes he doesn't try to make them feel better about interrupting our dinner. It's fine if everyone wants to take selfies the whole time, but why do they have to make it our problem? We were at this Mexican restaurant recently, and everyone was getting drunk on tequila and people kept coming over—like a constant stream—until John was like, "Come on, you're grown-ups, man, go away." One of the only places we've ever been where this didn't happen was when I finally managed to persuade John to go away somewhere without playing tennis and we took a trip to Cuba for a few days in December of 2011. It was no coincidence that going somewhere people didn't know him was one of the best holidays we've ever had.

John is never physical with his anger when people annoy him. I will lose it long before he does, and I have—believe it. But he's not going to do it, because he wasn't raised that way. They're not physical at all, John's parents—the only violence there is the yelling. And John doesn't have that either. I guess the neighborhood he grew up in wasn't so tough that you needed it, whereas mine kind of was. As brash a New Yorker as he is thought to be, his background is middle class. Whereas even though I only grew up a few miles from him, I was blue-collar to lower middle. That's the difference between us.

In a way it's interesting that John should be with someone who's got the anger thing worse than he has. John McEnroe is calming me down and that's the truth. He'll tell me, "Be smarter." Like if I'm losing it with the builders who took eight months to finish fixing a frozen pipe at our house, I'll be firing off all these angry messages and he'll be saying, "Don't send those texts," and even though I don't want to admit it, I'll know he's right.

21

"He keeps moving from city to city, country to country, moving through airports hidden behind shades and a baseball hat with a tennis bag on his back that is a part of him now, that carries his life in it future and past. The constant traveler covering ground, going miles across the planet alone, always alone, though he doesn't like being alone. It is the way he travels best, like a lone wolf and he can't stop. He does it for the family, he does it for the game, he does it because it's what he knows"

Patty Smyth

I'd been playing Ivan Lendl in Hong Kong in March of 2013 when Ivan's agent, Jerry Solomon, came up with the fateful idea of having an event back at the Garden where my brother Patrick and I would play the Bryan brothers. Mine and Ivan's matches aren't the life-and-death affairs they used to be—now we tend to let it get to 3–3 or 4–4 and then try all-out in the last couple of games—but the Bryans were probably the best doubles team in the world at that time, whereas my brother and I hardly get the chance to play together anymore, and on top of that, we're pretty old. I didn't want to be embarrassed—certainly not in my home city, at the place I considered my home court—so I'd responded with an emphatic "no." But Jerry kept on at me and over the course of the next few months somehow turned that "no" into a "yes."

Little did I realize then how this innocent-seeming three-letter word would enmesh me in a cruel web of destiny. From that point on, circumstances conspired like a sadistic puppet-master to set me up for one of the most painful ass-whippings of my entire tennis career. And the worst part of it was, I only had myself—and my reckless attachment to the word "Yes"—to blame.

In August 2013, Ray Moore had come to Malibu to discuss ways of bringing me back into the mix a little at the Indian Wells tournament. Ray, who used to be a good tour player back in the sixties and seventies, is a real old-school guy, a throwback to when tennis wasn't all about big bucks (unfortunately, his old-school ideas would get him fired in 2016 for some ill-considered remarks about the debt he thought women tennis players owed Nadal and Federer). Ray had been around way before I arrived on the scene, and when he was young he looked like a total hippy, with his straggly long hair, huge mustache and headband. He and I have always been friendly and he's one of the few guys in the world who still calls me "Junior," Peter Fleming being another (Nastase would have called me that too, if he hadn't chosen to call me "Macaroni" instead—which is typical Nasty).

"Junior," Ray told me that August, "we want to do something with the seniors and we think it would be great if you came up and played. We haven't quite ironed out the kinks, but we know we want you here more than anybody." I figured it was nice of him to offer and I wanted to make it work. The problem was that the match—for which my academy would also receive a share of the proceeds to go toward funding tennis scholar-ships—was set for March 1 in Palm Springs, two days before I was supposed to play the Bryan brothers on the opposite side of the country. "I'll figure it out," I thought. So I said, "Yeah, sure." Genius.

It was a potentially tricky but still just about feasible schedule that turned disastrous when the Jim Courier-backed Champions Tour, which I also played on, moved their dates. So instead of playing a twelve-city tour in October–November 2013, I was told it would now be February–March, wrapping right around the Indian Wells and Madison Square Garden dates. The idea behind this change was that hopefully we'd be playing at a time of year when people might be a bit more starved of tennis, not right after the US Open and all the summer tournaments, and that would make more commercial sense.

What would turn a theoretically amicable encounter between two generations of leading doubles performers into a full-scale grudge match were some comments I made at the December 2013 Royal Albert Hall event. When I was asked what I thought about the state of doubles and did it have a future, I didn't say anything in reply that I hadn't already said about a hundred times, for instance that doubles is for the guys who were too slow to play singles. Big surprise. Something I hadn't said was that maybe we should get rid of doubles and use the money to provide more prize money in the lower-tier tournaments, like the Challengers and the Futures, to give singles players more of an incentive to stay on the tour instead of bailing too early because they can earn more money teaching tennis than playing it.

I swear most people have never heard of the vast majority of doubles players. They can't identify with them because ever since tennis became so physical and so commercial that you couldn't seriously play both events—never mind the mixed—and give yourself a decent chance in either, the household names from the main singles draw barely even play doubles. Now I accept that if you ask the public, they always say, "Oh, we love doubles," especially in Britain, because most club tennis involves doubles. But when there's a doubles match on in a tournament, half the stadium empties. So much for loving doubles.

The reason I can say all this is because I was arguably a better doubles player than singles and, unlike most of my peers, I played both for most of my career on the tour. Peter Fleming once generously said, "The best doubles team in the world is McEnroe and anybody." Peter has always been too modest for his own good, but it's true that, overall, my record is better in doubles than in singles. I won nine Grand Slam doubles titles versus seven singles ones and I also finished number one in the world in doubles seven years in a row, versus four years in singles. So if anyone's going to defend doubles, it's going to be me. Don't shoot the messenger because, hey, I'm the one that actually *liked* doubles. Apart from anything else, it helped my singles game.

After making those comments in December 2013, I hadn't thought any more about it. But one day, midway through January 2014, I was in the lobby of an apartment in lower Manhattan on my way to a friend's birthday party, when my phone rang. I don't know why I took the call rather than ignoring it and going into the elevator, because it wasn't from a number I recognized or had saved on my cell phone. Anyway, for some reason, I answered. "Hey, John, man, it's Mike Bryan," said the voice on the other end.

He sounded unhappy. "Oh," I answered, surprised. "Hey, Mike, what's up?" "Listen, you know I really respect you—always have—but I just wanted to say that I'm a little hurt by what you said about doubles. The media is asking me all these questions and, uh, I don't know what to say." I was struggling to focus, let alone remember what I might have said that could have resurfaced. It turned out that Mike was at the Australian Open and the media had resurrected the stuff I'd come out with six weeks earlier. "I don't remember exactly what it is I'm supposed to have said, Mike, but you should say whatever you wanna say. Stand up for yourselves. Doesn't matter to me either way." Had he wanted me to say sorry? Yes, probably.

When I'd made those comments at Royal Albert Hall, it had in no way been meant as a personal attack on the Bryan brothers, who are probably the best thing that doubles has going for it, so I wasn't even talking about them specifically. They're twins, they bring some good energy to the court, people like them—I get it. And it wasn't like I was coming out and saying, "My brother and I are gonna kick your ass." I was just trying to have a sensible discussion, because as far as I'm concerned, doubles is on life-support.

In the weeks leading up to the Madison Square Garden showdown, the malevolent deities who were directing this whole shitstorm decided to use the weather against me. The Champions Tour of 2014 became known as the Snow Tour: almost every place we went there were incredible white-outs. We flew to Kansas City during a blizzard. Oklahoma City, we barely made it in. For the trip to Birmingham, Alabama, it was so bad they canceled every flight because it was unheard of to get any snow there at all and the place was at a standstill.

I was in New York the day before and my flight had already been canceled because of the terrible weather, so I was wondering how the hell I was going to get down to Birmingham anyway. I happened to be at dinner with some friends and Barry Sternlicht, the CEO of Starwood Capital Group, was there. I'd met him a couple of times; not only was he a big tennis fan but he also had a private plane. "I'm going to Miami tonight, you want a ride?" "Thank you very much, that would be great." Every once in a while I get lucky with that sort of thing and I appreciate it every single time, let me tell you (thank you Allen and Deborah Grubman for inviting us to dinner that night).

At least in Miami it would still be 75 degrees, so I figured Miami–Birmingham would probably be doable by the time we got there. Somehow we made it out of New York. But the winds were so bad that what should have been a two-and-a-half-hour flight turned into a very bumpy four-hour trip. Finally, we got to Miami at some crazy time like 2:30 in the morning. Thank God, my agent Gary, who lives there, was able to pick me up and drive me back to his apartment. The next day, I managed to get a regular flight out to Birmingham, even though it was still under three inches of snow. "Why the hell am I still doing this?" I thought. Especially as, right after Birmingham, I had to fly to Indianapolis and that was under a foot and a half of snow.

The worst part of it was knowing that the most exhausting week of an already-exhausting month was yet to come, and there waiting at the end of it were the Bryan brothers. Knowing that I was entirely responsible for my own imminent humiliation didn't help either. The schedule read as follows:

Saturday night—fly to Madrid to stand in for Maria Sharapova in an advertising shoot for Movistar. [I forgot to mention that I'd agreed to take Maria's place in a disastrously timed—but temptingly well-paid—last-minute extra European engagement. I know what you're thinking: "McEnroe for Sharapova, now that's what I call a like-for-like replacement!"]

Sunday morning—arrive Madrid, shoot the commercial all day until 10 p.m.

Monday—get up 5 a.m., fly to Paris, then on from Paris to Salt Lake City, Utah.

Tuesday—play, then fly to Sacramento, California.

Wednesday—play, then fly to Portland, Oregon.

Thursday—play, Portland.

Friday—fly to Palm Springs, California.

Saturday evening—play Palm Springs.

Sunday morning—fly Palm Springs to Dallas then Dallas to
New York for match at the Garden the following evening.

I held up OK in the beginning. The first day back after the Madrid trip I even beat Sampras, who admittedly was having some shoulder problems. The next day, I won a match against Courier, so that was good, too. I was actually playing pretty well. On the Thursday in Portland I played Agassi, and did well even though I lost.

The straw that broke this increasingly travel-weary camel's back was that the next trip, from Portland to Palm Springs, was one of the top-ten worst flights I ever took. There was so much turbulence—and Lord knows I've been in enough of it over the years—that at one stage I was thrown right out of my seat and hit my head on the ceiling, on the buttons that call the flight attendant, which I might have wanted to do if I hadn't been feeling too ill and too scared to move.

Palm Springs is not my favorite place at the best of times (and this was not the best of times). It's so hot, it's stuck out in the California desert, and it seems like people only go there when they're ready to die. Unfortunately, it happens to also be where the Indian Wells tournament is held, which is now probably the biggest tournament of the year outside of the four majors. Larry Ellison, the billionaire Internet entrepreneur and philanthropist, had bought the tournament a few years earlier and was pouring tens of millions of dollars into a new stadium to give the tournament even more credibility than it already had. I couldn't very well have not turned up to a seniors mini-tournament that was now (thanks to Larry and Ray Moore) called the John McEnroe Challenge for Charity, could I?

After what had happened on the flight down from Portland, the prospect of getting back on a plane to New York via Dallas wasn't that appealing. My agent assured me that I'd be on a bigger plane, so I wouldn't get the turbulence, but I was still wary. "Are you sure? Because I really don't need that again." "No, no, don't worry." So I grabbed a few hours' sleep and got up at 5 a.m. for my early morning flight out. Just as I was getting ready, Gary called me. "The flight's canceled. There's another storm coming in to New York."

So now we were scrambling to get me back in time to play this goddamn doubles match that I should have been preparing for all week, instead of crisscrossing the skies over America and the Atlantic, racking up an insane number of air miles and experiencing some of the worst weather conditions I'd ever flown in. Boy, how I wish, looking back, that I'd let that storm come in and not driven like a maniac for two and a half hours all the way from Palm Springs to LA to catch the last flight into New York before everything was canceled for the next twenty-four hours. Especially because when I got to LA I had maybe an hour and a half to kill, so I decided to go to my house in Malibu, which turned out to be a mistake, because when I got there and walked up into my room, I saw somebody in my bed.

It was like the children's fairy story with the three bears, except there was only one of me, and before I had time to ask, "Who the hell's been sleeping in my bed?" I could see it was my step-daughter, Ruby—who Patty had forgotten to tell me was supposed to be staying in this other little place nearby that we were trying to fix up—and she was with a guy we'd never even met before. I was calling Patty, saying, "Oh my God, you won't believe this!" As it turned out, this is pretty much the only part of the story that has a happy ending, because at the time of this writing Ruby's still living with the guy—his name is Michael—and I like him a lot, but on the morning in question, it wasn't doing my stress levels any good.

I swear to God, by the time I stepped off that flight in New York, I'd shrunk to about 5'7" instead of being nearly 6' tall. That's how stiff and sore and beat up I was after all the traveling I'd done. I was in no condition to do anything other than go to bed and sleep for twenty-four hours, let alone play a game of tennis.

At this point, I would like to be able to tell you that my brother and I crushed the Bryans with a barrage of aces, but it would not be true. Inevitably, the match itself was an unmitigated disaster. Patrick and I had barely played together since the Wimbledon seniors the previous summer, and stepping out onto the court that day was like walking the plank.

After all the months of negotiations, we'd agreed to play one eight-game set. For whatever reason, most of the balls weren't hit to me, even though I would have missed every one of them anyway because I could hardly stand up straight. I'd like to say that Bob and Mike—to give them each a first name, not that many people can tell them apart—sensed I wasn't exactly knocking them dead and cut me a break. But no, I think they'd figured that Patrick wasn't serving as big as me, and although he hit some balls that would normally be good enough in an over-45s doubles, these guys were just blocking, poaching and hitting everything all over the court. When they got to 7–0 after what seemed about seventeen minutes—the idea had been to play for around forty-five minutes to make it look like we belonged on the same court as them—it became one of the most embarrassing experiences I've ever had in tennis.

It wasn't the Bryan brothers' fault that we were both laying serious eggs out there. They were even nice enough guys to throw us a bone and let us win a couple of consolation games— come to think of it, we may even have won one legitimately. So the final score ended up being 8–3. The 15,000 people who'd paid good money to see us play probably weren't under any illusion that we stank. But I was so pissed at how bad they'd made us look that my thoughts about the matter were probably clear for all to see. By the end, I swear to God I was trying to find the nearest place to hide.

I couldn't blame the Bryan brothers for wanting to prove a point to me, or for letting their tennis do the talking. I might have done exactly the same in their position. But in a way I guess the fact that Patrick and I hadn't played so much as a practice set as a pair in preparation for a match which they had probably been building up to for weeks was the ultimate reflection of the insignificance of doubles.

Did we deserve that beating? No. And was it something of an empty victory on the Bryans' part—to come onto the court thinking "we're gonna show them," see that we were virtually cripples and then batter us anyway? I'd say so, maybe. It's like, "Are you happy now? What did that do for you?" But I guess at the end of the day they're still laughing all the way to the bank, because they're making millions of dollars a year playing doubles when nobody cares.

While I'm on the subject of doubles and what I'd do to try to breathe some life into them, I would definitely make some changes: firstly, it should be against the rules for players to stay back on their serves. Move up to the net, volley, do what so few singles players are doing, so that at least you're doing something differently and better than the singles. Also, you lose a point whenever you high-five your partner after missing a shot or double-faulting. It's such an annoying habit to me and I'm totally sick of it. I started doing a little bit of high-fiving when I played with Michael Stich at Wimbledon the year we won the doubles in 1992, but I sure as hell didn't do it when one of us double-faulted.

Nowadays, Lord knows, I'd be high-fiving my partner every few points if I was doing it after every missed shot or double fault. And by the way, I don't bother talking tactics either during my matches. In the past, sure, I'd be talking tactics at change-overs or at crucial moments in the set. Nowadays, there's no point. Unless we're saying, "Get the damn return in." I guess that's a tactic? When we're serving, "Could you just get your first serve in?" is about as far as us old-timers go tactically. But as for, "Shall we play the Australian formation?" That would be way too dangerous because it would involve one player crouching down at the net near the center line while his partner served, and he might need a chiropractor to get him back up again.

22

"I'm eighteen and I like it"

Alice Cooper

Our youngest daughter, Ava, turned sixteen in 2015. On March 28, to be precise. It was a milestone. For her, because she had a Sweet Sixteen party which Patty had of course planned in great detail. For us, because that's when Patty and I realized it won't be long before Ava flies the nest and we'll be left on our own for the first time ever. We were almost done raising six children (though you're never done, right?). How did that happen?

Any parent knows how fast those childhood years go by, especially when your work takes you away from home as much as mine did. When I was with them in New York, I'd drive or walk the kids to school whenever possible, because I wanted to let them know that, although I was away a lot, once I was back home I was there for them. In recent times I'd get up every morning to make breakfast for Ava, cutting up pieces of fruit for her and making her scrambled eggs on brown rice toast, long after she was totally able to do it herself. I just wanted her to have a little company in those early weekday starts, because I think it sucks if you're the only one who's up and everybody else is asleep—though as you get older solitude can become more appealing.

With six kids, it's not always been easy to feel like I've given the right amount of time to each one, to make sure I got to the concerts, the basketball games, the teachers' meetings, etc. But wherever I was playing tennis in the world, I'd always try to get the earliest flight home, and while I was away I'd be calling them the whole time to see how they were, doing the dad thing of, "How did that play go?" or "Whose party are you going to?" and their old favorite, "Be home by ten."

I always figured that having such a large family, there'd be maybe two kids that would be constantly saying, "Dad, we love you," and hugging me, two that were sort of in the middle, OK with me, and two who would be pissed; for whatever reason they'd just have a problem. Then I'd be thinking, "I'm going to hang around with the two that are hugging me, forget the other ones!" Is that so wrong? I should emphasize at this point that I am actually joking, in case any of my kids are reading and thinking, "I knew it!"

By the time this book comes out, Ava will be eighteen. When I was that age, I couldn't wait to leave home. I loved my parents, but I couldn't wait to go off and be independent—obviously I'd already done a fair amount of traveling by then, so I was used to being away. My mom and dad left me in no doubt about their ambitions for me: "Get a college scholarship," they'd tell me. No pressure. They were pushy parents, though maybe not by today's crazy standards, but there was always this expectation to succeed and, being a dutiful son, I obliged.

In spring 1977, I got the news that I'd gotten into Stanford University, on the West Coast—with a scholarship, thank God—and my parents couldn't have been prouder. Even though I only ended up staying there for a year, going to college was still one of the best decisions I ever made, because it allowed me to grow up as a person, be surrounded by an atmosphere of learning, and most of all to learn how to live on my own—and let's not forget the partying. As it was, not long after the news came through that I was going to Stanford, I got that generous $500 grant I mentioned earlier from the USTA to travel to Europe for the summer of 1977 and play the French and Wimbledon juniors, and I quickly found myself having to learn fast in a couple of different and highly pressured situations.

Talk about a steep learning curve! Paris was a total eye-opener in itself. And not just because I was in a city where, despite my many years of taking French in school, I couldn't understand a word of what people were saying, though I was pretty sure the famously surly Parisians weren't exactly complimenting me too much of the time. But the real mindblower was when my friend, Mary Carillo, who I'd grown up with in Queens and who was now a pro, took me off to the Louvre and the Jeu de Paume Museum to see some amazing impressionist paintings, which started my slow awakening to what great art could be.

Back on court, I not only won the juniors but managed to get through the qualifying and a round of the main draw. This was a huge deal because it got me enough ATP points to get me into the qualifying round at Wimbledon. I also teamed up with Mary to win the mixed doubles in Paris, which gave me my first Grand Slam title when I was still only eighteen.

At that age, I was at my best on clay. As a junior, all my national titles were won on that surface. It was only after I got to Stanford that I became bigger and stronger, all six feet (OK you assholes, five feet eleven and three-quarters) and 170 pounds of me, and it dawned on me that my natural style was serve-volley. The fast courts of the West Coast definitely didn't hurt as far as that realization was concerned. Even though I've often been thought of as having an all-out attacking kind of game, I've actually always been a percentage player and don't like to take chances. I've never been a big hitter, but relied on quick hands, good movement and a smart tennis brain to overcome opponents—my style was to try and help the guy on the other side of the net to beat himself. I didn't take big swings or big risks on my returns. Block it back, come in if I see a quick opportunity, attack.

My Paris trip must have given me a lot of confidence because I got through three rounds of qualifying at Wimbledon and suddenly I was into the main draw. How the hell had that happened? I was still an amateur and only supposed to be playing the juniors. Meanwhile, London turned out to be only slightly less strange than Paris. The main difference was that I understood most—though not all—of what was said to me. But the warm beer, the English reserve, the grass courts, all of that took some getting used to.

The funny thing about it was that—as stuck in its ways as England seemed to be to me—it was going through some big changes at the time. That first Wimbledon I played, the whole punk scene was crazy. The Sex Pistols had made it to the top of the charts in the week of the Queen's Silver Jubilee, and I was walking down the King's Road as a total unknown. At first I was thinking "these kids are a bunch of freaks," but then, the more I thought about it, the more I started to feel some connection with them. Not long after, I would find myself being called "the punk of tennis." I should've dyed my hair pink and gotten a Mohawk—they'd have loved that on Centre Court at Wimbledon. Just kidding!

I got through the first four rounds without too much trouble, including a win against a future top-ten player, Sandy Mayer, an

After his opponent had to default at the US Open, Novak Djokovic called me out of the commentators' booth to show him how it was done.

Guess who's not the comedian in this group – with Conan O'Brien, Kevin Nealon, Jack Black, Colin Quinn, and Jimmy Fallon.

Hamming it up at a charity event in Florida with former president George Bush, Chevy Chase, and Chris Evert. (© 1999 Alese/Morton Pechter)

Showing Boris Becker how to wear a jacket.

With my wife, my parents, and my kids at the Hall of Fame induction ceremony, 1999.

The last full McEnroe family photo.

Horror hair at the French Open – I've learned that lesson now.

With my friend the great Ranger hockey goalie Henrik Lundqvist, Oscar-nominated actor Edward Norton, and Novak at my charity event on Randall's Island, 2014.

In Kuala Lumpur, in front of one of the world's tallest buildings, with James Blake, Roger Federer, and Björn Borg.

Ivan's manager made sure we all had recent photos on the laminate except him – talk about going the extra mile!

Having some fun with Andy Murray playing a doubles exhibition at the London O2 Arena in 2014. (Getty/Andrew Couldridge)

Standing in front of Royal Albert Hall in London – one of my favorite buildings in the world to play in. Thankfully for the audience, it's tennis I'm playing, not music.

ex-Stanford player, and found myself among the big guys in the quarters, on Court One. For the first time, I'd be playing a seed. Phil Dent, the tough Aussie who had beaten me at Roland-Garros. As it turned out, I'd learned a lot from that defeat, not least how to figure out his game, which came in handy when I was two sets to one down and a break down in the fourth. For some reason, unlike in Paris where I'd been the one two sets to one up, I didn't get tight, whereas Phil, who would have been desperate at twenty-seven to make it to his first Wimbledon semi-final, started to tighten up a little.

Meanwhile, the crowd really got into the match, particularly after I'd broken a racket at the end of the first set and started to complain to the umpire about some of the bad line calls the sleepy line judges had made. The crowd was obviously shocked that a teenage nobody should behave like this in the temple of tennis, so they started to boo me, something that had never happened to me before. But instead of folding or getting mad at them, I actually found it funny that this normally reserved gathering of uptight Brits was starting to make some noise.

Here I was, playing in front of the biggest crowd I'd ever had, and the New Yorker in me loved how much I was getting under their skin. I was pretty pumped up, let me tell you, and I was desperate to keep this incredible run going, knowing I'd be the first qualifier to get this far in the tournament. When I shook hands with Dent after coming through in five tough sets, it felt both crazy and natural that I should have won. I remember thinking, "Either these guys are a lot worse than I thought, or I'm a whole lot better."

Clearly, Jimmy Connors, my semi-final opponent, was going to show me how wrong I was by crushing this total upstart. Having made it into the quarters, I'd finally been moved into the main locker room, the one reserved for the top players. This was a big deal. Getting ready before my semi-final, I spotted Connors in a corner. By then he and Borg were the two superstars of the tour, and I was in awe of him. Despite that, I decided I'd try to say "hi" because I'd never actually met him. The long and short of it was that he literally did not even acknowledge my existence or my attempt to introduce myself in any way. Connors was in no mood to give me an inch in either the mental or the physical matches that we were about to play.

He won both battles, and looking back I think that was probably the best result for me too. Getting this far in my second ever major tournament changed my life enough as it was, but if I'd actually got to the final? Or won? I would have missed out on going to college completely to turn pro right-away, which would have put me even more in the glare of the media and built a potentially unbearable pressure of expectation.

I don't mind admitting that by the time I came back to New York after getting to the Wimbledon semis in the summer of '77, the whole thing had gone a bit to my head. I'd left for Europe that spring as a promising junior. When I came home a few months later, I was suddenly someone who people knew a little bit. It wasn't just me who'd changed either. My relationships with some of my old school-friends faltered, because they didn't know how to treat me anymore. There's a good line in that song "One Headlight" by Jakob Dylan's band, the Wallflowers—"I ain't changed, but I know I ain't the same"—that summed up how I felt.

I know that Borg won his first major, the French Open, at eighteen and Boris Becker won Wimbledon at seventeen. But they hadn't come from nowhere. They didn't win those titles as qualifiers. For my part, I'm glad in retrospect that I didn't have to cope with a situation that I didn't feel ready for. Still, I managed to get a set off Connors, and even if he hadn't wanted to acknowledge me back in the locker room, I'm pretty sure what I did on court that day was enough for him to notice me.

Our relationship since then has had its ups and downs, to put it mildly. But when I rejoined the Snow Tour ten days after the Bryan brothers match, I was actually happy to find myself playing Jimmy again almost forty years on—in a funny way, I'd almost missed him. Our match in Nashville, Tennessee was the first time we'd met on court since I'd beaten him 6–1, 6–0 at Royal Albert Hall fifteen years before. He stopped playing for a while after that, had an incredible three hip replacements and since then had bailed on a few occasions when we were supposed to play. He was sixty-one now, so I thought there was no way he was gonna show up this time either. But to my surprise, he did.

Connors walked onto the court wearing long pants and a sweater, looking like someone out of the 1920s—Bill Tilden. We started the match—or rather, the set we were scheduled to play—and he kept the clothes on. "Jimmy, are you going to take off your pants or your sweater at any point?" "No," he replied. Sure enough, he stayed totally covered up until the end. Maybe he was keeping his muscles warm, because his movement wasn't too great. Maybe he didn't have any muscles. Although he could still hit it and he was still Jimmy Connors, he was somewhat on slo-mo.

Looking back from the other end of my own career to the experiences I had as a boy on the brink of manhood, I'm not proud of the fact that I acted like a jerk more times than I'd like to remember. Was that because I was too young when everything hit me? Too spoiled? Did I feel guilty about my success? Did I think I didn't deserve it? Soon after I turned pro, my dad, who looked after my finances at that stage, told me that I'd earned more in the previous year than he'd earned in his entire life. My dad, who'd worked his way through night school to become this successful lawyer, was now out-earned by his teenage son? Even I—cocky as I was—could see how insane that was (and sometimes I wished he hadn't pointed it out).

As I've watched my own kids battle to find their own way across the threshold into adulthood, I've seen how the very advantages that my success has brought them have put pressures on them that I never had to deal with. The McEnroe name follows them everywhere they go, and that can be tough to live up to, because they're scrutinized the whole time and it's hard for them to establish and maintain their own identities.

For example, if my daughter Emily tries to get a waitressing job in LA, she'll get asked, "Hey, if you're McEnroe's daughter, why are you waitressing?" As if it's not a decent way to earn some money, and as if I should be bankrolling her for everything. If she's willing to earn her living while pursuing an acting career, it shouldn't matter what work she does, and people should respect her even more because she's not too proud to do that sort of work. Overcoming the obstacles that growing up in the public eye presents is every bit as much of a challenge for my kids as it was for me to gain the renown that put them in that situation in the first place.

A sad marker of the way our family dynamic was changing as we drew nearer to the time when Ava would move away came when our little white part toy poodle, part Maltese, Lulu, passed away in June of 2015. She had been with us since August 2002 and from the minute we got her, we all fell in love with her. All four of my girls and Patty had wanted a dog for a while, because they all loved animals. I'd been much less enthusiastic because, truth be told, I've had some bad experiences with dogs. And the larger animals downright scared me. Plus, I knew what would happen when we got one. As much as the kids loved that dog, none of them was exactly asking to walk her at seven in the morning. They dropped the ball pretty fast on that and, guess what, I got stuck with that task.

Luckily, Lulu turned out to be the friendliest and most low-maintenance dog in the world, and soon I found myself in a routine: after getting the kids up for school and before sorting out their breakfast, I'd set off with her on our early morning walk, nodding hellos to everyone else out there with their dogs. I hadn't realized that having a dog was such a great ice-breaker. There was just this one little Napoleon-type guy I never said hello to. He lived halfway down our block and had a crazy pit bull-like beast he always seemed to be hanging on to for dear life as it snarled its way down the sidewalk. I swear to God, I was afraid for my life and for Lulu's whenever we came across that animal. Every morning, I'd be going, "God, please, I don't want to run into this dog," and my heart would be jumping out of my chest as he approached. I had the whole story worked out: the guy was a nut, he lived on his own, was totally miserable. In the end, of course, having built this whole thing up, I finally plucked up the courage to say "hi" to him, and he was perfectly friendly and seemed like a nice guy. His dog was still out of control, though.

Lulu was a lot easier to handle—she'd roll on her back and let herself be cuddled by everyone. The funny thing is, if you've got a dog like that, people think its owners must be like that too. Once people got used to seeing me around the place with Lulu, they started looking at me differently. "Here's this guy with a cute, fluffy dog. Maybe he's like that too. Maybe he *is* human after all."

Lulu was part of our family life the whole time that the kids were growing up. She was small, so we'd take her with us whenever we flew out to LA. We'd stick her under the seat and she was a great traveler. But when Patty and I got back to New York between the French Open and Wimbledon in 2015 she noticed Lulu wasn't herself and was having trouble breathing. Long story short, Patty took her to a hospital and they sent us home saying it was early diabetes. Four hours later she went into respiratory distress.

Patty took her to a different hospital but, as it turned out, it was too late. None of us thought she was that sick, which is why it was such a shock. I came over at once, along with Anna, who was in tears, and we were just deciding whether to operate—my main concern was that she shouldn't be in pain—when a nurse knocked on the door and had a quiet word with the veterinarian. He disappeared for a few minutes while we were left on our own. Lulu was elsewhere in the building so we didn't know what was going on. Five minutes later, the doctor came back and told us that he was sorry but she had passed away. "Would you like to see her?" So they brought her back in, wrapped up in this little blanket, and put her in my arms. And that's when I cried. Yes, I admit it, I did. Maybe I've got to thank Roger Federer for that, but I've become more of a crier now in my old age.

I've got to be careful not to overstate this, because Patty has accused me of using my emotional reaction to the loss of our first dog as a way of stalling on us getting a second one, but I never thought I was going to love that dog quite so much or that her death would affect me quite as badly as it did. It was horrible. Within two minutes, though, someone came into the room and went, "How are you paying for this, Mr. McEnroe?" As in, "Will that be Visa or American Express?" "Do you think we could talk about this tomorrow?" I suggested. Welcome to America.

23

"If it ain't broke, don't fix it"

approximately one million viewers of the BBC's early
evening Wimbledon highlights show, 2015

A few days after Lulu died, I flew to London for the start of Wimbledon. I love that time of year and I've been staying in the same hotel in Chelsea Harbour every June for the last twenty years. One of the things I like about it is that it's got a great pool and a good gym. I've got my routine all set: I either swim or work out every morning, or both if I can, then head down to SW19 and the All England Club to start my day's work.

I never know until the night before which matches I'm going to be calling or for which broadcaster, because it depends on the following day's schedule and the draw. If Murray is playing, the chances are the BBC will want me. Currently we don't have an American equivalent of Murray; there's no big-name draw. But if we had, say, an Agassi or Roddick, the Americans would want me for that and they'd take priority over the BBC. The producers on both networks get along well, so they talk and sort it out between them, which I appreciate. Believe it or not, I mostly do what I'm told.

For the last ten years or so, I've also done a once-weekly

phone-in, *606*, on the BBC's Radio 5 Live early evening drive-time slot. They've recently put Tim Henman with me because he's a good foil and has got that dry sense of humor. Andy Roddick and Boris Becker have been on with me a few times too, and we end up with a fun, relaxed type of show. I don't know which questions are going to come through, but to be honest they don't tend to stray too far from the fairly predictable. It's not as if I'm being asked to comment on anything out of left field. The people who phone in also tend to be fans, which is a whole lot better than if I had total assholes coming on. Or no one phoning in at all.

The evening Wimbledon highlights show at the BBC has changed over the ten years or so that I've been involved. It used to be fronted by John Inverdale, who I've always thought was really good at his job. We don't have the sort of relationship where I've ever gone to dinner with him, but I've been impressed by what he does. I don't know what happened exactly for him not to be doing it in 2015 because he clearly knows his tennis. What's sure is—and I don't think it'll come as a surprise when I say this—the show we used to do with him was way better than the train-wreck 2015 show, lamely called *Wimbledon 2Day*.

As bad as the title was, the show itself was even worse. If you'd said to me, "We're thinking of doing it with a live audience," I would have thought, "OK, potentially that could be cool." But it turned out not to be cool at all because I swear the audience looked like mannequins. I don't know who came up with that idea but it didn't work. Then I was told we'd be trying a new set. Turned out it was way over somewhere in the parking lot, nowhere near the media center where we used to be.

How the hell would that make it any better? Particularly given the phony set, with its fake ivy and grass and this pathetic tiny table we were supposed to stand around. Because let's not forget the worst bit of the total disaster: the idea that we'd all be standing up for the entire show. I was told that Clare Balding, the new host, liked to move her hands a lot, so was more comfortable standing. I went, "Well, I move my hands a lot as well, but, guess what, you can move your hands when you're sitting down." Clare Balding is obviously a very good, experienced commentator, but she seemed nervous and it felt like she was in a bit over her head.

When I did the first show, I thought "Oh my God, what *is* this?" We were standing around this dumb awkward set, huddling around this ridiculous table, and they kept having us do all these embarrassing things. It reminded me of the stupid stuff I'd had to do on my own talk show all those years before. Those ideas never work. The whole thing was wrong from the start.

"This is pitiful, you've gotta change it," I told the producer early on. Luckily, I wasn't the only one. About a million other people complained too and, credit to the BBC, they realized pretty quickly it couldn't stay like that and quietly moved the show back to a decent studio in the grounds and a format more like the old one: a highlights show, with a lot of tennis, for people who've come back from work and just want to see the best parts of the matches they've missed plus some expert analysis, not some dumb-ass clips of babies playing tennis that had nothing to do with the tournament.

The good news for John Inverdale was that he was sent to the commentary booth instead, and he turned out to be a natural. In fact, he was so good that he called the women's final. That's amazing for his first year. I did that match as well—along with Lindsay Davenport, and as it happens I think the three of us did fine. For John, I guess it was the icing on the cake. He was even gloating a little, because he knew people were missing him as the face of the evening round-up show, plus he'd shown he could do the commentating really well.

It's more or less normal now both for the BBC and for American networks to have men and women calling each other's matches. I'd gotten myself in trouble in the past by saying that there were certain things about men's tennis that only a man could know and the same for women. Partly because if you've been in that locker room, you potentially have that insight into the players' mindset and what goes on behind the scenes that an outsider wouldn't have. But I now realize that it's more important to be a good commentator. If you're terrible, you'll still be terrible, whatever match you're calling.

The 2015 tournament started a week later than usual—at last the powers that be had decided to listen to players' pleas for an extra week to recover between the French Open and Wimbledon—so it was the first time in all the years we'd been together that Patty's birthday didn't fall during Wimbledon itself, so I could finally do something a bit different on her birthday, rather than just having a drink in the hotel bar.

A couple of days beforehand, I had an exhibition match to play against Yannick Noah at the British Embassy in Paris, but right after that I flew down to the South of France to meet Patty and Ava on a friend's yacht for a few days as it sailed around the Mediterranean, and we went to Portofino on the actual day. I was a bit nervous about it, to be honest; for a guy who gets seasick, spending his first night on a yacht was always going to be a challenge. Poor me. Luckily I managed to keep my dinner down, and I was hoping that would make up for a few of the terrible birthdays Patty's had to put up with, but I nearly spoiled it all because beforehand she'd told me, "Under no circumstances give me my presents in front of everyone." So what did I do? Exactly that. I guess I've still got a bit to learn.

Patty and I have always had an intense relationship but we talk a lot, and we're definitely best friends—I used to think that would be the end of our romance but she said we could have both, and that is the way it turned out. When we met, I think she had lost the belief that true love can last, but I hope I proved her wrong. And being totally loyal and faithful to each other is everything to us. She often says that I wore her down with my love for her, but I think she accepts now that, as much as I need her in my life, she needs me too.

Patty has always been incredibly supportive of whatever I've wanted to do—even music. Well, she told me that I should stick to tennis, but she's kind enough to put up with my incessant guitar playing in the house. So now that she has more freedom, with the children needing less of her time, I'm pushing her to do more of the songwriting, recording and performing that she loves and excels at. Not long after we first got together, she had an Academy Award nomination for a song she'd co-written. In the end, it was Elton John who won that year, so when he came on my talk show a few years later I reminded him that he was responsible for my wife *not* getting an Oscar.

Patty has written tons of good songs over the years, and whereas I can't move like I used to when I was twenty-five, she can still hit the notes. She proved that when she went out on tour in the summer of 2014, and a year later released her first album since we'd been together, which happened to be a Christmas album. She donated the proceeds to an armed forces mental health charity, because her dad was in the army, so she knows how much psychological support veterans often need and how much work still has to be done out there to destigmatize these problems. The good news is that there's a whole lot more stuff she wants to be doing now that she has some time to do her own thing again. The bad news is: however hard I practice, I know I'll never be part of her band.

My kids—along with Patty—are the best thing that's ever happened to me outside tennis, no question, but I admit that I'm really looking forward to being an empty-nester, whereas Patty's got mixed feelings about it. On the one hand, she likes the idea of us being able to go on vacation on our own together, but on the other, she thinks it's going to be a tough adjustment. Plus, as she's always reminding me, she's gonna have to put up with me the whole time.

Of course she will get the occasional day of respite, for instance when I'm off playing golf with Roger Waters. Golf is a game a lot of tennis players tend to get into later in life. It's a good way to catch up with someone you don't see a lot. You have three or four hours to talk, and that's part of what I like about it—you can't do that with tennis, because you're on opposite sides of the net, running around.

There have been long periods when I haven't played at all. For example, when I initially had kids, it seemed like that wasn't cool, to go off and play golf—"Hey, honey, I'll be back in six hours, take care of the kids." But over time I realized that's actually why some people do it—to get away from their wives and kids. And by the way, sometimes the wives and kids are happy with that arrangement too.

It's not like that now, obviously. I'd never want Patty to be a golf widow, and she wouldn't stand for it even if I did. But you don't have to be around each other 24/7, and it's not a bad thing to play a little golf. I'm not usually a gambler, but as a general rule I'll play golf for money—even if it's only five bucks a hole. For some reason, I've never played for money with Roger Waters. Maybe he'd have strong views on that, the same way he does about everything else.

I'd always been really into Pink Floyd—I'd seen them doing *The Wall* the original time at Earls Court in 1981, when I was over for Wimbledon, which was great. I was only in my early twenties the first time I met Roger, so I was still pretty angry at the time, but I remember thinking, "Man, this guy's *really* angry—I'm nothing compared to him."

We didn't see too much of each other for a while, until he married a girl from the Hamptons, about fifteen years ago—he's divorced her now, but when they first got together he bought a place out there literally half a mile from ours. So I think there was a sense of, "We should get together," and we started to meet up for dinner here and there. I'm not going to pretend it was a lot, but we got along well.

The first time we ever played golf together was at this charity event Mats Wilander used to put on. He got Roger to play, and we auctioned off eighteen holes with Roger and me. Yeah, I know . . . the second prize was thirty-six holes.

Since then we've played together a number of times, and I really enjoy it. Of course, I'm so bad at golf that I start to get pissed—and I have a feeling that if I got better at it, I'd get even worse. Because when you finish a round, it's not like you're sweaty and you feel like you did something. OK, maybe you've been for a walk, but most of the time we don't even do that—we take the cart. At least when you play tennis, even if you lose you've had a workout. But I still find golf quite addictive. You hit two or three bad shots and you're starting to get in a terrible mood and you want to quit the game, then you get one lucky bounce and you're like, "Oh yeah! I'm back!"

Roger loves to talk shit about his old bandmate David Gilmour, who played in New York recently. At first I was going to attend that concert, but then out of loyalty to Roger, I decided not to. I don't know why, because Roger didn't ask me not to go, and Gilmour's an incredible singer and guitarist. So I definitely missed out on that one. Yeah, he played some new material, but it's worth sitting through that for "Wish You Were Here" and "Shine On You Crazy Diamond," among other classics.

At least when Roger does *The Wall*, he's just playing *The Wall*, and he can get other people to sing and play David Gilmour's parts (which are about 85 percent of it!).

Last time I saw Roger do that show it was great—the guy who played the "Comfortably Numb" guitar solo duplicated it pretty much note for note, close enough to the point where you'd think, "Yeah, I can hear that over and over—if I closed my eyes I could be back at Earls Court."

It is funny when Roger and I play golf together, but he has mellowed a bit over the years and now he even laughs occasionally. I'll tell him, "Look, Roger, life's not that bad. I mean, just try to look on the bright side." Obviously it's ironic, for me to be the one telling him that, but it's nice to have found someone I can play that role for.

Life's not going to be all smooth sailing when you've got six kids—any time you think you're in the clear, you're never more than one phone call away from a crisis. On top of that, times were tough for my dad in health terms over the past few years, but he never lost the power to surprise. Like the time when, at the start of Donald Trump's campaign to get the Republican nomination for the 2016 presidential election, my dad sent him a letter of support asking if there was anything he could do to help.

Of course at that point, no one thought Trump had a chance of winning. But whatever you think about Donald Trump's politics, you can't deny he's a very good salesman and he can come across well in person. I've known Donald a little over the years, and at least he didn't bear a grudge (good salesmen never do) when I turned down his offer—in Trumpian terms, an "unbe-lievable" offer—of a million dollars to play one of the Williams sisters.

Trump has had a box right next to the broadcasters' booth at the US Open ever since the Arthur Ashe Stadium opened. Even before he became President, you didn't see him there as much as he used to be—it's a sign of tennis losing popularity that Donald's not around to get his mug on TV. But at the 2015 tournament he was very much in attendance and Mike Tirico, one of the best play-by-play guys on ESPN before he moved to NBC, said, "You know Trump, right? Let's go over and say hello," because he wanted to meet him.

Patty and Ava were with me, and they were telling me, "Don't you dare go over there. He's a misogynist and a blowhard, among other things—it could hurt your reputation." But I said, "Hey, come on, it's no big deal." So I took Mike over, and sure enough ESPN showed it on TV—me hugging Donald like we were long-lost brothers or something. Trump did seem more pleased to see me than he usually would be, and I only realized why when he started saying, "John, thank you so much for the letter you wrote. I've already got it up on the wall in my office!" I hoped this was fake news, because I didn't want everyone who went into Donald Trump's office during the election thinking I was his number one fan. Thanks, Dad. I owe you one. Now that Donald has been elected President of the United States, there might be an ambassadorship in this for me.

24

"The art world is like tennis on steroids"

John McEnroe

Maybe the most exciting art purchase I ever made was over twenty years ago, when I bought the Lucian Freud that is still on the wall at the foot of our stairs. Apart from how beautiful the painting itself is, and the fact that I'd been eager to get a Freud for a long time, what made this acquisition particularly satisfying was snatching this artistic masterpiece out from under the noses of the British. That was money well spent. OK, it was a *lot* of money, but sometimes a man's gotta do what a man's gotta do.

My old friend Bill Acquavella, one of the greatest art dealers ever and one of the few guys I trust in the art world to this day, had originally promised the painting to a London museum—I'm not sure which one—but the deal was they had to raise half of the cost in public donations. I was sitting with him in his office one day and he asked me, "Do you want this piece?" I said, "Hell, yeah." So he said, "If the museum can't get the funds together in six months, then you can buy it." I don't know if it was a bad time for the UK economy in 1996, but either way, thanks very much, England. You had your chance and you blew it.

One of the things I did at my gallery that I was proudest of was the first show I ever put on, which was *War Murals* by a guy named Bruno Fonseca, who I thought was a really good artist but who sadly got AIDS and ended up passing away at thirty-five. He was in pretty bad shape by the time we put it on, but his parents wanted to do something for him, and I was glad that I was able to bring a bit of light to a dark time for them, as well as showing some great work which had never previously been seen. That show packed a real emotional punch.

I've always loved work that inspires a strong response, and some of the work I've collected over the years by outsider artists certainly fits that bill. Outsider artists are the guys who exist outside of the gallery system and even society itself. A lot of them seem to be in and out of insane asylums, and the ones who aren't are often out on the streets making art from any materials they can get their hands on.

James Castle is a good example. He was a deaf guy from Idaho, who used soot, saliva, pieces of old chewing-gum wrapper—literally anything he could find—to create these amazing artworks. Martín Ramírez would be probably another of the top five names in outsider art at the moment. He was a Mexican schizophrenic who had a fixation with trains, and his paintings are simple—childlike, would be one description—but so real they're awesome.

The African-American artist Bill Traylor is—in my opinion—another of the real greats. The first piece of outsider art we bought was one of his, because Patty liked him—it was her idea. Bill Traylor was born a slave, and didn't start doing the work he's known for until he was in his eighties, when he took up a pencil and a scrap of cardboard and spent the last three or four years of his life doing these amazing drawings on the streets of Montgomery, Alabama. I often wonder what he could've achieved if he'd been given the chance earlier in life.

If you looked at the critical hierarchy of outsider art in tennis terms, Henry Darger would be Andy Murray to Traylor's Djokovic at the moment—they're definitely the two at the top of their game. I've got two Henry Dargers. To me, that is unbelievable art. The guy wrote a 15,000-page book about a kind of *War of the Worlds* situation where these six little girls were like the superheroes, and then he did about three hundred illustrations. One of my favorite things about them is that they're double-sided, so you get two artworks for the wall-space of one. Some of them are pretty hard-core, but the one that's hanging on the wall over our bed isn't as pervy as some of the others.

If you were going to try and analyze why I'm drawn to these guys and their work, you might think it's because I identify with their outsider status, but I don't think it is that. First and foremost, Patty liked them. Plus, I suppose some of the bad experiences I've had in the art world have led me to see that these guys have been short-changed and deserve a bit more respect. They're actually way better artists than a lot of the household names who maybe do a better job of promoting themselves. At least you can be sure it's more about the art than it is about the business with them, which is what matters most to me.

Their work doesn't tend to be the kind of investment you'd get a huge return on. Darger's stuff has gotten more respect from the art world over the years—a piece sold for a record price in France recently, which would lead you to believe that his art, and outsider art in general, has broken out beyond the US and it's going to become a multimillion-dollar enterprise. In general, I believe the prices will creep up over time and you'll do OK if you buy wisely, but that's not all it's about.

One of the most interesting pieces of contemporary art that

I own is by an artist named Fred Tomaselli. His unique way of constructing a portrait is by asking you to fill out a six-page questionnaire detailing all the drugs you've ever taken in your life. Talk about getting up close and personal! He then takes that information and uses it as the basis for a kind of solar system where the planets represent all the different substances you have ingested—medicines, painkillers, cortisone, sleeping tablets, tea and coffee, alcohol, everything—with size varying proportionately according to consumption. It's a real conversation piece.

There's nothing that would really surprise anyone on mine, although maybe caffeine should be less of a moon and more of a sun these days. But I'd be willing to bet there are a few professional tennis players whose chemical profiles would be eye-openers. When I say—as I have been known to—"the art world is like tennis on steroids," that doesn't mean I think performance-enhancing drugs are unknown in my sport. Far from it.

Let me be clear, I still think tennis is one of the cleanest topline sports, and I hope to God no one playing it is on any type of illegal drug. I'd never heard of Meldonium which was what Sharapova failed a drug test for. That was kind of legal on one level but at the same time not. It's a medication which she'd been taking for ten years. Even though it's not FDA approved, the Russians clearly thought it helped them, as 250 of their athletes were using it, and it was only made illegal in tennis at the start of last year.

Maria didn't do herself any favors by having two different excuses. On the one hand her people were saying they weren't sure how long it takes to leave your system, and it could still show up for sixty days, which would only matter if she'd stopped by the end of December. But then on the other she was saying, "I take full responsibility, I didn't know it was on the list," which would mean she had taken it after January 1, right? Either one of those explanations could sound plausible—well, not to me, but maybe to someone—but they didn't work together. I think that's why she ended up with a fifteen-month ban.

With some of these super strait-laced tennis players who never seem to do anything to wind down in terms of a beer or even a glass of wine every now and again, I can't help feeling they must be doing something else. Because the highs of playing are so high, you feel like Superman. There's got to be something to soften your landing when you come back down to earth. That's the only way I think you can survive, emotionally—if you can occasionally tell yourself, "Oh thank God! I'll have a beer." Or whatever else your thing is, right? Chocolate, fried chicken—something.

Maybe I think that because I wasn't the kind of person who could give up everything. I mean, obviously that's my fault, and I believe it cost me in terms of my career, but for me to have completely given up alcohol and a little marijuana when I was playing would've been like, "Whoa, man, this is rough." Even though I wasn't as disciplined as I could or even should have been, I was still way more disciplined than a lot of people— than most human beings, even. I tried to find a balance between sometimes burning both ends of the candle, but also getting the best out of my body on the court. What I was looking for was a middle ground between someone like Vitas, who really liked to party, and a fitness machine like Lendl. But when you look at things on an elite sports level and you see how these guys live now . . . jeez, they sacrifice a lot, even if the financial rewards *are* greater than ever.

Nowadays when I'm in the UK, for example, I love to drink Carlsberg Special Brew. It may be my favorite beer, even though it's very strong and has a bit of a stigma attached because apparently a lot of street-drinkers used to favor it. I managed to shock Chrissie Hynde once—which takes some doing—by stopping the car at a liquor store on my way into London from the airport to stock up on Special Brew. I should add that I wasn't doing this at the height of my playing career—it's a more recent thing, over the past twenty years.

There are so many gray areas between the dependencies that are tolerated and even encouraged and the ones that aren't. For instance, for me, competing, performing and getting applause for what I do will probably always be the ultimate drug. I know very few pro athletes are lucky enough to be able to continue enjoying that for as long as I have, and leaving behind that disciplined structure of professional sports can cause problems—problems to do with finding substitute highs and replacement ways to feel good about themselves that can lead to all sorts of bad decisions that have terrible outcomes.

As I've gotten older, I hope I've done a pretty good job at weaning myself off the applause drug because I'm mature enough to realize and accept that one day the supply will stop. But in the early days after I left the tour in the early nineties I did try to fill the space by smoking more marijuana than I care to admit. "Hey, I'm not a professional athlete anymore. I'm not trying to win Wimbledon now, and I'm going through a painful divorce. Why shouldn't I have a smoke if I want to?"

Obviously that wasn't the smartest move I've ever made—for reasons I'm about to explain—but the funny thing was, if you look at the art I was buying over that period of a couple of years, I was totally acing it, man! Maybe that was just a coincidence that I'm sort of talking my way into, but I do feel there was a connection. Either way, Patty used to say, "How about taking some time off the weed every now and again?" But I wasn't having it.

The thing that finally got me to stop was having to take tests for the court, because in the custody battle over my kids which was going on at that point, my ex-wife Tatum was accusing me of being a drug addict. In addition to that, my kids—who were in their early teens at the time—had started stealing grass off me. I probably wouldn't have noticed if Patty hadn't brought it to my attention.

When I found out, I was understandably angry, but the aggressive way I acted toward my older kids over this reminded me of a football player who had bullied me when I was in college, and that made me feel bad. It probably didn't help them in the long run either. Obviously this was not the right way to handle things, and at that point I knew it was time to call it a day on being stoned. As it happened, stopping turned out to be a lot easier than I expected. I'd thought it would be tough, but basically I gave up and that was it.

Flash forward to a couple of summers ago, and Kevin got arrested for what was thought to be possession of cocaine and prescription meds. I was with him the night he was arrested. We'd just had a dinner to celebrate the fact that he had gotten a publisher for his novel, loosely based on the turbulent life of his grandma on his mother's side. It was a proud night, but a strange one, because on the one hand Kevin was literally saying, "This is the happiest day of my life," and yet his mood seemed really erratic. Patty had been concerned for almost a year that something wasn't right, but we couldn't put our finger on what it was, and obviously I hadn't looked into it carefully enough.

Next thing we knew, Kevin was on the front page of the *New York Post*. I'd gone to LA for a vacation and to visit the studio of this amazing artist named Mark Bradford, and I was at the baggage claim when I got a text from Patty saying, "Call me immediately." That sounded serious, and it was. Apparently Kevin had been arrested. I was flabbergasted. He'd allegedly tried to buy cocaine, but it turned out it was all baking soda—zero percent cocaine. That was good news, in terms of the law, although it didn't look great in the newspaper.

At a time like that, any parent will ask themselves what they've done wrong. If you went to Patty or the kids, they would probably tell you that I was too tough on them, whereas my instincts tell me that I went too easy, at least compared with the strict parental controls I grew up with. I guess that's the problem in a nutshell—the gap between my own desire to be an authority figure and the fact that I was someone who was always seen as bucking the system.

For all my "bad boy of tennis" reputation, I was actually a very respectable kid when I first came into the game—my dad had scared me straight as far as drugs were concerned. But not all my sons' familial role models took such a strict line, and I'm not just talking about my own recreational marijuana use. I don't want to go into details about my ex-wife's side of the family, but let's just say if you were looking for a stabilizing influence as a grandparent, you probably wouldn't choose Ryan O'Neal.

Kevin was always such a good person that it's been painful to watch him struggling, but I'm proud of how hard he's worked to get his life back on track over the last couple of years, and I was proud of the book he wrote, too. At the time of this writing, things are tougher with my other son, Sean. When his mom was going through troubled times, Sean was the one who gravitated most to her—who tried to be there for her—but maybe a certain amount of damage was done in that process too, and his relationships with the rest of his family have been quite turbulent as a consequence.

The day back in early 2007 when he nearly drowned after going paddle-boarding in rough seas at our house in Malibu has stayed etched in my mind throughout some of the tough times we've had lately. There were so many "ifs" left hanging in the air that day—if the coastguard hadn't come out so quickly when the other two emergency services refused to help us, if one of our neighbors hadn't gone upstairs at the precise moment they needed to be there to see Sean was in trouble—and the consequences of events unfolding even slightly differently would've been too horrible to think about. That was a frightening day with a good ending which I hoped might mark a turning point in my son's life. Unfortunately, these things don't always work out the way you want, even though you try your best as a parent and always hope for the best for your children.

The real challenge is to keep the things that are most important to you in your mind throughout the normal stresses and strains of everyday family life, instead of only remembering them in times of crisis. The phrase "unconditional love" is easily written down, but it's not an easy idea to put into practice. I always saw myself as sympathetic, because I knew I would always try to be there for my children. But in terms of my own shortcomings as a parent, I can see where I could have done better when it came to understanding how my kids—especially my sons—were trying to live up to something and feeling pressure to get over the bar I'd set.

One of the things you have to be able to do as a professional athlete is shut out everything that might stand in the way of achieving your goals. The downside of having this ability is that it makes it harder for you to see situations from other people's point of view. I can remember how much motivation I seemed to lose in 1984, when I first signed the deeds on the beautiful top-floor Central Park West apartment that Patty and I and (for the moment) Ava are still lucky enough to live in. And I can't be sure how much less driven a person I would have been if I'd lived in a place like that all my life.

The problem is identifying the point at which continually making allowances for someone who is behaving destructively stops being an act of kindness and starts holding them back from taking responsibility for themselves. I wish you could buy a parenting manual that showed you where that line was.

25

"Maybe you could beat Serena and maybe you couldn't, I'm not sure"

Milos Raonic

Part of putting the whole Larry Salander debacle behind me once the second appeal was finally kicked out in 2015 was realizing that the tennis world was the one I belonged to most of all, and therefore the one I wanted to devote the vast majority of my time to. At the start of the new year—even three months into 2016—there was nothing specific on the horizon in terms of affirming that commitment. The revelation that within a few months I would be on the coaching team of a player in Queen's and Wimbledon men's singles finals would certainly have come as a surprise to me.

My first forays into coaching—brief and somewhat fruitless entanglements with Sergi Bruguera and Boris Becker (who I'm still friendly with, so at least we didn't fall out over it) in the early 1990s—had been such a pain in the ass it took me a decade to get over them. The feeling may have been mutual, because no one called me for the next ten years. And the fact that I didn't get paid a cent either time was the icing on the cake. My unofficial 2004 attempt to help out the 6'4" Aussie (and two-time

Grand Slam finalist) Mark Philippoussis—whose serve had earned him the nickname "Scud"—didn't end much better.

Mark had handwritten me an extremely heartfelt letter asking for my help, in the knowledge that at twenty-eight this was probably going to be his last chance to get it right. I was so touched by this that, despite being tied up with the talk show at the time, I decided I would give it a try. Unfortunately, once we got together, things didn't go so well. The problem was, everything I said, Mark seemed to do the opposite. I got him to come to New York so I could take a look at his game, but I ended up working harder on court and in the gym than he did, which was a bad sign. Especially as he'd put on about fifteen pounds and needed to get back in shape fast. Mark was apparently going out with an actress and was regularly in the gossip columns because he's a good-looking guy. I suggested that he might like to fly under the radar a bit, avoid the press for a while. The next thing I know, he's supposedly had a fling with Paris Hilton. Paris Hilton, the most notorious party girl of that time!

"Mark, if you're gonna do this, you'd better have slept with her!" I half-joked. "Because this is absolutely the last thing you wanna be doing right now." "No, no, I didn't!" he assured me. "Listen," he went on, in what he thought was a lightbulb moment, "I'm gonna call this Australian radio station and I'm going to explain to them that we're just friends." "No! Whatever you do, do *not* do that, because it'll only keep the story going."

Of course that's exactly what he did. "Oh my God," I thought, "this guy is unbelievable." I mean, he was the one who'd come to me for advice, yet now I felt like begging him, "Could you just listen to *something* I say, because, I promise you some of it really does make sense?" I liked Mark a lot—I still do—but the experience of coaching him fell into the category of "If it hadn't been so sad it would've been funny."

With this disastrous track record to call on, a move into coaching on my part did not look like the obvious next step. But right from the start with Milos Raonic it felt like something that could possibly work. He's a very smart kid—Canadian now but from Montenegro originally. His family had gone through a lot to help get him in a position where he was one of the best players, and he'd decided he wanted to further invest in his career to see how much higher he could go. One of the things I admired about him was that he was doing everything in his power to become the best tennis player he could be. Why else would he hire me?

When Milos's people first approached me a few weeks before the French Open to ask if I could work with him over the grass-court season, the timing was perfect for me. From the moment ex-Grand Slam champions started to do the coaching thing part-time on a more advisory basis, I knew that it was something I could do, and at this point I was primed for a new challenge. To me, Milos was clearly one of the five or six players with the potential to win at Wimbledon that year—I wouldn't have taken the job on otherwise—and he also had a clear idea of what he wanted from me, which was to help him express himself a bit more in the course of a match, and translate his undoubted physical power (he's 6'5" and has one of the deadliest serves in the game) into a more commanding presence on the court.

Milos thinks about the game a lot, and has a completely different temperament to me. In a way, that's why we're a good fit: we're like the Odd Couple—I'm Walter Matthau, he's Jack Lemmon. If I was going to be coaching someone people would think I'd have more in common with, Nick Kyrgios would be the obvious choice, but I'm not sure if two nutcases together would work so well.

The whole Wimbledon 2016 jigsaw came together in a very entertaining way, as if an unseen hand was putting the pieces down for maximum dramatic impact (but with a happier ending than when this happened with the Bryan brothers). First there was the fact that, shortly after I was taken on, Andy Murray brought Ivan Lendl back as his coach. Given that he'd won two majors with him, and none without, that seemed like a logical move. Next was the fact that my first tournament on Milos's team (alongside his full-time coach Riccardo Piatti—his other coach, the former French Open champion Carlos Moya, was to join us the following week) was at Queen's, the traditional pre-Wimbledon warm-up competition.

Now I've had some great times at Queen's—winning a record-equaling four times, which qualified me to be part of a special trophy presentation for four-time winners, shortly before Andy Murray invalidated the whole ceremony by winning his fifth—but also some not so good ones. During Wimbledon, we used to go there to practice, and one time in the late eighties I had a court booked there at ten thirty or eleven in the morning for a practice session before a two o'clock third- or fourth-round match. But I got there ten minutes late, and by the time I arrived this lady had taken my slot—or at least, she was still on my court.

Obviously, I was hyped because I had a big game coming up and I needed to practice, but even after I'd explained the situation to her quite politely, she wouldn't budge, to the point where eventually I was forced to tell her, "Get the fuck off my court." As luck would have it, she turned out to be the wife of the club's president, and my membership was rescinded—not that I was too happy to hang around there after this had happened. I remained in the wilderness as far as the Queen's Club was concerned until that president finally keeled over from old age, probably ten years ago, and a new guy came along and brought me back into the fold.

So here I was, back at Queen's as an *éminence grise* (very *grise* in my case) and it was sort of nice to be there. The whole thing was working out well, with Milos 3–0 and a set up against Andy Murray in the final. It would have been perfect if it was 7–6, 6–3—oh, my God, why didn't it end like that? The simple reason was that the champion took things up a notch.

Milos had beaten several tough players to get there, though, and he did some really good things in his first grass-court final. One of the best was the runners-up speech he made afterward, where he wished Andy Murray "Happy Father's Day"—which was cute and went down well with the home crowd—and then added, "Hopefully, I'll be seeing you in a few weeks for a re-match." At the time, even I was thinking, "Hmmm, maybe not *that* likely, given that Djokovic is playing at this incredible, insane level," but as it turned out, that was exactly what happened, which only goes to show that the guys who have the confidence to impose their own story-line on events are often the ones things work out for.

The sideshow of Ivan and me renewing our rivalry got a lot of attention from the media—to the point where Andy Murray got a little riled about it, at one point telling Sue Barker, "It's about me playing Milos, not about Ivan playing John"—come on, Andy, give the old guys a break! The funny part of it, which no one knew at the time, was that right before the match I was in the bathroom with Ivan, and he said to me, "Shall we have a bet about who needs to go to the bathroom first to take a piss?"

That's why Andy ended up making another slightly irritable comment when his coach wasn't there for his winner's speech—because I'd broken Ivan's spirit and he'd had to go and take a leak. I wouldn't have minded a bathroom break myself by that stage, but I wasn't going to let him beat me. Ivan's player might have won the battle out on the court, but my bladder had won the war that really counted. I just wish we'd bet $20 on it.

Raonic's great achievement at Wimbledon was beating Federer in the semi-final. He found another gear in that match, and it was very satisfying to think that I'd managed to make the 2 or 3 percent difference that I'd hoped for. We knew facing Murray with a home crowd behind him in the final was going to be tough. The one thing I was telling him beforehand—and Carlos was saying the same thing—was: "The only way you're going to win this is if you can match his emotional intensity. You got it?" And Milos was like, "I got it."

I think what he was looking to pick up from me was some of my understanding of how to be aggressive, and my awareness of the geometry of a court, so that he could use his weapons to their best advantage. Milos's best asset is his serve and the fact that he's a big, imposing guy. So I'd be telling him: "Look, your opponent doesn't want to see you coming into the net—he wants you further back." Now Milos is actually pretty good at the baseline, but it's not the same thing. If you see huge animals—elephants or giraffes—far away, you'll be saying, "Wow, that's impressive." But it's only when they get closer that you'll really think, "Whoa!" For Milos to beat Murray or Djokovic—which I'm convinced he can do—he needs to impose his size and physicality on them.

Unfortunately, in this particular Wimbledon final, he didn't quite manage to do it. Milos did some good things, and he certainly didn't freeze, but he also didn't bring it in the way he had against Federer—which was disappointing to me, and no doubt to him too. It's a difficult balance to get right as a coach before the game. You don't want to freak someone out by saying, "This could be your only chance to win a Slam." But as I watched the match unfold, I felt Milos's body language was saying, "It's OK to lose, this is only my first final and I'll be back next year."

I was up there in the commentary booth thinking, "Why didn't I tell him he may never be here again?" because maybe that would have given him more of a sense of urgency. At one stage, when Milos almost seemed to be flat-lining, I texted Carlos from the box to say, "You've got to wake this guy up!" Carlos could see what was happening as clearly as I could, but there was nothing we could do about it by then. (And let's give credit where credit's due: Andy was playing at his very best.) It was tempting to open the commentary booth window and start screaming "You cannot be serious!" at him, but I resisted. This wasn't about me, it was about Milos.

Overall, Milos gave a great account of himself in the tournament as a whole, to the point where I had guys like John Newcombe—who must be in his seventies now—coming up to me and saying, "Raonic is going to win this one year," which I hope he will. John and I never really saw eye to eye about anything, because he thought I was a total ass and I thought he was too smooth for his own good. So it was funny to have this guy who rarely speaks to me because he didn't like the way I behaved come up and tell me, "Milos is a fine young man . . ." He didn't have to say the words " . . . not like you" at the end of that sentence for me to hear what he meant.

I did get a bit of a hard time for combining the roles of commentator and coach at that tournament, but I'd signed the broadcasting contracts before Milos took me on, so he knew I was going to have to be in the booth for some of his games, and he was fine with that. Personally, I didn't feel there was a conflict of interest, because when you're working with someone, you're trying to give him an edge, but as a commentator, I'm trying to explain the game and help people understand what these guys are thinking, so having that extra involvement actually helps. Even if the critics were right and there was a conflict of interest, so what! At least that would be a talking point, which is exactly what I think tennis needs more of at the moment.

Those seven weeks I spent in Europe—from before Paris to after Wimbledon—were the longest I'd been away from home since my Grand Slam debut in 1977. This time around wasn't quite so earth-shattering, but I really enjoyed it.

Apart from anything else, it was good to be able to make use of Milos's support staff. When I played on the tour I had an entourage of one—me, myself and I. So I enjoyed getting a little free care from the four other people Milos had in his team—"Look, will you check me out so I can be ready for the practice, because I don't want to fall apart just when Milos needs me most."

The only aspect I could've done without were the inevitable conversations about whether I could beat Serena. As you know, my own family has no faith in me, but even when I was with Milos, he was analyzing what we'd both bring to the match and saying, "Maybe you could beat Serena and maybe you couldn't, I'm not sure." Then Carlos Moya was saying he didn't think I could—he didn't say it to me, but apparently that's what he said to Milos. So since we're nearly at the end of the book, why don't I round things off by saying what everyone seems to want to hear? "OK, I don't know if I could beat Serena."

Are you happy now?

AFTERWORD

The excitement of helping Milos go almost all the way at Wimbledon in 2016 brought my story full circle. It had been reaching the semi-finals of that tournament thirty-nine years before that changed my life forever. That was where the media, God bless them (and OK, I did give them a little help), built up an image of me which still shadows me every step I take to this day. The Brat became Superbrat, and wherever I went, expectations followed of what I might do or who I might be. I polarized opinion: people loved me or hated me. I'd say the establishment was freaked out by me, where the average sports fan liked what I did and what I stood for, but there were definitely exceptions on both sides.

A lot of people say they used to love me yelling at the chair umpire. It was almost as if I was doing it on their behalf: shouting at authority, fighting back, even representing the subconscious desire we all have to push against those people who make the rules, especially when those rules suck and are totally meaningless. But the level of petulance that might be indulged in a teenage athlete would not be such a good look on a fifty-eight-year-old man, so the big challenge for me in the years since I left the main tour has been managing to reinvent myself without—as they say in England—"throwing the baby out with the bathwater."

Commentating definitely helped me in terms of public perceptions. Suddenly I was able to show a side of myself where I wasn't so serious, I wasn't screaming and, Holy Moses, it turned out I was quite a self-deprecating guy with a sense of humor. When the BBC came calling—and who would ever have thought I'd be hired by them?—even the Brits started seeing that I was reasonably articulate and that I could make the sport more fun and accessible. By then, I'd gone through some very public personal problems, and I think people could relate to the fact that I'd had some hard times. That helped them to see me more as a real person, not that curly-haired loudmouth cartoon character with the red headband.

Don't laugh, but one area where I've definitely changed is on the anger front. Although I wouldn't yet describe myself as a Zen master (are you crazy?!), the whole "angry man" image is one I've come to accept because it pays the bills. Cops, security guards, passport officers—anyone with a bit of authority, in other words—as well as the general public, they all go, before I've even said a word to them, "You're not going to yell at me, are you?" Most people say it in a positive, funny way, but sometimes I think, "Oh my God, is this ever going to stop? Am I going to be a caricature of myself for life?"

I'm afraid I know the answer to that. If a whole day passed when someone didn't say "You cannot be serious!" to me, that would be amazing. Half an hour going by without it sometimes seems unlikely. My feelings about that are a strange juxtaposition of embarrassment and pride: on the one hand, that this is what I represent to people; on the other, at least I represent something. Ultimately, pride wins out.

Funnily enough, the only time now when I play along some-what and fake the anger thing is on court. When I was on the tour, every single complaint was totally authentic—or at least that's what I told myself. Not one part of me was acting up for the crowd; unlike Nastase, for example, who I think sometimes did pull some stuff as part of "the Nasty show," and his perfor-mances suffered as a result. Nowadays, when I question line calls when I'm playing seniors tennis, it can be a bit of a show because, while people are curious as to whether I can still play, they're definitely more excited by the prospect of me getting mad at the umpire.

I'm very aware of how lucky I've been in life. As a player, I came along on the crest of a huge wave in tennis, one with enough power to allow some of us oldies to continue riding it long after we ever thought we would. Then I started commen-tating at exactly the time when the TV networks were looking for a less formal style, and I fit that bill perfectly, so that was another lucky break. Consequently, I count my blessings very regularly, believe me. I used to be a glass-half-empty person when I was younger, partly because I always felt I could play better and win more (with my mom's words to my dad ringing in my ears, "If you'd worked harder . . ."). Now, I'm definitely in the glass-half-full camp. And I'm trying to get it to inch its way up to being a little fuller all the time.

One of the benefits of getting older (and I'm as surprised that there are some benefits as anyone else would be) is that you actually have to face down a lot of the things you thought were demons when you were younger, and then you find out that they're not so terrifying after all. It's not so much turning lemons into lemonade as realizing that maybe they weren't even lemons in the first place, or that they were but you learned to appreciate the bitter taste. Either way, although commentating on a Grand Slam final can't match the excitement of playing in one, it can still be fun. And helping to coach Milos Raonic has given me a new way to reconcile the individualism of tennis with working alongside other people, which was something I always loved about team sports. It turns out that being a small part of a bigger thing can be almost as satisfying—but perhaps even more enjoyable—than being out there on your own. Definitely so at this stage!

It's funny that after all these years of chasing other possible identities—as an art dealer, a rock guitarist, a TV talk-show host, even a politician—here I am, back where I started, finding new ways to compete with Ivan Lendl! "John McEnroe, Mr. Tennis." But if that's my destiny, then I'm happy with it.

Around Halloween of 2016, my father became very ill and had to go into the hospital in New York. He never came out. Over the next three months or so, I managed to fulfill my commitments while struggling to come to grips with what was seemingly inevitably going to happen. I played my seniors matches, flew to Korea, went to the Australian Open in January, but whatever I did it felt like my heart wasn't fully in it. Yet at that first Grand Slam tournament of 2017, I was privileged to experience another demonstration of the power great sport can have to elevate you out of your circumstances.

Whatever the odds were at the start of the Australian Open on the first Serena versus Venus final in more than a decade, and Roger Federer playing his first tournament of any kind since Milos had beaten him at Wimbledon, and actually beating Rafa in the final, I guarantee you that no one was taking them. Serena beating Steffi Graf's record to become the all-time biggest Grand Slam winner in the women's game and Roger achieving something so spectacular that I don't think even he would've predicted it was a truly historic combination in the open tennis era.

The excitement of watching these events unfold brought me—albeit temporarily—out of the sadness of my dad's illness and back into the excitement of the moment. As I walked the hallways of the Rod Laver Arena, I found myself hugging Rod himself on a number of occasions, in fact, almost every time I bumped into him. I even hugged Ken Rosewall, who I used to dislike because he was my hero Laver's great rival. Why? I guess just because I could, and maybe because I needed to, given the state of my father's health. Flashing back to 1976, I remember getting whipped 6–4, 6–3, 6–2 by Rosewall in a practice match at Madison Square Garden. I was only seventeen at the time, and I recall being amazed to realize afterward that Ken was then six months older than my father (he'd won the Australian Open when he was two years older than Federer is now!) and yet still able to play at this incredible level.

Flying back to New York after Federer's amazing victory, I felt like I'd been in suspended animation. However small our phones and other electronic devices can make the world feel at times, I was very conscious of having been on the other side of the planet. And the sad reality of my dad's deteriorating health situation brought me crashing back to earth.

On my fifty-eighth birthday, I went to see him in the hospital with my son Kevin. We asked if he'd watched any of the Australian Open, and my dad just looked back at us blankly. Knowing how much he loved tennis, that was the point when I knew it was nearly over for him. It was tough to take, but my dad's answer to Kevin's follow-up question brought us smiles through the tears.

Kevin asked, "Did you see me and Dad at the New York Knicks game on the TV?" My dad's reply was barely audible, so we both leaned in closer to hear it. "Not 'me and Dad,'" he corrected, "'my father and I.'"

Well, that's Dad. He was never going to change—still correcting our grammar until the very end. And sadly, that was pretty much the last thing we'd hear him say. Two days later, he was gone—the man without whom I wouldn't have been writing this book (or at least, if I was, you wouldn't want to be reading it), the man who made me what I am—for better and worse . . . but mainly better.

Thanks, Dad, for everything. You were a good man, a good agent, a good singer (for a lawyer!), a good storyteller—if maybe a little too prolific—but above all, to me at least, a great dad. I'll love you always.

"Dad"

by Emily McEnroe

Oh dad, my dad
When was the last time I told you I loved you dad?
7:15 every morning you wake up to your alarm clock.
You come into my room "Good morning," you always say
I push your face away.
You try to talk to me to wake me up and I scream, "get
    out!"
You open the blinds and I pull my blankets over my head.
You have to go through so much just to wake me up.
A grapefruit is always waiting for me on the kitchen table
    to be eaten.
You're truly the only one who can cut a grapefruit dad.
You take time every day to drive the whole crew to
    school.
You take me to school early on Tuesdays.
When was the last time I told you I loved you dad?
I go to school and come home to usually see you there to
    greet me.
"How was your day," you always say. "Fine."
Oh dad you really are a D A D
Doing Always Doing is you.
Always trying to do more for us more like.
You call me beautiful or shorty,
I like both of them but I prefer beautiful.

John McEnroe

You take Anna and I to tennis on Fridays.
Tennis is your thing I guess.
Oh dad, my dad,
You were there when I first saw the world,
And said my first word,
You were at the hospital when I broke my arm,
and when I got my braces on.
You were there throughout the entire roller coaster of my
    life,
bumping around here and there but pretty much going in
    somewhat of a direction.
Oh yeah by the way
when was the last time I told you I loved you dad?

April 29, 2004

ACKNOWLEDGMENTS

To Patty, for making my life better and better when, for an athlete, it usually gets worse and worse; to my kids for keeping me on my toes and making me realize there is no more rewarding and tougher job than parenting; to my mom and dad for making me the person I am today; to my brothers, Mark and Patrick, and my in-laws, nieces and nephews, for keeping the family name going. To all my friends who have helped make my life an incredible journey: you know who you are (I hope!), thank you and I love you all. Special shoutouts to Ron Perlman, Ron Delsner, Bjorn Borg, Matteo di Fontaine (you are a true inspiration), Milos Raonic (for making me think I can coach!), Ron Meyer, Tim Commerford, and Gary Swain, who has been with me every step of the way. To all my friends at the Malibu racquet club, and everyone that's left of the Malibu mob: Chris Chelios, Nate Heydari, Don Wildman, John Mcginley, Marshall Coben. Everyone at Randall's Island: Lawrence Klieger, Nate Emge, Ben Schlansky, Fritz Buehning; and all the pros who have beaten up on me, especially those who haven't!, with a special shoutout to Jay Karl - thanks for taking such good care of me and my family. Everyone at InsideOut Sports & Entertainment, especially Jim Courier and Jon Venison, for giving me work and making me feel somewhat young! All my friends and cohorts who have taken such good care of me over the years on TV: John Mcguinness, Jackie Smith, Paul Davies, Jamie Reynolds, Bobby Feller, Caroline Davis, Bob Mansbach, Ken Solomon, Bob Wylie, Gordon Beck, Steve ('Sticks') Dinkes, Ted Robinson, Dick Enberg. All my music buddies and old, old friends: John Martorelli, Jimbo Malhame, Doug Saputo, Chris Scianni, and Andy Broderick, and the guys who tried to get in my band and couldn't: Chris Cornell, Eddie Van Halen, Dave Grohl, Josh Homme, Eddie Vedder, Buddy Guy, Lars Ulrich, Keith Richards, Mick Jagger, Jimmy Buffett, and of course, Paul McCartney! The trainers and physios who have tried to keep me in one piece: Kimberly Caspare, Dr Rob de-Stefan, Mike Rollins, Clary Sniteman, and especially Pat Manoccia at La Palestra and Gary Kitchell. To my tennis and sports buddies, especially Peter Fleming and Chris Mullin. To everyone at MSG, I love you all and I love the place. Especially Ann-Marie Dunleavy. You're the best. Thanks for taking such great care of me over the years.

And finally, to all the people who tried and helped get this book to the finish line: Alan Samson, Michael Stone, my son Kevin, Debbie Beckerman, Gillian Stern, Lucinda McNeile, Reagan Arthur, John Parsley, Sarah Wooldridge, Clare Reihill, and a special thanks to Ben Thompson for finally getting it done, a big hug to Chrissie Hynde for pushing me and recommending Ben, Patty for her writing expertise, and Michi Kakutani for her valuable insight and advice.

i want to kill myself